AF656183

FISCAL POLICY FOR UNIVERSITY DEVELOPMENT

About the Author

Dr. M M Ansari is Joint Director & Head (Research Cell), Association of Indian Universities, New Delhi. He is the author of Unit Costs of Higher Education: An Efficiency Study of Universities 1993; Economics of Distance Higher Education (1992); University-Industry Interaction: Exploring Areas and Forms of Collaboration (co-author) 1990; Studies in Distance Education (co-ed) 1988; and Education and Economic Development 1987. Besides, he has prepared a number of important study reports for national and international agencies. He has to his credit numerous articles and papers published in reputed Journals. His areas of specialization are: Public Finance and Economics of Education.

Fiscal Policy for University Development

Retrospection and Prescription

M.M. ANSARI
Joint Director & Head
Research Cell (Eco. of Edn.)
Association of Indian Universities
New Delhi

Foreword by
A.M. KHUSRO
Editor
Financial Express
(Formerly Member, Planning Commission)

CONCEPT PUBLISHING COMPANY, NEW DELHI-110059

All rights reserved. No part of this work may be reproduced, stored in a retrieval system, or transmitted in any form or by any means, electronic, mechanical, photocopying, recording or otherwise, without the prior written permission of the copyright owner and the publishers.

ISBN 81-7022-501-9

First Published 1994

©M M **Ansari** (*b.* 1952)

Published and Printed by
Ashok Kumar Mittal
Concept Publishing Company
A/15-16, Commercial Block, Mohan Garden
NEW DELHI-110059 (India)

Lasertypeset by
Printing Express
H-13, Bali Nagar
NEW DELHI-110015

Dedicated to
my parents
Haji Ahmed Ali
and
Medina Begum

FOREWORD

Institutions of higher learning consume a significant and increasing share of nation's resources, though that is not exactly the case in India. Insufficient provision of resources for higher learning detracts from development and inefficient utilization represents economic loss as much as the benefits sacrificed elsewhere in the economy owing to misallocation of resources. Besides, lack of cost-effectiveness of university programmes constitutes a major drag on productivity gains of other sectors of the economy which employ educated and trained manpower and use the research results produced by institutions. In the present era of knowledge-intensive and technology-propelled economic development, universities and colleges are facing an unprecedented challenge of facilitating adjustment to technological, economic and social change as well as meeting individual needs for personal development. In this sense, the study of costs and of the financing aspect of higher education is no different from other sectors of development like industry which have, in the recent times, attracted the attention of policy planners for exploring the possibility of greater efficiency in allocation of resources. In a diverse and complex socio-economic setting, which has given rise to multifarious activities of higher education institutions in countries like India to meet the manpower requirements of all kinds and levels of specialization, the exercise of resource allocation becomes complex as it involves various competing interests and issues. This requires that the limited funds be distributed and managed efficiently so as to seek the value for money without unduly sacrificing the equity considerations.

The on-going economic reforms in India are oriented to achieve this objective by way of increasing cross-fertilization among different inter-related socio-economic sectors including higher education. While in the recent past various measures have been initiated to raise efficiency in resource use by promoting competitiveness among various productive sectors, there is no appreciable effort either to rationalise educational subsidy or to improve performance and accountability of higher education institutions under the aegis of the Central and State Governments. The credibility of University system requires to be improved as most institutions largely cater to the needs of better the off-sections of society and thus hamper the efforts to equalize educational opportunities. The approach of funding higher education is regressive as about three-fourths of the financial requirements of higher education institutions are met by the Government out of the revenues collected mainly from indirect taxes, the incidence of which largely falls on the poorer sections of society. Most of the un-motivated students who enter into the university portals end up with low academic performance as merely 60 per cent of them pass and those who do so merely 25 per cent score more than 50 per cent marks. Due to the rising pressure of social demand for higher education and the corresponding growth in expenditure on education, the problem is how to provide for financial sustenance of the system which is becoming cost prohibitive. Whereas most economic activities such as those relating to transportation and communication as well as service sectors like health care have taken advantage of technological breakthrough for achieving greater efficiency, there is hardly any perceptible change in the method and technology of teaching to ensure the application of effective and low cost ways of imparting knowledge. As a result, students' learning attainments are much less than desired to cope with the challenge of development as we confront today. Due to low standard of education and lack of relevance of teaching and research programmes, a significant majority of graduates remain 'unemployables'. The expenditure on their education constitutes an economic waste and a counter productive phenomenon owing mainly to the subsequent non-participation of unemployed graduates in gainful activities and their drift towards unlawful activities which create social tensions.

In the regime of high ratios of poverty, illiteracy and income inequality, as is true in India, public support for higher education or its subsidization to the extent being done today is inefficient without being equitous. The literature on economics of higher education has not adequately focussed on the issues pertaining to resource allocation policy for the promotion of higher education institutions. In this book on 'Fiscal Policy for University Development: Retrospection and Prescription', Dr. M.M. Ansari has made a pioneering effort to examine in some detail the entire gamut of issues relating to costs and finance aspects that affect performance and accountability of the university system. The publication of this book is most timely as most developing countries including India are making concerted efforts to accelerate the pace of development through enrichment of human resources. The significance of this contribution is to be viewed against the backdrop of linkages between education and development. The relative level of development of a country vis-a-vis other countries is largely determined by the extent to which a country has comparative advantage in human resources, mainly in terms of qualified scientific and technical manpower. Most countries of the world including India have in recent years, revised their educational policies to cope with the challenge of education to meet the manpower requirements of the economy. Even at the individual level, knowing full well the social and economic value of education, the parents of every successive generation want for their children a higher level of education than they had with a view to ensuring a better future for them. As the ratio of educated manpower in the total labour force is one of the lowest for India, which explains the cause of lower productivity in the economy, there is an urgent need to rationalise the funding policy for university development to ensure proper correspondence between the supply of an demand for educated manpower of a reasonably high quality.

Dr. Ansari has done commendable work in indicating the areas and forms in which financial accountability of the university system could be improved to suit the developmental requirements of the country. Some of the major recommendations which have emerged from findings of his study are worth recapitulating. First, the distribution of funds should be linked to the performance of higher education institutions in teaching and research. Since the best and worst performing institutions simultaneously exist today as they receive government funds on the basis of past trend rather than scientifically determined requirements, the scope for improving the quality and the relevance of programme is limited. Without modifying the existing resource allocation policy to eliminate diseconomics, the system's responsiveness to the nation's socio-economic needs cannot be improved. Second, indiscriminate subsidization of higher education ought to be minimised and financial incentives to economically backward regions be provided to nullify their fiscal deficiency. Similarly institutions promoting education in frontier areas of knowledge and/or catering to socially deprived communities should be provided with special grants. Such a step is necessary to reduce inter-personal inequalities in income and wealth by empowering the deprived sections. Third, expansion and diversification of higher education should be planned in relation to manpower requirements of all kinds and levels of specialization. The motivated students who have demonstrated their ability to benefit from new knowledge should be admitted to higher education programmes and their education should be financed by the government on the sound principles of public finance which duly regards equity and efficiency criteria of financing social services. Fourth, financial dependence of higher education institutions on government funds should be gradually reduced to the extent possible by providing a separate window wherefrom the students could take interest-free but inflation-adjusted loans to pay for the cost of their education. The author's suggestions for establishing an independent financial agency named as Educational Opportunity Bank is worth considering. The reduction in financial dependence would minimise Government interference and ensure greater autonomy in the functioning of universities; and, at the same time a part of the costs of education could be shifted on to the beneficiary groups by levying appropriate rates of user charges for different services. Also, the limited public money could be ploughed back for reinvestment in the education of future generation. Fifth, resources should be efficiently utilized with a view to ensuring cost-effectiveness of various programmes. The factors which have been identified as major hurdles in achieving economies of scale, as revealed from variations in unit costs of education as estimated by Dr. Ansari, are worth examining by the individual institutions if, at all, they wish to stay in the business in times to come. Last but not the least, the various measures indicated in the book to economise expenditure and to augment resources for higher education require due consideration of the funding agencies as well as the universities. Since the policy measures recommended in this book are based on rigorous empirical work, the follow up of these suggestions by the concerned Government departments and universities and further research on various issues raised in the book would greatly help improve the financial health of universities – which is a pre-condition for ensuring their greater contributions to national development.

I congratulate the author for pioneering work done with painstaking effort and commendable analysis. I trust that his contribution would be an extremely useful addition to the literature on economics of public finance in general and economics of education in particular.

June 29, 1993 A.M. KHUSRO

PREFACE

India is the Union of States which encompasses considerable diversity of socio-cultural and politico-economic conditions. This diversity is reflected from the States' varying stages of economic development, composition of various shades of political parties sharing power, linguistic and ethnic differences, variations in educational efforts and achievements particularly in terms of active involvement of different sections of people in promotion of education of all types and levels. In such a diverse socioeconomic setting as is the characteristic of India, the system of higher education is developed such that the diversities of culture of all the federating States are duly preserved without unduly sacrificing modernisation of the society and growth of economy. The system, therefore, strives for promoting the pursuit of knowledge and innovation of technologies to satisfy the educational demands of every section of the society and to meet the manpower requirements of every sector of economy. The endeavours in this direction are deemed necessary not merely to make the country economically prosperous but also to ensure equitable distribution of benefits of development among a cross section of people. In order to fulfil its obligations of ensuring human development through education, the demands of the system on the national exchequer have been rising and is already heavy so much so that the Central and the State Governments are unable to meet the financial requirements due to competing claims of other priority areas of development. The exigency of financial constraints has become even more acute because the Governments at both the levels have to accord high priority to such unfulfilled commitments as to ensure decent standards of living by eradicating poverty, liquidating illiteracy, providing drinkable water and ensuring minimum health facilities. The question of human resource development which is a means as well as an end in itself, therefore, looms large, especially of reasonable standard of which India can boast of in due course of time. How far the costs and finance aspects of higher education are important to the task of expediting educational progress for human development could be a debatable issue among educationists mainly in terms of priority but for fiscal economists and planners a clear picture for the purpose of resource allocation surely emerge from answering such queries as to : how the programmes of education are financed from the current funding policy and with what consequences? Are the contemporary developments in higher education consistent with social and economic policy of the Government? If not, what could be the proper approach that could successfully tackle the challenges faced by the higher education system?

As the impact of higher education on societal development is positive and negative as well, the use of fiscal tools to rectify the system to put it on the right track is crucial to the task of preparing a cadre of human resources for building a healthy and wealthy society. While there is no denying that a multidimensional approach needs to be adopted to streamline the functioning of universities and colleges such that their contributions to national development could be increased, it is however not possible to deal with all the relevant issues at one place. Nor one can proclaim to be competent to duly thrash out all the pertinent issues. The question of funding higher education has, therefore, been chosen by us for a comprehensive discussion and rigorous analysis with a view to developing sound perspectives on the policy of resource allocation and efficient utilization of funds. Since the tradition of higher education in India is one of the oldest and that it has gone through many transformations overtime from ancient to the modern India, the contemporary developments particularly with regard to funding would be of interest to not only the researchers and policy planners but also to funding agencies. The study would be of particular interest to the States which largely finance the universities and colleges in India as well as the Central Government which plays a crucial role in setting the pace and direction of higher education development, mainly through the University Grants Commission. This Commission was constituted in 1956 with such laudable objectives as to inquire into the financial needs of universities and to allocate and disburse grants for maintenance and development of universities. Yet, even after the lapse of about four decades, there exist no scientific approach of funding of higher education; as a result of which considerable distortions are observable that adversely affect the cost-effectiveness of university programme. Due to erosion in credibility of university system, there is considerable deceleration in allocation of funds for higher education in the current Eighth Plan as compared to previous Plans. Since the universities and colleges acquire their legitimacy from different agencies of the Centre and the States, they are, therefore, governed by different Acts and Statutes of the respective Governments. Accordingly, they are governed by different norms or grants in aid codes as evolved by the Centre and States for financing plan and non-plan expenditure. Even though there is notional parity in the degrees/diplomas awarded by different universities, there are notable differences in the level of financial inputs for comparable programmes of study. Irrespective of the channel through which financial resources flow into the university system, they are largely drawn from the national pool. Why should, then, the institutions of higher education are given inequitous treatment in allocation and distribution of funds by the different agencies of the Government, particularly when the concern for enrichment of human resources of every region in the Indian federation is equally important as recognised by the Constitution of India? Is it possible to pursue the Constitutional objective of establishing a 'socialistic pattern of society' without ensuring effective equality of educational opportunity for individuals and institutions? Against the backdrop of these issues, this study is devoted to examine various aspects of financial problems facing the higher education institutions and to explore possible strategies to deal with the emerging issues, which include changing the method of resource allocation so as to ensure efficiency in use of funds as well as cost-effectiveness of programmes; diversifying the sources of funds not only to meet the additional requirements but also to shift the burden of costs on the beneficiary groups for equity reasons; and to reduce financial dependence on the Government so that infringement on the university autonomy could be duly minimised.

As most developing countries like India suffer from common problems like fiscal deficiency, high dependence of universities on the Government, rapid increase in enrolments in higher education, increased demand from public and private sectors for highly trained personnel of all type and levels, and successive failure of Governments to provide for basic human needs including elementary education to the citizen, etc., it may be hoped that the framework of analysis, the approach of diagnosis of problems and the prescriptive measures that have been suggested in the study would provide an aid to formulate policy on funding of higher education institutions in whose context the study has been accomplished.

In finalisation of this study, I was immensely benefited from the support and assistance of many more people than can be acknowledged here. In particular, I would like to thank Professor A.R. Rizvi, my supervisor for doctoral dissertation, in providing superbly effective guidance for completing this study. His keen intellectual interest and academic expertise on the subject not only enabled me to improve my analytical ability to carry out rigorous empirical exercises but also provided a great deal of motivation for its timely completion. Had he not provided considerable academic support, this study would not have been completed.

I express my enormous thanks to Professor A.M. Khusro, my mentor, who was always very willing to discuss the issue of exploring the possibility of greater efficiency in allocation of resources for university sector as well as improving the planning of higher education for meeting the requirements for educated manpower in the country. The analysis of data and interpretation of results have immensely benefited from discussions with him which I have had on a number of occasions. He was also kind enough to accede to my request to write the foreword to this book.

On various issues dealt with in this book, I had the privilege of having enlightened discussions with Shri Anand Sarup, Prof. G. Ram Reddy, Prof. Moonis Raza, Prof. S.K. Agrawala, Dr. V.C. Kulandai Swamy, Dr. P.R. Panchmukhi, Dr. J.L. Azad, Dr. P.B. Tripathi, Shri M.R. Kolhatkar and Dr. J.B.G. Tilak. I am extremely grateful to them for sparing their valuable time.

At various stages of the work, Shri S.K. Barua, Mrs. Zeenat Shafi, Dr. Adarsh Dubey and Dr. T.C. Sharma, rendered valuable research support. They did a commendable job for which I am extremely grateful.

I am indebted to the Concept Publishing Company for undertaking the responsibility of the publication arrangement of this book.

Finally, I appreciate the co-operation which I received from my wife, Mrs. Rukhsana Begum, in writing this book. Without her help, it would not have been easy to concentrate on such a serious study as this, especially in a joyful environment created by our children playing around the study table. It was she who helped in many capacities to complete the book.

None of the above mentioned, I need hardly add, can be held responsible for the errors and omissions that might have still remained in the book.

July 1, 1993 M.M. ANSARI

CONTENTS

LIST OF TABLES

LIST OF APPENDICES

1

INTRODUCTION

More than four decades ago, the University Education Commission (1949) under the chairmanship of Dr. S. Radhakrishnan observed that 'we have a wider conception of the duties and responsibilities of universities. They have to provide leadership in politics and administration, the professions, industry and commerce. They must enable the country to attain, in as short a time as possible, freedom from want, disease, and ignorance by the application and development of scientific and technical knowledge'. After about four decades, the National Policy on Education (NPE) 1986, too, has duly recognised the significance of higher education in human development. The NPE has stated that "higher education provides people with an opportunity to reflect on the critical social, economic, cultural, moral and spiritual issues facing humanity. It contributes to national development through dissemination of specialized knowledge and skills. It is, therefore, a crucial factor for survival". Such perceptions, as above, about the role of higher education in economic growth and social progress and the consequent high social demand for education have led to considerable expansion and diversification of Higher Education Institutions (HEIs), particularly since the beginning of planning era in 1951.

The factors like the growth of population, widening bases of elementary and secondary education, equalization of educational opportunities, the growing realization among the people about the socio-economic value of education and the growing need for higher level manpower are mainly responsible for raising the demand for higher education. By the end of the century, it is likely that the total enrolment at tertiary level would reach to about 6 million as against 4 million in 1988-89. However, even though the rate of growth of enrolment is high and rising, the share of students who benefit from higher educational facilities would remain merely 6 to 7 per cent of the total age-specific population; which, in itself, is the indicator of a lower level of human capital formation. It also means that the quality of human inputs into all the industrial and other productive enterprises would continue to be invariably low as compared to the standard of the foreign economies with which India would have to compete. The quality and quantity of output would therefore remain below the expected level which, in effect, would impede India's efforts to develop a self-reliant and prosperous economy. This has, therefore, aroused considerable skepticism about the operation of HEIs and their abilities to overcome the difficulties facing the nation in as short-time as possible. More specifically, even though higher education has been assigned the key role in improving country's future, the development in this field have been extremely uneven as discussed below.[1]

1.1 The Issues

First, the social accountability of most HEIs, as assessed from quality and relevance of educational programme, has been much below the expected level. Of the total enrolment, only 60 per cent manage to pass and of these less than a quarter score marks above 50 per cent. A large number of graduates, are therefore categorised as 'unemployables' which is a pointer to the poor quality of higher education. Second, infrastructure facilities which have been created with them by making huge investments are inefficiently utilized. The evidence shows that in most institutions utilization of facilities like classrooms, labs, library is as low as sixty per cent of the capacity. Also, the average hours of teaching is much less than stipulated by the UGC which demonstrate uneconomic use of resources. Almost 50 per cent of over 7000 colleges in the country have however been established without the necessary facilities for quality education. All these have added to the diseconomies in management of HEIs. Third, HEIs have been characterised as elitist and inflexible in their mode of operation since instead of acting as instrument of remedying some of the pressing national problems like high incidence of poverty, illiteracy, socio-economic disparity and shortages of manpower in crucial areas, they have rather aggravated these problems as the beneficiary of the schemes of HEIs have largely and traditionally been the better off sections of society. As the private benefits of subsidised (to the tune of 85 per cent or so) higher education are more than the corresponding benefits from the lower levels of education[2] the questions like who benefits from higher education, how and to what extent the costs of education are shared by the beneficiary groups, etc., naturally, become debatable and require clarification. Fourth, in a democratic country like India which also happens to be economically backward, there are social pressures, political compulsions as well as economic rationale for making a somewhat more judicious use of public funds by ensuring that the education of rich is not unduly subsidized and that adequate resources are released for hitherto neglected programmes like eradication of widespread adult illiteracy and sufficient provision for elementary education to which the Constitution of India is committed. In this context, it has been observed that 'there is no justification for subsidising higher education to the extent it is being done today'[3]. Fifth, in the regime of unprecedented fiscal crisis as is currently experienced and the interplay of economic forces like the recent deregulation of the economy, huge Central Government deficit to the tune of 8.5 per cent of GNP and excessive dependence on foreign loans and aids for financing the development plans compel the Government to initiate appropriate measures to effect economy in public expenditure.

In view of the foregoing observations, a critical assessment of fiscal policy for the development of higher education become an interesting area of investigative research, particularly from the view point of adequacy and efficiency in the use of resources. In this respect, the major questions which are always required to be answered are: (a) Where have funds for higher education come from? (b) For what purposes has this money been spent; and (c) where in the educational system have the funds been allocated? The answers to these questions can be found out by analysing such aspects of education as the sources of funds for education, the different components of costs such as capital and recurrent costs and the break-up of these by levels and types of education, etc. An analysis of these aspects lend sound perspective on resource allocation policy especially for gaining an idea about the purposes and uses of funds.

1.2 **Review of Related Literature**

A considerable amount of time and effort have been devoted to examine various aspects of educational finance especially the sources and methods of providing funds for the development of higher education. A brief survey of literature on the subject reveal that till the beginning of industrial revolution, money was hardly considered as an important factor for educational development. This is attributable to the fact that the demand for higher education was low and that there was not much use of capital intensive infrastructure facilities as are being done in the modern institutions. Through time, however, when an increasingly large number of people began to realise the economic value of education especially because of the crucial part played by knowledge and new technology in economic progress, the demand for higher education steadily picked up. The level of education and training emerged out to be the major determinant of life-long earnings. The question that arose from such evidences was that as to who benefits more from higher education, the society which largely bears the costs of education or the individuals who seek to enhance their levels of education and training with a view to improving the prospects of their earnings. From the point of view of public finance of education, an idea of such aspects, as above, is imperative with a view to sharing the costs of education by different beneficiary groups. While there is hardly any worthwhile attempt to quantify the extent to which different economic categories of people benefit from higher education and the degree of financial burden shared by them, a number of studies have dealt with the aspects of the sources, methods and adequacy of resources for higher education. The major studies in this category are briefly reviewed here with a view to providing a background about the objectives, methodology and major findings of the studies which have been completed on the subject during the last three decades.

Rizvi F.H.(1960)[4] examined the pattern of expenditure on higher education against the backdrop of economic development and concluded that the public funds and fees were the main stay of higher education finance and the proportion for total educational expenditure allocated to higher education was much below the expected level of investment. The study suggested that the government subsidisation of education would remove the element of unduly low level of investment in education, while allowing private initiative and free flow of resources for investment in human capital. The study however, did not explore the possibility of augmenting resources from non-government sources nor it indicated the extent of financial burden to be shared by the government and other beneficiary groups.

Mishra, A. (1967)[5] made an intensive study of educational finances from 1698 to 1956 and assessed the policies, purposes, lapses and lacuna involved in their handling by the public and private agencies. While the allocation of resources for education was examined in historical perspective, the study did not make any attempt to describe a rational system of financing higher education, whereby adequate resources could be channelised while ensuring equity and efficiency considerations in creating the provisions for higher education. While the study recommended for higher allocation of funds mainly through revision in fee structure, there was no attempt to examine the pattern of utilization of funds either to indicate under investment in certain areas or to identify the areas in which economy in expenditure could be affected.

Azad, J.L. (1975)[6] made a critical study of the patterns, procedures and policies of providing financial support to the institutions of higher education. A major conclusion that emerged from this study was that the expenditure on higher education increased at the expense of primary education. Of the various policy measures, the study suggested that rates of fees should be revised and students should be provided grants and loans through a separate agency so that, to the extent possible, higher education could be made both equitious and self-financing.

Nanjundappa, D.M. (1976)[7] in his study on the working of University Finances tried to determine: (a) how much money should go into the financing of higher education and (b) how a given amount should be distributed as between the various competing demand heads of university expenditure. The study focused on the problems of finances of Karnataka University. The study has tried to provide an economic cum functional classification of the university budget and explored the possibility of devising indirect system of financing whereby repayable loans are to be given directly to all prospective students instead of giving grants to universifies. The study offers suggestions regarding the criteria for fixation of grants and restoring stability to university finances, pleads for a change in the funding pattern of University Grants Commission, suggests a new format for the presentation of the Budget, emphasises the need to allocate more funds for academic services of the University and suggests guidelines for optimal inter-functional allocation of funds, advocates the setting up of a Planning Committee for universities at the State Government level and a Planning Advisory Board and Planning Cell at the University levels, pleads for a closer alignment between the costs and fees so as to make the beneficiaries pay the full costs, suggests giving restricted powers to borrow with government approval for specific purposes and pleads for introducing an indirect system of loans, in place of the existing grant system, to all eligible students with the condition of repayment from their future earnings.

Panchamukhi, P.R. (1977)[8] made an attempt to evaluate the use of the resources of the University of Bombay and developed general principle of resource mobilisation and resource use in the non-profit institutions of higher education. The study made an in-depth analysis of the sources and patterns of expenditure in the university. The relevant comparisons with some other universities were also made. Even though the study confined largely to one university, the recommendations have significant policy implications for other universities.

Singh, A. and Sharma, G.D. (1981)[9] have put together a number of papers on university finances which were presented at the Seminar jointly organised by the Association of Indian Universities and the Indian Council of Social Science Research. The various papers have dealt with different aspects of university and college finances. The main focus of most research papers having been on the methods of resource allocation and their implication for university development, the major recommendations, that emerged from the discussions on various issues and findings of individual papers, stressed on the need to rationalise the funding pattern so as to eliminate differences in unit costs of education, to recover the costs of education from beneficiary groups while providing due protection to weaker sections of society and to ensure efficient utilization of resources.

Singh, P. (1982)[10] studied the aspects of financing universities in Bihar. The study pointed out that most universities in Bihar suffered from under investment. The funds provided by the State Government and other Central agencies like UGC were much less than the requirements for realizing the university objectives of providing quality education and meeting manpower needs of the State economy. The study, however, did not attempt to quantify the extent of under funding and the degree of its adverse impact on university education. Of the various suggestions; the study recommended that the State should provide adequate funds for university development while the individuals benefiting from university education should be made to pay for their education.

Garg, V.P. (1985)[11] studied the case of Punjab University and examined the pattern of expenditure for the period 1952-82. The study attempted to work-out the institutional and private costs of university education. The results of various excerises carried out in the study indicated that the costs of education increased overtime. As may be expected, the costs varied a great deal across the departments, a relatively higher in laboratory based courses as compared to other courses. The estimates of private costs emerged out to be much higher for the university teaching departments as compared to the Government colleges and other affiliated colleges under private management.

Mridula (1985)[12] analysed the opinions of Finance Officers of universities and Education Secretaries of the State Governments about the methods of providing maintenance grants to the State Universities. While the university authorities mainly Vice-Chancellors and Finance Officers expressed dis-satisfaction over the manner in which resources were provided to the universities, the funding authorities were generally critical about the manner in which funds were utilized, particularly by circumventing the relevant guidelines for management of resources. The study suggested that in allocating the resources the cardinal principle of adequacy and equity should be adhered to and accordingly grants in codes should be revised. Also, private initiative in mobilisation of resources and desirable financial autonomy should be granted for realizing educational goals of universities.

Chalam, K.S. (1986)[13] analysed the pattern of financing higher education in the State of Andhra Pradesh (AP). Apart from examining the major sources of revenue and items of expenditure, the study attempted to work out the institutional as well as private costs of higher education in AP. An interesting aspect of higher education which the study examined, relates to the assessment of internal and external efficiency of university system in AP. The study revealed that while there was improvement in internal efficiency i.e. use of resources in relation to the output of students, external efficiency i.e. returns to investments as measured from earnings of pass-out students, deteriorated during the period of the study. An overall assessment of the study was that the allocation of funds for higher education in AP was not based on rationally devised criteria. The study suggested that the focus of higher education policy should concentrate on providing quality education in professional areas and accordingly adequate funds should be provided on realistic basis.

Azad, J.L.(1988)[14] analysed various facets of financing higher education at the States as well as institutional levels, mainly colleges of four states. Based on the views of college Principals, the study concluded that 'even the none-too adequate resources made available for educational development do not tend to be utilized fully. Moreover, the 'declining trend in non-salary expenditure is indicative of the slow progress in modernization and the introduction of high-tech equipments and, therefore, low quality of education. The study has suggested that in view of general paucity of funds, the prospect for higher allocation of resources for university and college development are not very encouraging and, therefore, alternative sources of finance like private philanthropy and students' fees should be explored. The above observations made in the study are based on qualitative information which were collected in the form of responses from the college Principals.

Mathew, E.T. (1991)[15] attempted to study the aspects of income and expenditure of private colleges in Kerala. The study pointed out that inspite of substantial amount of collection of donations on account of appointment of teachers and admissions to various courses, the colleges were dependent on Government grant to the extent of 90 per cent or even more. A major share of donations/capitation fees was generally received by the management to evade audit of accounts by the Government; and, it was not possible to ascertain the extent to which the money, thus collected, formed the part of colleges finances. The relevant comparisons revealed that rates of tuition fees in Kerala, however, emerged out to be one of the lowest in the country. The study also pointed out that while it was difficult to establish whether or not appointment of teachers and admission of students on donations basis affected the academic performance of colleges, such practices have had demoralising effects on the academic atmosphere of colleges. For improving the finances of colleges, it was suggested that fees structure should be revised and linked to the ability to pay of the beneficiaries of education.

Sulochana, M. (1991)[16] examined the financial problems of Osmania University. The patterns of income and expenditure of the university are discussed in historical perspective and the impact of various changes in the constitution and powers of university bodies on the university autonomy are also examined. The study stressed the need to augment revenues from internal sources like fees and other user's charges as well as to rationalise the system of budgeting such that a close correspondence between the available resources and effective utilization is established. Finally, audit control in universities should be made effective, the study suggested.

Sharma, M.M,. (1992)[17] examined the aspects of financial management of universities and tried to identify the factors which could be said to be responsible for efficient use of resources. The study has analysed the views of a cross-section of university authorities, namely Vice-Chancellors, Finance Officers and Heads of Departments of different universities on the issues pertaining to the method of providing finance, planning and budgeting of resources, accounting and auditing system, etc. For improving effectiveness of financial management of universities, the study suggested a model approach for distribution and utilization of funds. The study however, revealed diverse practices of financial administration and auditing and accounting system among the universities.

In addition to the major published books on university finances, as reviewed above, a number of papers have been contributed by many scholars. Some of the important contributions based on empirical exercises include: Ansari, M.M.[18] (1989, 1991) and Tilak, J.B.G. and Varghese, N.V. (1991)[19] which have essentially attempted to focus on the problems of higher education and have indicated the relevant policy options. In general, however, while all these studies differ in their basic objectives, scope, coverage and time frame, they have attempted to examine the aspects of the growth of educational expenditure in relation to the increase in aggregate national income and expenditure, the sources and methods of resource allocation, the assessment of the adequacy or otherwise of the machinery of financial management in different institutions. A general consensus which has emerged from the above studies is that system of financing universities in India is inequitous, inefficient and the provisions for funds are not based on requirements of HEIs. As HEIs differ a great deal in respects of administrative, financial, and academic structure, the generalisation of conclusions derived from the study of specific institutions, for purposes of appropriate policy interventions have always been somewhat less acceptable for want of rigorous and comprehensive analyses of financial data. Also, without an extensive and intensive retrospection of the policy of pricing higher education particularly against the backdrop of prevailing socio-economic milieu and political considerations, it is not possible to suggest prescriptive measures for reforms of higher education, which fall under the purview of the Centre and the State Governments ruled by different shades of political parties. More importantly, most studies have however not been able to quantify the nature and extent of deficiency in funding higher education, mainly because appropriate statistical techniques and approach of analysis were not employed to the data drawn from a wide spectrum of institutions which represent Indian system of higher education. The present study is an humble attempt to overcome the above shortcomings of the researches done on the subject, a part from covering some new grounds, employing a rigorous approach of analysis to a reasonably larger sample, etc., as discussed later, to shed light on the aspects of fiscal policy for university development.

1.3 Objectives of the Study

India is a country of striking diversity among the federating States including Union Territories. This study explores an interestng aspect of that diversity, namely the system of higher education and attempts to draw lessons for development of university system particularly concerning the issues of costs and its financing. More specifically, the objectives of this study are as below.

(i) To outline the significance of higher education in the context of national development and to assess the nature and extent of relationship between the promotion of higher education and socio-economic progress over the last of our decades;

(ii) To examine the trends in allocation of funds for the development of HEIs by the funding agencies. An endeavour would be made to describe the mechanism of distribution of funds and to quantify the extent of financial dependence on various sources of funds and that with respect to different types of HEIs. This would be done against the backdrop of the theory of investment in human development and the long-term fiscal scenario of the country;

(iii) To study the pattern of utilization of funds and to ascertain the extent to which resources are devoted to different components of expenditure so that an idea could be gained on inter-institutional comparative basis, about the areas in which economy in expenditure could be effected;

(iv) To work-out the unit costs of higher education by discipline and to identify the factors, and the degree to which, they account for the total costs of education. An attempt would also be made to compare the costs of comparable programmes of a cross-section of universities so as to examine the extent of internal-efficiency in management and utilization of funds by different university departments. Such as analysis of costs, apart from providing the much needed data on institutional costs or the extent of Government subsidy (per student) in different disciplines would lend perspective on financial planning at the institutional level;

(v) To develop a methodology of forecasting financial requirements and to estimate the budgetary needs on account of implementation of the continuing and new schemes in higher education during the current Eighth Five Year Plan;

(vi) To identify and discuss the nature of fiscal deficiency from which HEIs are suffering and to suggest the ways and means of using the mechanism of resource allocation as a tool for ensuring accountability of HEIs to the society which finances them. In fact, alternative methods of funding higher education would be discussed in the light of the recent economic reforms so as to improve academic performance and accountability of HEIs to the society;

(vii) To prepare an agenda for reforms of higher education and to indicate the areas which require immediate attention of policy planners for vitalizing the HEIs; and

(viii) To indicate the areas and to suggest the manner in which economy in expenditure could be effected and also to recommend various policy options for mobilising additional resources for financing university programmes. The changes in the fiscal policy instruments would be deemed and formulated such that should be compatible to both national policy on education and the growth oriented demands of the national economy for educated manpower.

All these objectives would be examined, in this study, in *seriatim.*

1.4 Overall Approach and Framework of the Study

The expansion and diversification of higher education programmes over the last four decades have been accompanied by a concomitant rise in government spending. As a result, not only the share of government has increased but the Government contributions consitute the single most important source of funds for financing higher education, even though the parallel practice of establishing institutions under private management and shifting the costs on beneficiary groups are well developed in India. Since the exigencies of fiscal situation of the governments have been adversely affecting the maintenance and development of universities, this study concentrates, in terms of the above objectives, on Government spending on higher education at the Centre, States and institutional levels.

While a long term perspective of four decades since 1950-51 has been taken into account, our analysis is confined to the relevant data for the period 1970-71 to 1985-86 for which reliable time-series data at all India level are available. The case study of various universities, as mentioned below, is based on cross-sectional data for 1985-86. Care has also been taken to use and interpret relevant information for the latest year i.e. 1990-91 to develop a realistic perspective on university finances. The focus is largely on the recurring expenditure both under plan and non-plan which together comprise 90 to 95 per cent of the total expenditure on higher education. In order to ascertain the validity of macro-level observations at the micro-level, the case studies of a select number of important universities from every region of the country and that of all categories – unitary and affiliating as well as types of universities namely Central, State and 'deemed to be' universities have been included in the sample. The inclusions of a university in the sample is purposive, based on the major considerations like availability of reliable data for inter-university comparisons of costs, a reasonably long years of establishment so as to assess the potential increase in economies of scale, a representative institution within the types of universities and diverse activities of teaching and research. Thus, in addition to all India and inter-State analysis of a relevant financial data, the cases of 24 univesity level institutions have been studied. These incude seven, of the ten, Central universities, namely University of Hyderabad, North-Hill East University, Aligarh Muslim University, Banaras Hindu University, Viswa-Bharti, University of Delhi and Jawaharlal Nehru University. In all, there are ten State Universities drawn from the major Indian States. These include the Universities of Andhra, Gauhati, Sardar Patel, Kurukshetra, Karnataka, Kerala, Dr. H.S. Gour, Vikram, Bombay and Poona. Likewise there are seven 'deemed to be' universities which include Central Institute for English and Foreign Languages (CIEFL), Indian School of Mines, Gujarat Vidyapeeth, Tata Institute of Social Sciences, Birla Institute of Technology and Science, Gurukul Kangri and Jamia Millia Islamia (now a Central University). All these institutions represent a broad spectrum of university system in India and truly represent the respective group and the geographic regions for the purposes of all the meaningful analyses.

At the time when the concern for development of higher education is duly high whereas the prospects of increased level of government funding, due to poor macro-economic outlook and keen inter-sectoral competition for resources, are not very encouraging, a comprehensive comparative exercise of the type contemplated in this study would lend the desirable perspective on fiscal policy for university development. The main focus of the study having been on economic and financial issues, several other aspects like management, pedagogical, socio-cultural and political facets, which are not easily quantifiable, have not been examined. Besides, the aspects of privatisation of higher education and allowing free play of market forces and its implications for shifting the burden of funding on students or non-government sources are also not examined. Since higher education everywhere is largely financed by the Government, irresepctive of the stage of development and structure of the economy, the view taken in this study, it may be noted, is that the responsibility of financing higher education should largely be vested with the Central and the State Governments, which, in turn, might devise its own mechanisms of distribution of funds among the students or institutions such that equity in provision of resources and efficiency in delivery in educational services could be ensured. This approach is consistent with the relevant provisions of the Constitution of India, under which the development of education is deemed as a joint responsibility of the Central and the States. Moreover, since the outcome of educational attainments of students and the consequent returns to investment in the form of earnings over the entire working span of life might vary for different reaons, it is not possible to charge a uniform price for the education as the end results of education and training for all the students would not be the same. In view of this, at the most what funding agencies can and should do is to adopt a more scientific approach of allocation of limited funds such that cost-effectiveness of university programmes could be ensured. To this end in mind, special attention was paid to the compilation of data and financial indicators that satisfy, to the extent possible, two requirements: comparability across the universities in different States and consistency within the group which a university represented.

In terms of each of the objectives, as set out before, appropriate statistical technique was applied to the relevant data as explained, wherever necessary, in each of the ensuing chapters. Broadly speaking, in the case of time series data, the approach of regression analysis has been employed. This approach establishes the relationship between two or more variables and indicates the extent to which different explanatory variables have the deterministic influence on the factor whose behaviour is being studied. The approach of regression analysis is the most important scientific method to study the degree of inter relationship between different variables having significant bearing on one another. In the case of cross-sectional data, standard deviation from mean value and coefficient of variation (CV), etc., were estimated to demonstrate the differences with respect to each indicator across the sample universities. In a diverse system as characterised by university institutions in India, it is indeed difficult, and sometime impossible, to indicate as to what should be the absoloute or relative level of expenditure on a specific input item. In such a situation, the average level of allocation of funds as obtaining for a group of comparable institutions and the extent of variation from the mean, as measured by CV, provide the needed clue for making a sound judgment about the area, form and degree of required policy interventions. In view of such considerations, as this, relevant statistical computations have been carried out to assist the planners and decision makers to delineate the trend overtime and to identify the areas of over or under spending with respect to various components of costs of higher education. Besides, against the backdrop of fiscal policies and practices of various countries including India for educational development in general and higher education in particular, appropriate inferences are drawn to bring about desirable changes in the approach of funding higher education. Without making any distinction between the two economic terms, namely, cost and expenditure, these terms have been used interchangeably.

In brief, the framework and the approach of analysis have largely been tailored to suit the requirements, as would be necessary, to desirably comply with the objectives as set out for this study.

1.5 The Plan of the Study

Education and development are inextricably linked with each other. The experiences of most countries demonstrate that development of education is tending to precede economic development. In this context, the theoretical aspects of the relationship between higher education and national development are examind in Chapter 2. The relevant evidences with regard to the indicators of educational and economic development are also presented to show the extent to which the theoretical perception about the significance of higher education in national development holds true for India.

Chapter 3 discusses the theory of investment in education in general and higher education in particular. Against the backdrop of macro-economic scene and exigencies of financial situation, the process and mechanism of allocation of resources are described. Also, the relevant results are analysed and interpreted to indicate the trend in distribution of funds at the national, States and institutional levels. This chapter, thus, presents a comprehensive picture about the structure and method of financial allocation for educational development.

Chapter 4 deals with the expenditure side of the fiscal policy. An indepth and detailed analysis of the growth of expenditure on higher education have been carried out to reflect *inter alia* the pattern of utilization of funds so as to isolate the factors that account for the costs of higher education at the Centre, States and institutional levels. The extent of variations in the weights exercised by different components of costs in different types of institutions are duly revealed which help the planners to gauge the financial performance of an institution vis-a-vis the other institutions.

The usefulness of the analyses of costs of higher education for effective planning and efficient management of resources hardly needs to be stressed. Chapter 5 is devoted to work out the per-student costs of higher education, by institutions and major disciplines, as obtaining in different types of universities. The relevant comparisons demonstrate wide variations in different components of unit costs due to ineffective planning of educational facilities and unscientific methods of allocation of funds for different university programmes.

Chapter 6 attempts to workout the budgetary needs upto 2000 A.D. for higher education. An endeavour has been made to estimate the financial costs of the implementation of policy on higher education for which the nation is committed. The methodology of projection of enrolment has been developed and appropriate financial norms have also been worked out and applied to the physical data to arrive at the total financial requirements. This exercise aims at providing the much needed assistance to the funding agencies, if they are indeed serious to properly execute the policies approved in 1986 (revised in 1992) by the National Parliament.

Chapter 7 recapituates the major shortcomings of the prevailing methods of distribution of funds for the development of higher education and discusses alternative methods of funding higher education such that performance and accountabilty of HEIs could be improved. It argues that funds should be provided on the basis of performance in teaching and research for the planned number of students in various fields of study. Alternatively, instead of providing block grants to the HEIs funds should be directly provided to the eligible students who should buy education out of the funds thus provided, from the institutions which are offering a package of high quality and relevant programmes of education and training. The application of either of these methods could help seek value for money by promoting competitiveness among the HEIs.

Chapter 8 focusses on the major areas, forms and direction of reforms of higher education with a view to raising its contributions to the national development. It discusses policy issues and prepares a list of agenda for appropriate reforms. Besides, the measures for effecting economy in expenditure and mobilisation of additional sources from different sources have also been identified with a view to vitalizing the financial health of universities.

Chapter 9 summarises the main conclusions that have emerged from the discussions in the preceding chapters.

REFERENCES

1. See Author's 'Assessing the Extent of Use of Educational Infrastructure Facilities in the University Sector *Journal of Higher Edu.* Vol. 15, 1990.
2. The relevant evidences are provided in Chapter 3 of this study.
3. *Challenge of Education : a policy perspective*, Ministry of Human Resource Development, 1985, Para 3.40.
4. Rizvi, F.H. (1960) *Financing of Higher Education in Less Developed Countries*, Aligarh Muslim University, Aligarh.
5. Mishra, A. (1967) *The Financing of India Education*, Asia Publishing House, New Delhi.
6. Azad, J.L. (1975) *Financing of Higher Education in India*, Sterling Publishers Pvt. Ltd., New Delhi.
7. Nanjundappa, D.M. (1976) *Working of University Finances*, Sterling Publishers Pvt. Ltd., New Delhi.
8. Panchmukhi, P.R. (1977) *Economics of University Finances: Basic Principles and Practice*, Centre for Multi-Disciplinary Research, Karnaaka Historical Research Society, Dharwar.
9. Singh, A. & Sharma, G.D. (1981) *University and College Finances*, Association of Indian Universities, New Delhi.
10. Singh, P. (1982) *Financing of University Education*, B.R. Publishing Corporation, Delhi.
11. Garg V.P. (1985) *Cost Analysis in Higher Education*, Metropolitan, New Delhi.
12. Mridula, (1985) *State Funding of Universities : A Study of Maintenance Grants to Universities*, Association of Indian Universities, New Delhi.
13. Chalam, K.S. (1986) *Finances, Costs and Productivity of Higher Education*, Inter-India Publications, New Delhi.

14. Azad, J.L. (1988) *Higher Education in India: The Deepening Financial Crisis*, Radiant Publishers, New Delhi.
15. Mathew, E.T. (1992) *Financing Higher Education: Sources and Uses of Funds of Private Colleges in Kerala*, Concept Publishing Company, New Delhi.
16. Sulochana, M. (1992) *Financial Management of Higher Education in India*, Chug Publications, Allahabad.
17. Sharma, M.M. (1992) *Financial Management in India*, Concept Publishing Company, New Delhi.
18. Ansari, M.M. (1989) 'Financial Health of Universities: A diagnostic Study', *Journal of Higher Eeducation* and University Finances: Determinants and Implications in *Development of Higher Education* by Moonis Raza (Ed), AIU, 1991.
19. Tilak, J.B.G. and Varghese, N.V. (1991) 'Financing Higher Education in India', *Higher Education*, Vol. 21.

2

HIGHER EDUCATION AND NATIONAL DEVELOPMENT
A Theoretical Perspective

This chapter seeks to (i) underscore the significance of Higher Education (HE) in enrichening human resources which plays a decisive role in accelerating the pace of development; (ii) delineate the trends in growth and expansion of HE; and (iii) examine the extent to which HE has helped or hindered the national efforts to cope with the challenges of emerging technocratic society.

2.1 Education for Human Development

The development of human resources is both a means as well as an end in itself; and, therefore, the thrust of almost every enlightened policy has been to create conditions for human development. Human development is defined as the process of enlarging people's options. 'The most critical choices that people should have include the option to lead a long and healthy life, to be knowledgeable and to find access to the assets, employment and income needed for a decent standard of living'.[1] Thus construed the human development, encompass people choices to make it more democratic and participatory which is imperative for enhancing individuals satisfaction and enlarging the scope for social progress. Human development is however, inextricably linked with a number of socio-cultural and politico-economic factors; and is largely determined by three indicators: life expectancy, education and income. Of these, education is the most crucial factor having a bearing on all aspects of human action. Briefly, the evidence has established that literacy is a decisive factor in liberating individuals from ignorance and exploitation. The countries with high illiteracy have high mortality and short life expectancy rates and a large proportion of population below poverty line. Most children in such countries are under-nourished; and the minimum basic needs for a decent human living are hardly met. The effects of literacy and continuing education programmes convincingly show that more of education leads to more income, a narrowing of income differentials, reduced level of fertility, better health and nutritional standards and high life expectancy. Since the relationship between education and factors like the availability of new crop varieties, fertilizer, exposure to extension services is strong and positive, the more educated not only produce more from a hectare of land but also make larger income in off-farm activities. Likewise, when the gross output and earnings of industrial enterprises having manpower with varying levels of education are compared, it emerges that enterprises having more educated manpower maintain higher productivity than others. The relationship of education to health, nutrition and fertility is similarly positive. In general, more educated people, especially women, tend to have not only fewer children, and better health and nutrition standards but also create conditions for expediting the process of learning and generating income. Education is indeed very effective in the development of social, political and personal values. It can thus be argued, *a fortiori*, that human development through education is a must for social upliftment and economic progress of the country. In developing countries like India, the dimensions of the twin problems of poverty and illiteracy are complex. Therefore, a multifaceted and integrated approach has generally been adopted to overcome them. It is in this context that higher education and research, which provides the necessary feedback for planning and management of resources, including of education system, play a crucial role in giving direction to national development. A critical level of balance between all types and levels of education is however required to be maintained for ensuring manpower development, which is most important among all the variables that determine social progress and economic growth.

In economic sense, capital and natural resources are passive factors of production, whereas human resources are the active agents who accumulate capital, exploit natural resources, build social, economic and political organisations as the human beings alone have the ability to generate knowledge, analyse information, innovate technologies and utilize the same in their routine activities which provide them some kind of satisfaction. Obviously, if a country is unable to develop the skills and knowledge of its people and to utilise them effectively in various socio-economic activities, it would be unable to develop anything else. In brief, it is the development of human resources of a nation, not its capital nor its material resources, that ultimately determine the character and pace of economic and social development; which, in effect, influence the quality of life of people. In this sense, human development is dependent on itself. The National Policy on Education (NPE) 1986 has, therefore, emphasised the need to 'intensify the nation-wide effort in human resource development with education playing its multifaceted role'.[2] To this end in view, the NPE has categorically stated that 'development oriented objectives of Indian society can be realised only by making investments on education of an order commensurate with the nature and dimension of the task.'[3] This, therefore, stresses on the need to examine the educational fiscal policy which has significant bearing on human development.

2.2 Higher Education and National Development

In the context of higher education, the NPE has rightly observed that 'higher education provides people with an opportunity to reflect on the critical social, economic, cultural, moral and spiritual issues facing humanity. It contributes to national development through dissemination of specialised knowledge and skills. It is, therefore, a crucial factor for survival'.[4] It follows that it is indeed difficult to realize the objective of building up a sustainable and prosperous society without the development of human resources which, in turn, is dependent on the health and vitality of higher education. Thus, higher education and economy are tightly linked with each other. For instance, while the economy provides for necessary resources for promoting the system of higher education, the system prepares, in turn, a cadre of manpower with varying degrees of specialization and levels of skills for increasing productivity of various factors of production, which consequently generate employment opportunities, enhance income and improve quality of life of people. Moreover, the programmes of higher education, pertaining especially to the theoretical and applied fields of studies, provide desirable perspectives and necessary framework for formulation of appropriate policies with a view to ensuring long-term sustainable development. In view of this, the planners and policy-makers are genuinely concerned about the strength and vitality of the system of higher education to ensure maximum contributions of the system to the fulfilment of changing and growing needs of the society. Such a concern is justified even more strongly in developing countries like India which suffer not only from deficiency in physical and financial capital but also the abundance of labour force having much less than desired level of education and training as may be necessary to earn and maintain a decent standard of living. In order for creating such conditions as would be conducive for ensuring a reasonable level of standard of living, the promotion of human resources by way of strengthening education system, in which the programmes at tertiary level are to determine the quality and relevance of educational service is *sine quo non* for national development. The experience of most of the developed countries reveal that they have thrived owing largely to the increase in threshold of education, training and skills formation. It has been observed that 'for the first time in the history of humanity, development of education on a worldwide scale is tending to precede economic development'.[5] As the economies of both developed and developing countries become more knowledge and technology intensive, human resources would continue to become more central to economic progress. Almost in every country, though in varying degrees, the search for knowledge and new technology has become the major concern of national economies since productivity is increasingly determined by the knowledge and skilled workers put into their tasks. Human knowledge is the moving factor behind productivity change and when the requisite knowledge and appropriate technology are missing, output suffers; however much finance and hardware are supplied.

There are at least two fundamental implications and policy issues emerging from such situations as above. Firstly, the minimum competence threshold for being able to function in the economy is moving upward. That is to say, it is becoming more and more difficult for the individual to perform in the emerging economy if he does not have the necessary skills. This is one of the key factors behind recent and renewed interest in education and training everywhere. The second implication is that there is a great risk that the new economic situation, if the necessary investments in education, training and skill formation are not made, will create a dividing line between those who can and those who cannot perform because of their level of skills. Therefore, the demands of new technology upon system of human resource development have to be seen in the perspective of a more knowledge intensive economy. Hence, when new technologies lead to an increase in skills requirements, both within the work place and within the economy as a whole, systems of education and training must increase the quality and relevance of their programmes.

2.2.1 *Expansion of Higher Education*

In view of the foregoing, commendable progress in respect of expansion and diversification of higher education system has been made; as a result of which the system has emerged out to be the second largest in the world after the USA. The factors like the growth of population, widening base of elementary and secondary education, equalization of educational opportunities and the growing realisation among Indian people about the socio-economic value of education have spured the demand for higher education. By the end of the century, it is likely that the total enrolment at tertiary level would continue to rise at around 10 per cent per annum and reach to about 6 million as against 4 million in 1988-89. Tables 2.1 through 2.6 present the detailed picture in terms of institutions, teachers and levelwise break-up of enrolment in higher education since 1950-51 to date.[6] However, even at this high rate of growth of enrolment, the share of students who benefit from higher educational facilities would remain merely about 6 to 7 per cent of the total age-specific population (18 to 23 years) as against 25 to 40 per cent for most of the European countries. If this ratio is taken as a major indicator of skills formation, it would mean that quality of human inputs in the form of new knowledge and technology into all the industrial and other productive enterprises would continue to be invariably low as compared to the corresponding levels of the economies with which India would have to compete. Thus construed, the quality and quantity of socio-economic service or outputs would remain below the expected level which, in effect, would impede India's development efforts to occupy a place of prime importance in the comity of nations. Obviously then, the system of higher education ought to be developed such that desired results are ensured.[7] A great deal of care should however be exercised in deciding the content and clientele group of higher education since those aspects would have significant bearing of varying nature on societal development as discussed below.

2.2.2 *Use and Mis-use of Higher Education*

Universities and colleges are the main establishment of higher education and research, the major functions of which are to preserve, generate and disseminate knowledge as well as to prepare a cadre of manpower with varying degrees of training in skills and specialization into frontier areas of knowledge. The educated and trained manpower, in

TABLE 2.1: Quantitative Growth of Higher Education in India

Year	No. of Universities/Colleges			Enrolment (in 000's)			No.of Teachers		
	Universities	Colleges	UC	Total	AC	% in AC	Total	UD/UC	AC
1950-51	28	695	-	174	-	-	21264	-	-
1951-52	30	762	-	199	-	-	23880	-	-
1952-53	30	797	-	215	-	-	25553	-	-
1953-54	30	824	-	238	-	-	27680	-	-
1954-55	31	912	-	260	-	-	30112	-	-
1955-56	32	1025	-	295	-	-	33208	-	-
1956-57	33	1107	-	327	-	-	36504	-	-
1957-58	37	1171	-	371	-	-	39872	-	-
1958-59	40	1291	-	428	-	-	43631	-	-
1959-60	40	1405	-	482	-	-	49549	-	-
1960-61	44	1542	-	557	-	-	55460	-	-
1961-62	46	1783	107	664	-	-	63053	9313	53740
1962-63	54	1938	133	752	-	-	66370	11044	55326
1963-64	55	2111	128	842	690	82.0	68634	11522	57112
1964-65	62	2360	147	950	781	82.2	77120	13637	63483
1965-66	64	2572	163	1067	881	82.6	84676	14291	70385
1966-67	70	2749	166	1191	990	83.1	93251	14900	78351
1967-68	70	2899	170	1370	1135	82.8	103180	17456	85724
1968-69	76	3112	181	1566	1306	83.4	110943	19058	91885
1969-70	79	3297	185	1793	1522	84.9	119052	19757	99259
1970-71	84	3604	206	1954	1655	84.7	128876	21619	107257
1971-72	86	3896	208	2065	1773	85.9	139204	22842	116362
1972-73	90	4158	229	2168	1855	85.6	145524	24704	120820

(Contd.)

TABLE 2.1 (*Contd.*)

Year	No. of Universities/Colleges			Enrolment (in 000's)			No.of Teachers		
	Universities	Colleges	UC	Total	AC	% in AC	Total	UD/UC	AC
1973-74	95	4308	230	2234	1905	85.3	156562	26659	129903
1974-75	102	4388	240	2367	2013	85.0	161782	27830	133952
1975-76	102	4508	305	2426	2059	86.0	167623	31624	135999
1976-77	105	4569	302	2432	2069	85.1	169615	32142	137473
1977-78	105	4375	351	2565	2160	84.2	178344	37142	141202
1978-79	108	4460	352	2618	2178	83.3	181659	38835	142824
1979-80	108	4558	352	2649	2210	83.5	188502	39838	148664
1980-81	112	4722	411	2753	2299	83.5	193341	39964	153377
1981-82	118	4886	495	2952	2455	83.3	199904	42186	157718
1982-83*	120	5039	501	3133	2610	83.3	209017	44596	164421
1983-84*	124	5246	-	3308	2749	83.1	216500	46859	169641
1984-85*	125	5590	-	3404	2846	83.6	220101	47382	172719
1985-86*	132	5816	-	3571	2975	83.3	226909	49008	177901
1986-87*	136	6512	-	3682	3067	83.3	234388	51150	183238
1987-88*	142	6647	-	3814	3177	83.3	241973	53165	188808
1988-89*	144	6912	-	3948	3293	83.4	249068	54973	194095

* Estimated ** Excluding Pre-university/Intermediate/Pre-professional level 1977-78 onwards. Number of colleges excludes junior colleges and colleges having only diploma/certificate courses.

Source: University Grants Commission's Annual Reports as quoted in 'Higher Education in India' by Moonis Raza.

UC = University Colleges; UD = University Department; AC = Affiliated Colleges turn, increase the productivity of resources in all the sectors wherein they are deployed; which, in effect, enhance national income and improve quality of life of people. While the education system generally assist the process of accelerating the socio-economic development, the specific relationship between higher education and economic growth has, however, been difficult to quantify owing mainly to the conceptual and statistical problems since the factors which influence the costs and benefits of education are not easily susceptible to measurement. In fact, the nature and strength of relationship between higher education, social progress and economic growth are inextricably linked with each other and they differ because of the complex nature of interaction between the variables characterising different stages of development, social settings and cultural milieu.

TABLE 2.2: Decennial Growth Rate of Enrolment in Higher Education

Period	Annual Growth Rate
Five-yearly Index	
1950-51 to 1955-56	11.2
1955-56 to 1960-61	23.5
1960-61 to 1965-66	14.0
1965-66 to 1970-71	12.8
1970-71 to 1975-76	4.4
1975-76 to 1980-81	2.6
1980-81 to 1985-86	5.3
1985-86 to 1988-89*	
Decennial Index	
1950-51 to 1960-61	12.4
1960-61 to 1970-71	13.4
1970-71 to 1980-81	3.5
1980-81 to 1988-89	4.7
Thirty-year Index	
1950-51 to 1988-89	8.6

* Estimated
Source: As in Table 2.1

TABLE: 2.3 Levelwise Enrolment in Higher Education (1950-51 to 1988-89)

Year	Undergraduate		Postgraduate		Research		Total Enrolment	
	No.	%	No.	%	No.	%	No.	%
1950-51	145389	83.7	19992	11.5	1434	0.83	173696	100.00
1951-52	166935	84.1	21903	11.3	1774	0.89	198543	100.00
1952-53	182775	84.9	23751	11.3	1715	0.80	215250	100.00
1953-54	201258	84.7	26191	11.0	2071	.0.87	237668	100.00
1954-55	219917	84.5	27801	10.7	2464	0.95	260121	100.00
1955-56	248690	84.4	30866	10.5	2692	0.91	294815	100.00
1956-57	276999	84.7	33516	10.3	2992	0.92	326926	100.00
1957-58	314783	84.7	38298	10.3	3087	0.83	371446	100.00
1958-59	359829	84.1	45543	10.6	3745	0.87	427868	100.00
1959-60	407415	84.6	52244	10.8	4867	1.01	481534	100.00
1960-61	471658	84.7	58908	10.6	5083	0.91	556559	100.00
1961-62	571485	86.1	67610	10.2	5249	0.79	663661	100.00
1962-63	651805	86.7	71297	9.5	5297	0.70	752095	100.00
1963-64	739607	87.8	76685	9.1	5895	0.70	842110	100.00
1964-65	835804	88.0	84201	8.9	7104	0.75	950277	100.00
1965-66	944015	88.5	91830	8.6	8633	0.81	1066884	100.00
1966-67	1053750	88.5	101798	8.5	9668	0.81	1190713	100.00
1967-68	1211083	88.4	117250	8.6	11479	0.84	1370261	100.00
1968-69	1388335	88.6	135469	8.6	12145	0.77	1566103	100.00
1969-70	1603898	89.5	146804	8.2	12474	0.69	1792700	100.00
1970-71	1746090	89.4	161182	8.2	13311	0.68	1953640	100.00
1971-72	1835077	88.9	180343	8.7	14995	0.73	2065041	100.00

(Contd.)

TABLE 2.3 (*Contd.*)

Year	Undergraduate No.	%	Postgraduate No.	%	Research No.	%	Total Enrolment No.	%
1972-73	1920364	88.6	195307	9.0	16443	0.70	2168107	100.00
1973-74	1964432	88.0	214691	9.6	16417	0.70	2234385	100.00
1974-75	2075039	87.7	234114	9.9	17977	0.80	2366451	100.00
1975-76	2146919	88.5	219826	9.1	18381	0.70	2426109	100.00
1976-77	2141542	88.1	218128	9.0	21910	0.90	2431563	100.00
1977-78	2255306	87.9	233644	9.1	26659	1.10	2564972	100.00
1978-79	2294789	87.7	249528	9.5	30078	1.10	2618228	100.00
1979-80	2307924	87.1	265251	10.0	29570	1.10	2648579	100.00
1980-81	2401485	87.2	273337	9.9	32171	1.20	2752437	100.00
1981-82	2588759	87.7	285892	9.7	34558	1.20	2952066	100.00
1982-83	2757893	88.0	296103	9.4	36731	1.20	3133093	100.00
1983-84*	2912487	88.0	313110	9.5	36249	1.10	3307649	100.00
1984-85*	2999621	88.0	322541	9.5	38160	1.10	3404096	100.00
1985-86*	3142389	88.0	339235	9.5	39280	1.10	3570897	100.00
1986-87*	3240046	88.0	349778	9.5	40500	1.10	3681870	100.00
1987-88*	3356687	88.0	362370	9.5	41958	1.10	3814417	100.00
1988-89*	3474171	88.0	375053	9.5	43427	1.10	3947922	100.00

(*Estimated)

Source: As in Table 2.1

TABLE 2.4: Decennial Growth Rate of Stagewise Enrolment (1950-51 to 1988-89)

Period	Undergraduate	Postgraduate	Research
1950-51 to 1960-61	12.5	11.4	13.0
1960-61 to 1970-71	14.0	10.6	10.6
1970-71 to 1980-81	3.2	5.4	9.2
1980-81 to 1989-90	4.7	4.0	3.8

Source: As in Table 2.1

Whereas higher education is a vital instrument to bring about improvements in the techniques of productivity and production through the relevant research and innovations, some of the characteristics of the education system and its influence on the society create obstacles in realization of even such laudable objectives as social and economic justice and equality of opportunity for individual development. The impact of higher education, for instance, can be disastrous if the relevant programmes are not undertaken to impart education in universal human values, to inculcate scientific attitude and temper, to ensure equality of educational opportunities among a cross-section of socio-economic groups. Such deficiencies in educational programmes, as above, tend to generate social tensions and pose considerable political and administrative problems which impinge upon developmental efforts by way of diverting physical and financial resources from growth oriented schemes to unproductive activities. While examining the nexus between higher education and national development the Education Commission (1964-66) expressed the view that–

> "a system of university education which produces a high proportion of competent professional manpower is of great assistance in increasing productivity and promoting economic growth. Another system of higher education with the same total output but producing a large proportion of indifferently educated graduates of arts, many of whom remain unemployed or even umemployable, could create social tensions and retard economic growth. It is only the right type of education, provided on an adequate scale, that can lead to national development. When these conditions are not satisfied, the opposite effect may result."

TABLE 2.5: Facultywise Enrolment in Higher Education (1960-61 to 1988-89)

Year	Percentage to the Total Enrolment										
	Arts	Sc.	Com.	Engg./ Tech.	Med.	Edn.	Agri.	Law	Vet.Sc.	Others	Total
1960-61	44.9	30.0	10.2	3.6	2.7	1.5	1.3	2.3	0.5	3.0	100
1961-62	44.3	29.1	10.9	5.0	2.5	1.9	2.1	2.5	0.5	0.3	100
1962-63	42.2	30.8	9.6	5.4	3.9	1.9	2.9	2.2	0.5	0.7	100
1963-64	41.9	31.5	9.4	5.2	3.9	1.9	2.9	2.2	0.5	0.5	100
1964-65	42.1	31.3	7.7	5.2	4.0	1.9	2.9	2.1	0.4	0.5	100
1965-66	40.9	32.8	9.6	4.9	4.1	1.9	2.9	2.2	0.4	0.5	100
1966-67	40.5	33.7	9.5	4.9	3.9	1.9	2.7	2.3	0.4	0.4	100
1967-68	41.5	32.3	9.9	4.7	3.8	1.9	2.4	1.9	0.3	0.4	100
1968-69	42.8	32.5	10.4	4.0	4.1	1.9	2.2	1.9	0.2	0.4	100
1969-70	43.7	32.8	10.6	3.5	3.5	1.8	1.5	2.0	0.2	0.4	100
1970-71	44.3	31.7	11.5	3.0	3.3	1.8	1.4	2.3	0.2	0.4	100
1971-72	45.3	30.4	12.2	2.7	3.2	1.9	1.3	2.5	0.2	0.5	100
1972-73	45.9	29.3	12.6	2.5	3.1	1.9	1.3	2.9	0.1	0.6	100
1973-74	44.9	21.2	15.2	3.9	4.6	3.2	1.2	5.0	0.3	0.5	100
1974-75	44.6	19.6	16.5	3.8	4.5	3.3	1.2	5.7	0.3	0.5	100
1975-76	44.5	19.1	17.1	4.0	4.3	3.2	1.2	5.8	0.3	0.5	100
1976-77	44.4	18.2	17.7	4.1	4.6	3.0	1.3	5.8	0.3	0.6	100
1977-78	43.7	18.4	18.1	4.0	4.4	2.9	1.4	6.2	0.3	0.6	100
1978-79	42.3	18.8	18.8	4.3	4.3	2.7	1.5	6.4	0.2	0.7	100

(*Contd.*)

TABLE 2.5 (*Contd.*)

Year	Percentage to the Total Enrolment										
	Arts	Sc.	Com.	Engg./ Tech.	Med.	Edn.	Agri.	Law	Vet.Sc.	Others	Total
1979-80	40.6	19.2	19.5	4.5	4.2	2.8	1.5	6.7	0.3	0.7	100
1980-81	40.5	19.4	20.1	4.7	4.0	2.6	1.4	6.3	0.3	0.7	100
1981-82	40.3	19.6	21.3	4.4	3.9	2.4	1.3	5.9	0.3	0.6	100
1982-83	40.2	19.9	21.4	4.5	3.6	2.4	1.3	5.8	0.3	0.6	100
1983-84*	40.4	19.7	21.3	4.6	3.6	2.4	1.3	5.8	0.3	0.6	100
1984-85*	40.3	19.7	21.7	4.7	3.5	2.2	1.2	5.7	0.3	0.7	100
1985-86*	40.3	19.7	21.5	4.6	3.6	2.3	1.3	5.8	0.3	0.6	100
1986-87*	40.3	19.7	21.5	4.6	3.6	2.3	1.3	5.8	0.3	0.6	100
1987-88*	40.3	19.7	21.5	4.6	3.6	2.3	1.3	5.8	0.3	0.6	100
1988-89*	40.3	19.7	21.5	4.6	3.6	2.3	1.3	5.8	0.3	0.6	100

*Estimated

Note: In this Table, enrolment in Intermediate classes affiliated to the Board of High School and Intermediate Education, U.P. is included upto the year 1972-73 and from 1973-74 onward excluded.

Source: As in Table 2.1

TABLE 2.6: Facultywise Number of Ph.D. Degree Awarded (1961-62 to 1987-88)

Year	Ph.D. Degree Awarded										
	Arts	Sc.	Com.	Edn.	Engg./ Tech.	Med.	Agri.	Vet.Sc.	Law	Others	Total
1961-62	314	401	15	9	20	14	41	-	1	-	815
1962-63	389	489	22	8	23	20	38	-	1	1	991
1963-64	408	510	15	14	26	17	52	-	1	1	1044
1964-65	477	519	25	22	32	21	127	3	2	2	1230
1965-66	541	683	20	17	39	39	92	3	1	1	1436
1966-67	695	838	34	17	50	16	102	9	4	-	1765
1967-68	769	984	31	28	66	20	89	21	4	3	2015
1968-69	667	1017	35	24	75	26	123	18	4	4	1993
1969-70	788	1103	46	36	98	24	157	25	3	-	2280
1970-71	876	1103	58	42	99	33	216	26	5	3	2461
1971-72	929	1168	47	45	76	46	182	39	8	7	2547
1972-73	-	-	-	-	-	-	-	-	-	-	-
1973-74	1093	1327	58	60	95	46	276	56	4	41	3056
1974-75	1258	1515	55	77	163	50	281	60	5	14	3478
1975-76	1282	1516	41	82	136	42	289	44	14	19	3465
1976-77	1364	1671	70	98	152	49	334	66	15	24	3843
1977-78	1677	1901	96	92	168	51	329	81	5	44	4444
1978-79	1811	2044	87	105	134	48	364	58	10	14	4675
1979-80	1831	2261	118	120	176	56	422	58	13	21	5076

(Contd.)

TABLE 2.6 (*Contd.*)

Year	Ph.D. Degree Awarded									
	Arts	Sc.	Com.	Edn.	Engg./ Tech.	Med.	Agri.	Vet.Sc.	Law	Others	Total
1980-81	2246	2792	105	173	139	44	466	60	13	42	6080
1981-82	2347	2846	173	178	190	66	471	93	14	26	6404
1982-83	2422	2892	175	191	160	71	575	64	20	27	6597
1983-84	2678	2890	177	187	192	59	648	65	8	30	6934
1984-85	2754	2922	185	239	210	70	576	102	25	56	7139
1985-86	2886	2838	263	219	194	61	627	155	34	69	7346
1986-87*	2910	2840	244	212	215	77	592	98	43	64	7295
1987-88*	2933	2842	225	205	236	93	557	74	51	59	7275

*Estimated.

Source: As in Table 2.1

In order to develop a sound perspective on various aspects of educational programmes that contribute to (or retard) the process of development, a brief background about the nature, content and approach of promoting education may be provided.

The concept of national development encompass the effects of a variety of factors pertaining to social settings, cultural milieu and economic and political predilections of leaders. One of the crucial factors which has considerable bearing on all these aspects, as discussed above, is the human resources, the development and utilization of which determines the capability of a nation to forge ahead of other countries in respects of economic, social and cultural advancements. The choice of strategies for developing and utilizing the capabilities of its people are, however, incumbent on the relevant and adequate level of education and training. The role of education, as an instrument of change, in different spheres of human activities may be briefly described below.

Education is a social activity aimed at the realization of social values as well as individual self-realization. Education may be thus defined as the art of acquisition of knowledge, the application of which contributes to individual personality development and self fulfilment. This, in turn, generate intrinsic power to live a better life. In regard to polity, education plays the crucial role of laying the very foundation upon which democratic principles and democratic institutions are based. Specifically, education serves as (i) a primary means of political socialization which brings about national integration through strengthening the sense of national identity and developing the historical perspective of the people and their cultures; and (b) the major vehicle for supplying the political and administrative personnel needed by the country. Without the enlightment of the public, in general, especially through the promotion and choice of appropriate study materials, the internalization of democratic values and the building up of high moral character of the leaders, the development of a sound political system, etc., are not possible. Likewise, in the sphere of economic development, education has been the major source of providing trained manpower of various kinds and levels of skills including technicians, craftsmen and engineers as well as managerial personnel – which are pre-requisite for promoting entrepreneurial capacity that stimulate economic growth.

Higher education system being at the top of educational pyramid oversee the overall health and vitality of education system; and, thus, in essence facilitate national development through its manyfold task of preservation, dissemination generation and utilization of knowledge. The preservation and dissemination of knowledge both, normative and positive takes place, first of all, in the form of teaching which also includes publication and use of the means of mass communication by the university staff. The generation of knowledge is mainly manifested in research activities. The utilization of knowledge is concerned with problem – illumination, extension programmes, relevant analysis of information and policy formulation on specific issues confronting policy makers. Obviously, all these functions of HEIs are crucial for vitalizing the human resources that make their impact felt on all the development activities.

Higher education plays a negative role also, as pointed out before, in strengthening the forces which aggravate socio-economic disparities across various groups and regions, and in contributing to degradation of moral character and social disturbances. If HEIs are concentrated, for instance, in urban areas, this would reflect in-built bias in education system in favour of urban industrial sector. In such circumstances, the manpower requirements of the urban sector could be catered relatively more suitably than rural sector. And, as a consequence, the rural-urban differences in the levels of economic development might widen due mainly to differences in creative and productive abilities of human resources. Even if distributive measures are taken, their impact may not be desirably effective owing largely to inequality in educational achievements of rural-urban people; thereby influencing, their earning capacities over the entire span of working life. Such conditions, in effect, may tend to concentrate income and wealth in the areas or groups characterised by high enterprenuerial capacity of manpower as measured by the level of literacy, skill formation, health and other indicators of human development. Likewise, inter-personal differences in quality of life which is largely determined by the factors like education and health may also get accentuated if educational opportunities are not reasonably equalized among the people in different income brackets and social groups. Moreover, lack of proper orientation in various courses of studies in respects of national heritage, cultural ethos, social tolerance and the faith in the future of the country, may create obstacles in promotion of national integration and harmony among various socio-cultural and economic groups.

It has been observed for a number of countries that inequality between the education of boys and girls increases with the successive rise in the levels of education.[9] If adequate facilities for attracting and retaining the female students in the university system are not provided, the disparity in educational attainments between the two sexes might persist; and, social taboos and income constraints of parents might work against female education which would consequently retard participation of female in bringing about rapid reforms for social progress and economic development.

The inter-generational inequity between the rich and the poor section of the society may get similarly perpetuated due to inbuilt biases in the system of education in favour of affluent class which can afford, unlike others, to provide education to their wards without much economic hardship. The fact that the students who drop out of schools are predominantly from poor families and that the majority of students who complete college and university education are from relatively rich families suggest that the pattern of inequality in educational accomplishments is largely attributable to differences in income groups of the beneficiaries of education. This is corroborated by the fact that of the gross number of beneficiary of higher education in India about 80 per cent are drawn from the top 30 percent of income group.[10]

Obviously, such developments in educational system circumvent the economic and social policy of equitable distribution of income and wealth. As long as educational opportunities are unequal, the realisation of the Constitutional objectives of establishing a 'socialistic pattern of society' would be difficult. In this context, it is worthwhile to point out that the fiscal policy for the development of HEIs have come into sharp criticism for the following reasons. HEIs are largely financed about 85 per cent, by the Centre and the State Governments and that a major proportion of Government's revenue, about 80 per cent is derived from the indirect taxes, the incidence of which, as is well known, mainly falls on relatively poor people. HEIs have thus become a means to transfer resources from the poor majority to the rich minority. Such developments are attributable to the lack of proper perspective and insight into the nature and types of education that are provided through the network of educational programmes which influence the people of different categories in varying respects and degrees. A sound educational system ought to be, therefore, free from the deficiencies described above, lest the objective of human resource development which is a means as well as an end in itself of all the national policies would be difficult to realize. A great deal of care has to be exercised, therefore, in expanding and diversifying the post secondary level of education so that the benefits of educational network are reaped by the people of all the groups and regions so as to ensure economic justice and harmonious social progress.

2.3 Impact of Higher Education on National Economy: Some Evidences

In the following discussions, we shall examine the extent to which university education in India has contributed either to ameliorate or aggregate the socio-economic conditions in India.

The developmental efforts, that are being made through the strategies as outlined in the Five Year Plans, have largely concentrated on pursuing such laudable objectives as eradication of nutritional as well as health poverty, liquidation of illiteracy and reduction in inter-personal and inter-regional disparities in social and economic development. In all the Plan periods, an endeavour has, therefore, been made to improve efficiency of various factors of production so as to increase the volume of output or income with a view to raising the quality of life of people.

The attempts to attain these laudable objectives have been envisaged within the policy frame of a mixed economic structure, federal set up and democratic polity. The Five Year Plans have, therefore, focused on such aspects as correct identification of the people's need and proper selection of policy measures which, when implemented, can accelerate the pace of development. As discussed above, the successful execution of social and economic programmes is crucially dependent on the quality of human inputs, which when deficient, yields poor results. Infact, relevant and adequate level of education, technological know-how and training in skills have been one of the major needs of the Indian people; the lack of which has impinged upon the effectiveness of the chosen policy instruments. This has, consequently, adversely affected the performance of the Indian economy. The observed shortfalls in the achievements, as compared to the targetted rates of growth, during the different planned period amply prove the point. Whereas the long-term rate of capital formation in the Indian economy has been as high as 5.5 per cent, the growth of GDP has recorded 3.5 per cent per annum over a period of four decades. Comparatively speaking, less than stipulated degree of plan performance cannot be ascribed merely to paucity of financial resources and infrastructure and adverse natural calamities that occur from year to year. There are reasons to believe that the administrative and managerial inefficiencies and inadequacy of such inputs as are generally derived from research and innovation, which form the basis for formulation and implementation of social and economic policies, are equally responsible for the low rate of growth of Indian economy.[11] As argued elsewhere in this chapter, the quality of human factor is responsible for husbanding physical and financial resources and is, therefore, much more important than any factor of growth; and it is this factor which has been deficient due to the lack of proper coordination and integration of educational, manpower and economic planning. As a result, considerable distortions (or mismatch) are caused between supply of and demand for educated personnel by different sectors of development.[12] Also, the needed research feedback for policy formulations and for monitoring of ongoing programmes are hardly forthcoming from HEIs as they suffer from such problems as inapt management of physical and financial resources and the lack of accountability to the society. The vitalisation of higher education and research is therefore imperative to contain the adverse effects of certain factors or to stimulate the productive activities and the agents that have significant bearing on the management of resources as well as efficiency of various factors of production. The need for the expansion and diversification of higher education has been duly recognised and deemed essential by the planners ever since the beginning of the planning era in 1950-51, with a view to fulfilling the national objectives as couched in the Constitution of India. During the first decade of the planning, a number of universities and colleges came into being and this process has continued ever since. For instance, in 1950-51, there were 28 universities and 695 colleges which together enrolled 1.74 lakhs students and employed 21.26 thousand teachers to teach them (Table 2.1). Over the last four decades, there has been phenomenal increase in the number of HEIs. In 1990-91 there were 193 universities including 29 and 10, respectively, deemed to be universities and institutions of national importance. There were as many as 7121 colleges affiliated to these universities, which together enrolled 44.25 lakhs students for graduate, post-graduate and research degrees and employed 2.62 lakhs teachers to teach them.[13] This has thus recorded an increase of about 25, 12, 10 and 7 times in students' enrolment, teachers, colleges and universities respectively. The allocation of financial resources for HEIs has similarly increased overtime. For instance, the magnitude of plan funds for university education was doubled in Second Plan and raised to 18 per cent of the total educational outlays as against 9 per cent in the First Plan. Although this proportion has recorded a great deal of fluctuations over the different successive plans, it has almost stabilised at around 20 per cent of the total education budget in all the subsequent plans. In all, about one per cent of GNP is currently devoted for the promotion of higher education and research. The increase in financial allocation for university education has obviously been in response to both the manpower requirements of industry and trade and the economy as well as people's aspirations for improving their social and economic conditions. The fact that student enrolment at university level has increased at a high rate of 9.7 per cent per annum, as against 7.8 per cent and 5.5 per cent, respectively, for secondary and elementary levels of education over the last four decades,[14] demonstrate the extent to which social choice for higher education development is linked with the people's expectations to ensure socio-cultural and economic mobility.

Yet the beneficiary of the system of higher education constitute less than 6 per cent of the age specific population i.e. persons between 18-23 years of age. Moreover, about 65 per cent of enrolment is in the category of general higher education and the remaining proportions are in the areas of science and technology. A considerable majority, about four-fifths, of the graduates pass with less than 50 per cent marks which explains for both the extent of wastage and the low quality of higher education. This is also ascertained from the fact that a large number of graduates are unemployed or unemployable. An unavoidable conclusion that emerges is that due to the narrow base of higher education as compared to the diverse needs of the vast population as well as the low standard of teaching and research in HEIs, various socio-economic factors responsible for bringing about desirable changes in the society, have not got duly transformed such that their influence could be maximised in the task of national reconstruction. As a consequence, the traditional social impediments like caste ridden structure of the Indian society and religious superstitions, technological backwardness, the use of obsolete technologies in productive and services sector, etc., have continued to be the major factors hampering modernization and industrialization of the country. As many as 48 per cent of the total population, as per the Census of 1991, is illiterate and almost equal proportion of people live below the poverty line. This has proved to be counter-productive as poverty-illiteracy are positively related and have a dampening effect on each other.[15] Needless to say, a commendable degree of progress could have been made in the fields of social, political and economic development, had there been a concerted approach to plan, manage and coordinate the programmes of HEIs with a view to promoting the formation of human capital such that the benefits of both new knowledge of building up a healthy society and the latest technologies for raising productivity of various factors of production could have been duly utilized. The developmental goals cannot be realized unless inbreeding of mediocrity from a majority of the existing institutions is effectively checked at every cost as the costs of not doing it would be even more which our future generations would have to pay in terms of the loss of freedom, culture and dignity of life.

This is, however, not to underrate the contributions of education to individual fulfilment and national progress, but to emphasise that vigorous efforts for strengthening higher education and research would have yielded both qualitatively and quantitatively better results than what we have had over the last four decades. For instance, the development of education, with whatever vigour and sincerity it has been pursued, has definitely shown positive results. As a pre-requisite for societal advancements, the process of individual development is being expedited. The progress in regard to internalization of the new values based on scientific outlooks of the Indian people has been commendable; as a result of which, they are getting future orientation and are able to get rid of the pre-modern value orientations of the traditional society. Education has, moreover, contributed to increased social mobility both horizontal and verticle which, in turn, has facilitated acceleration of developmental activities. The major thrust of all this has been to bring about a new synthesis of Indian culture as the common asset which will integrate and build every Indian for the common cause of improving the quality of life. In brief, education being a social activity has been helpful in realizing social values and individual self-realization that are essential for social upliftment. While much is yet to be desired in this direction, there are evidences and indications of changing peoples attitudes for socio-economic reforms. For instance, the commitment to resolve all the socio-economic issues within the frame of democratic system and federal polity of the country has been duly strengthened and the education system has contributed a great deal to fulfil this objective by laying the very foundation upon which democratic principles and democratic institutions are based. Without the enlightenment of the public in general, the 'internalization of democratic and social values as well as the development of leaders who uphold such universal values, the sustenance of democracy and federal set-up and secular traditions in the country would have not been possible.

In relation to economic development, the contribution of higher education has been substantial in providing trained manpower of various kinds and levels of skills – including technicians, craftsmen and engineers as well as managerial personnel – which have been an essential component of economic growth and industrial development. In the beginning of the planning era, a negligibly small proportion of educated labour force participated in various economic activities. With the passage of time and increased network of educational programmes, the proportion of labour force having varying levels of education has increased, whereas the percentage of illiterate labour force has steadily been declining. It can thus be deduced that the economic contributions of all types of educated persons, as judged by the increasing proportion of educated labour force, has been rising. The analysis of composition and pattern of labour absorption in different sectors of the economy prove the point. For example, the proportion of illiterate work force has declined from 73.6 per cent in 1960-61 to 57.5 per cent in 1980-81, whereas for persons having primary/middle level of education, it has increased from 6.3 to 21.8 per cent during the same period. Likewise, the proportion of persons having matriculation and above level of education has accordingly increased from 2.8 per cent in 1960-61 to the 11.7 per cent in 1980-81.[16] The rising share of educated persons in the total labour force obviously indicates their increasing contribution to the Gross Domestic Product (GDP). It may also be deduced that had there been speedy development of education and a relatively high intensity of utilization of educated labour force as well as new technologies, the growth of GDP would have been substantial and at a rate much higher than what has been observed during the successive plan periods.

In brief, the evidence show that the contributions of education to economic development has been rising,[17] a point which is duly recognised by the development experts everywhere and the evidences in the Indian context also conform to the *a priori* expectations. It could also be construed to mean that a concerted effort to rectify various deficiencies of HEIs,[18] would yield much better results in terms of human development. The different aspects of reform of higher education would be discussed in Chapters 7 and 8 so as to provide the necessary background for developing a sound perspective on the costs and finance aspects of higher education, which are essentially the subject matter of this study.

REFERENCES

1. *Human Development Report,* 1991, UNDP, p.1-2.
2. *National Policy on Education*, 1986, para 12.2, p.29.
3. *Ibid* para 11.1, p.28.
4. *Ibid* para 5.24, p.14.
5. *Learning to be*, UNESCO, 1972, p.12.
6. Since the dimension of quantitative growth are self-explanatory, the data is not interpreted.
7. For a detailed discussion on the Contemporary issues in higher education, please see *Higher Education in India: Retrospect and Prospect* by Moonis Raza (Ed) 1991.
8. Education and National Development: Report of the Education Commission, 1964-66, NCERT, 1959.
9. For a detailed comment on the pattern of educational development across the countries, see *Learning to be*, op cit, UNESCO.
10. See Author's *Education and Economic Development,* AIU, 1987.
11. Another dimension of deficiency in human resources due to degradation of moral values is the widespread corruption in public life in India. As suitably described by the former Prime Minister of India, Shri Rajiv Gandhi in one of his speeches; of the total allocation for various poverty alleviation programmes, merely 15 per cent reaches the targetted population while the rest is pocketed by middle men at various stages of implementation of programmes.
12. This should be amply clear from the fact that a large number of graduates are unemployed while the experts of requisite background in several professional areas are not available.
13. See Introduction in *Universities Handbook*. AIU, 1992.
14. See *Challenge of Education: a policy perspective*, Govt. of India, 1985.
15. See Author's *Education and Economic Development op cit.*
16. The corresponding figures for the recent year based on 1991 Census are as yet available. But the results of 43rd round of National Sample Survey for 1987-88 duly support the observation that the share of educated labour force in the total labour force has been rising, as may be expected.
17. It may be reiterated that in this part of the study what is being described is about the significance of education in development. No attempt has been made to work-out the extent for which education has contributed to economic growth.
18. As discussed in *Higher Education in India, op cit.*

3

RESOURCES FOR HIGHER EDUCATION
Structure and Mechanism of Financial Allocation

Resources are always limited. The developing countries like India suffer more than others due to acute shortage of funds and physical capital including trained and skilled manpower. The planners and decision-makers, therefore, exercise a great deal of caution in choosing a set of alternative productive activities which yield maximum returns on investments. As education has considerable economic value and the programmes of educational institutions have significant bearing on productivity and economic growth, the deployment of resources for the promotion of education and training is essentially treated as investment; the benefits of which accrue to the beneficiaries over their entire life span and even for a longer period to the society. Because of the prolonged stream of benefits in the forms of socio-cultural development and economic gains which accrue to individuals and the society, education in all the countries is regarded in its major part as a social responsibility. The task of making provisions for adequate and relevant education of all types and levels is, therefore, largely assumed by the Government everywhere. Obviously then, the responsibility of ensuring effective management of physical and financial resources devolve on the Government which formulates education policy and prepares its perspective plans. To this end in view, the planners make a thorough assessment of the interests of different sections of the society and the socio-economic objectives which the nation has stipulated for itself to attain within the given timeframe. A sound judgement with regard to all the stages of plan formulation i.e. beginning from inputs through its processes to outputs, is necessary for successful execution of the plan, which require that corrective measures should be taken at various stages of implementation. In view of this, the process of decision-making especially from the view point of optimising gains from investments in education is discussed below.

3.1 Educational Investments: The Process of Decision-Making

In order to play a justifiable role in expediting the process of educational development, the Government and its constituent bodies have to take a number of sound decisions, taking, of course, into account the manpower requirements of different economic and social sectors as well as the interests of a cross-section of people of the country for their cultural development. A wide spectrum of issues which always receive the attention of educational planners and decisions-makers, encompass such areas as: (a) public and private uses of current resources; (b) public expenditure on social welfare programmes including those relating to the promotion of economic growth and the necessary provision for such services as education, health, housing and national defence; (c) estimation of budgetary requirements of different socio-economic sectors of economy including sub-sectors like primary, secondary, vocational and higher – general and technical education, etc., and (d) determination of the combination of a set of inputs like teachers, laboratory, library, size of classroom and other necessary equipment, keeping, of course, in view the desired quality of educational output. The decisions in respect of all these, however, require a detailed information pertaining to: (i) the identification of factors which have significant bearing on the process of educational development and the extent to which each factor is exerting its influence in determining the course of the above process; and (ii) the alternative costs or losses which the society will have to incur if the appropriate decision is not taken to initiate action for the promotion and execution of educational plan. Obviously, such information are gathered through different means from individuals as well as institutions with a view to providing a sound basis for taking appropriate decisions in respects of planning, management and financing of education system. Since education has both consumption as well as investment value, the benefits of which accrue to both the individuals and the society, the investment decisions with regard to the nature, types and levels of education as well as the extent of sharing the costs of such educational provisions are accordingly borne by them. Therefore, the process of decision-making can be classified, broadly speaking, into three categories. One relates to individual decision with regard to buying or obtaining education of different kinds and levels. The decision regarding the sale or supply of education by the institutions constitute the second category. In the case of conflict of interest between the group of individuals and the society, collective decisions through appropriate means are taken, which may be referred to as the third category. For various reasons, the perceptions which influence and guide the decision-making processes with regard to acquisition of knowledge, training and technical know-how, however, vary not only for the above categories of buyers and suppliers of educational services but also between the groups of people in different income brackets and the various types of institutions which cater for varying educational requirements. It is precisely for this reason that the demand for various types and levels of educational services for different groups of society differ a great deal. Since the costs of the provision for various educational services also differ due mainly to the differences in levels, nature of courses of study and quality of teaching inputs, the educational costs are accordingly shared between the major beneficiary groups like the society or the Government and the individuals in accordance with the perceived gains accruing to such groups over a period of time.

In the context of the above, it must be pointed out that there is preponderance of evidence to show that (i) the overall contributions of lower levels of education to economic growth are relatively more than higher education; (ii) the social rates of return to investments on education are also higher for lower levels as compared to post secondary education; (iii) the social rates of return to higher education are lower than the private rates of return. Tables 3.1 and 3.2 duly corroborate these observations. More precisely, the following patterns are observed which are due to Psacharopoulous, G. (1981):[1] Pattern No.1 - The returns to primary education (whether social or private) are the highest among all educational levels; Pattern No.2 - The private returns are in excess of social, especially at the university levels; Pattern No.3 - All rates of return to investment in education are well above the 10 per cent common yardstick of the opportunity cost of capital; Pattern No. 4 - The returns to education in developing countries are higher relative to the corresponding returns in more advanced countries. These evidences would suggest *inter alia* that pricing education or deciding about the extent to which various levels of education is to be subsidized by the Government or in devising formula for sharing of the costs of education, the considerations about the extent of benefits which accrues from educational investments to different socio-economic groups lend desirable perspective for decision-making. In fact, the theoretical expectations about the impact of different types and levels of education, have led almost all the countries, including India, to incorporate in their national policies on education to provide free and compulsory education to their nationals up to specific level or age. The Constitution of India stipulate for providing elementary education, upto the age 14 i.e. VIIIth standard, free of cost. Article 45 of the Constitution provides that 'the State shall endeavour to provide within the period of ten years from the commencement of this Constitution for free compulsory education for all children until they completed the age of fourteen years'. Since this objective has not been realised so far, the policy of providing free education up to 14 years of age is still in vogue. The policy of financing education at successively higher levels particularly tertiary education, however, differs a great deal across the countries; and therefore, the extent of government funding of higher education differ from country to country. In general, however, HEIs are largely financed by the Governments though a significant number of such institutions are under the private management which mobilize relatively more funds from private sources than other institutions. In the recent past, the growing concern for ensuring accountability of HEIs, including the rationalization of costs and benefits aspects of higher education, has led many countries to establish university level institutions under the private control. There are already many such institutions in India under this category. More than two-thirds of colleges which enrol about 85 per cent of students in higher education are under private management. Many more colleges are being established every year and some of the university level institutions like a few 'deemed to be' universities are in this category. Thus, there exist a mixed system in which private enterprise as well as Government effort determine the direction and pace of educational development. In view of this, an attempt is made below to examine the different aspects of educational finance with a view to developing a perspective on the policies and practices pertaining to resource allocation for the development of higher education. As the various aspects of educational finances are an integral part of the overall fiscal policy of the country, a brief background about the record of performance of the Indian economy and the sources and methods of its financing economic development may be provided with a view to assessing the strength and weekness of the economy and its ability to finance the education sector. It must be reiterated that the costs and finance aspects of education should be assessed against the backdrop of the overall framework of development which the country has adopted for itself and the long-term economic performance, which alone can assure adequate resources for educational advancements.

TABLE 3.1: Returns to Eucation by Level and Country Type (90)

Country	Survey Year	Private			Social		
		Prim.	Sec.	Higher	Prim.	Sec.	Higher
Africa							
Ethiopia	1972	35.0	22.8	27.4	20.3	18.7	9.7
Ghana	1967	24.5	17.0	37.0	18.0	13.0	16.5
Kenya	1971	28.0	33.0	31.0	21.7	19.2	8.8
Malawi	1978					15.1	
Morocco	1970				50.5	10.0	13.0
Nigeria	1966	30.0	14.0	34.0	23.0	12.8	17.0
Rhodesia	1960				12.4		
Sierra Leone	1971				20.0	22.0	9.5
Uganda	1965				66.0	28.6	12.0
Asia							
India	1965	17.3	18.8	16.2	13.4	15.5	10.3
Indonesia	1977	25.5	15.6				
South Korea	1967				12.0	9.0	5.0
Malaysia	1978		32.6	34.5			
Philippines	1971	9.0	6.5	9.5	7.0	6.5	8.5
Singapore	1966		20.0	25.4	6.6	17.6	14.1
Taiwan	1972	50.0	12.7	15.8	27.0	12.3	17.7
Thailand	1970	56.0	14.5	14.0	30.5	13.0	11.0
Latin America							
Brazil	1970		24.7	13.9		23.5	13.1
Chile	1959				24.0	16.9	12.2
Colombia	1973	15.1	15.4	20.7			
Mexico	1963	32.0	23.0	29.0	25.0	17.0	23.0
Venezuela	1957		18.0	27.0	82.0	17.0	23.0
Intermediate							
Cyprus	1975	15.0	11.2	14.8			
Greece	1977	20.0	6.0	5.5	16.5	5.5	4.5
Spain	1971	31.6	10.2	15.5	17.2	8.6	12.8
Turkey	1968		24.0	26.0	8.5		
Yugoslavia	1969	7.6	15.3	2.6	9.3	15.4	2.8
Israel	1958	27.0	6.9	8.0	16.5	6.9	6.6
Iran	1976		21.2	18.5	15.2	17.6	13.6
Puerto Rico	1959		38.6	41.1	21.9	27.3	21.9

(*Contd.*)

TABLE 3.1 (*Contd.*)

Country	Survey Year	Private			Social		
		Prim.	Sec.	Higher	Prim.	Sec.	Higher
Advanced							
Australia	1969		14.0	13.9			
Belgium	1960		21.2	8.7		17.1	6.7
Canada	1961		16.3	19.7		11.7	14.0
Denmark	1964			10.0			7.8
France	1970		13.8	16.7		10.1	10.9
Germany	1964			4.6			
Italy	1969		17.3	18.3			
Japan	1973		5.9	8.1		4.6	6.4
Netherlands	1965		8.5	10.4		5.2	5.5
New Zealand	1966	20.0	14.7			19.4	13.2
Norway	1966	7.4	7.7			7.2	7.5
Sweden	1967		10.3			10.5	9.5
United Kingdom	1972	11.7	9.6			3.6	8.2
United States	1969	18.8	15.4			10.9	10.9

Source: Adopted from 'Returns to Education an updated International comparison', *Comparative Education,* Vol.17, No.3, 1981.

TABLE 3.2: Returns to Education by Level and Country Type (90): Summary Statistics

Region or Country type	N	Private			Social		
		Prim.	Sec.	Higher	Prim.	Sec.	Higher
Africa	(9)	29	22	32	29	17	12
Asia	(8)	32	17	19	16	12	11
Latin America	(5)	24	20	23	44	17	18
LDC average	(22)	29	19	24	27	16	13
Intermediate	(8)	20	17	17	16	14	10
Advanced	(14)	(a)	14	12	(a)	10	9

Source: Same as Table 3.I

(a) = Not computable because of lack of a control group of illiterate

N = Number of countries in each group.

Prim. = Primary educational level.

Sec. = Secondary educational level.

High. = Higher educational level.

3.2 The Framework of Financing Economic Development: An Overview

Ever since the inception of Five Year Plans in 1951-52, the programmes of development have concentrated on realization of such vital objectives as the elimination of poverty, the satisfaction of the basic needs of people in terms of food, clothing and shelter, attainment of universal elementary education, and access to health facilities for all. In formulating plans, the main aim has been to create conditions for self-sustaining growth in terms of both the capacity to finance development oriented schemes and innovation of relevant technology so as to ensure progressive improvements in efficiency of various factors of production. The realization of these objectives has, however, been much below the expected level owing largely to paucity of resources. As we know, the total of resources available for investment consists largely of domestic savings, and to some extent, inflow of capital from abroad. Due to the low stage of development, as is obvious from the level of per capita national income which is one of lowest in the world, it has been difficult to mobilize funds through various financial instruments like taxation and incentives for savings, etc., commensurate with the magnitude of financial requirements for investment purposes. As a result of which, almost all the Plans have suffered from a significant shortfall in real term of around 20 per cent.[2] Consequently, the realization of plan targets in terms of the rate of growth of Gross Domestic Product (GDP) has been adversely affected. "The actual rate of growth of GDP has generally been lower than the stipulated rates for various Five Year Plans. While the perpetuation of inflationary conditions and the approach of deficit financing have largely been responsible for erosion of real resources, the lack of proper perspective on resource allocation, especially in the regime of financial constraints, and the cuts in plan outlays, generally on pro-rata basis have, in effect, distorted both the priority areas of development as well as the appropriate linkages between different sectors of the economy'.[3]

Obviously, then the performance of education sector which is heavily dependent on Government for finance cannot be regarded as exception. Infact, of all the socio-economic sectors, education has suffered more than any other sector due to the *ad hoc* nature of allocation of funds which has largely depended on the availability of residual resources with the Government, after meeting the requirements of other sectors of development.

TABLE 3.3: Real GDP Growth Rates and Value Added in Major Sections

	1950-51 1960-61	1960-61 1970-71	1950-57 1989-90	1950-51	1960-61 Sectoral Shares	1970-71	1980-81	1989-90
		Growth Rates				Percent		
Agriculture	3.0	2.3	2.5	55.4	50.8	44.5	38.1	32.1
Industry	6.2	5.4	5.6	16.1	20.0	23.6	25.9	28.8
Services	4.1	4.6	4.8	28.5	29.2	31.9	36.0	39.1
Total	3.9	3.7	4.0	100.0	100.0	100.0	100.0	100.0

Sources: Computed on the Basis of Data from Basic Statistics Relating to the Indian Economy Vol.1: All India Centre for Monitoring Indian Economy, August 1991.

3.2.1 *The Record of Economic Performance*

An assessment of the long-term performance of Indian economy however reveal improved resilience. Table 3.3 demonstrate that the economy's growth in GDP has risen significantly from 3.4 per cent per annum in the period 1950-51 to 1975-76 to 4.9 per cent per annum in the period 1974-75 to 1989-90. The achievement of 5.5 per cent per annum growth rate during the last decade i.e., 1980-81 to 1989-90 would mean that the growth path has shifted upward again. The economy's recent good performance due partly to the recent deregulation of economy indicate the potential for higher growth in the foreseeable future. As is evident from the Table 3.3 mentioned above, almost every sector of development show a definite sign of improvement, which is essential for reversing the slow growth that characterise Indian economy.

As may be expected, the composition of sectoral shares in GDP has gradually been changing. Whereas the relative contributions of industry and services to GDP have increased by 12.7 and 10.6 percentage points, the share of agriculture and allied activities has considerably declined, by 23.3 percentage points, over the period of 1950-51 to 1989-90. Obviously, these trends will have significant bearing on resource allocation policy which ought to be oriented in such a way that the tempo of development in respect of all the sectors of economy is maintained at high level. This would, however, depend *inter-alia* on the extent to which quality of labour force or manpower resources is improved and re-oriented on continuing basis so as to ensure effective management of socio-economic situations that are emerging due to the knowledge and technology induced growth. In this context, it is imperative to gain an idea of the ways and means of financing development, keeping especially in view the sources of revenues and the pattern of distribution of funds across the major categories of expenditure.

3.2.2 *Sources of Revenue by Major Categories*

The different forms of taxes have contributed nearly three-fourths of the total revenues. The share of indirect taxes and other forms of levies and charges under the head of non-tax revenues have, however, declined (Table 3.4). It is expected that as the national income rises, the shares of income linked direct taxes should accordingly rise. As per the Constitutional provisions, the collection of tax revenues are shared

TABLE 3.4: Patterns of Revenue Receipts — The Centre and States*

(*Rs. in Crores*)

Year	Source	Tax Revenues: Direct Taxes	Tax Revenues: Indirect Taxes	Tax Revenues: Total	Non-Tax Revenues	Others	Total
		1	2	3=(1+2)	4	5	6=(3+4+5)
1950-51	a. Centre	128 (29.2)	229 (52.1)	357 (81.3)	82 (18.7)	0	439 (100.0)
	b. States	103 (27.4)	166 (44.1)	269 (71.5)	76 (20.2)	31 (8.3)	376 (100.0)
	c. Total (a+b)	231 (28.3)	395 (48.5)	626 (76.8)	156 (19.4)	31 (3.8)	815 (100.0)
1960-61	a. Centre	202 (20.1)	528 (52.7)	730 (72.8)	231 (23.0)	42 (4.2)	1003 (100.0)
	b. States	203 (19.5)	420 (40.3)	623 (59.8)	188 (18.1)	230 (22.1)	1041 (100.0)
	c. Total (a+b)	405 (19.8)	948 (46.4)	1353 (66.2)	419 (20.5)	272 (13.3)	2044 (100.0)

(*Contd.*)

TABLE 3.4 (*Contd.*)

			1	2	3=(1+2)	4	5	6=(3+4+5)
1970-71	a.	Centre	504	1947	2451	863	32	3346
			(15.1)	(58.2)	(73.3)	(25.8)	(0.9)	(100.0)
	b.	States	505	1796	2301	535	586	3422
			(14.8)	(25.8)	(67.3)	(15.6)	(17.1)	(100.0)
	c.	Total	1009	3743	4752	1398	618	6768
		(a+b)	(14.9)	(55.3)	(70.2)	(20.2)	(9.1)	(100.0)
1980-81	a.	Centre	1983	7405	9388	3094	2	12484
			(15.9)	(59.3)	(75.2)	(24.8)	(Neg.)	(100.0)
	b.	States	1285	9167	10453	1577	3006	15036
			(8.5)	(61.0)	(69.5)	(10.5)	(20.0)	(100.0)
	c.	Total	3268	16573	19841	4671	3008	27520
		(a+b)	(11.9)	(60.2)	(72.1)	(17.0)	(10.9)	(100.0)
1988-89	a.	Centre	6072	27726	33798	9777	10	43585
			(14.0)	(63.6)	(77.6)	(22.4)		(100.0)
	b.	States	4817	29484	34301	4208	10372	48881
			(9.9)	(60.3)	(70.2)	(8.6)	(21.2)	(100.0)
	c.	Total	9783	57210	66993	13985	10382	91360
		(a+b)	(10.7)	(62.6)	(73.3)	(15.3)	(11.4)	(100.0)

Notes: Includes Union Territories

'Neg' - Indicates less than 0.1 per cent.

* Figures within parenthesis indicate percentages.

Source: Indian Economic Statistics (Public Finance), Ministry of Finance, Government of India, December, 1991.

between the Centre and the States. The relative change in the share of collection of revenues by the two levels of Governments therefore reflect both the modification in the arrangement of sharing of revenues between them as well as the relative tax efforts in augmenting resources from various sources. A major share of indirect taxes was collected by the Centre till the seventies; thereafter, both the levels of Governments have been raising, about 60 per cent or so of their revenues through this source. In brief, the different forms of taxes constitute the major source of revenue for financing development in India and as a percentage of GDP, it is as high as 18 per cent in 1989, which compares favourably with other developing countries.

The implication of this pattern of resource mobilisation for the education sector, it may be argued, is that the growth in collection of income linked taxes, from which education is largely financed, would exert pressure on HEIs for greater cost recovery mainly by way of increased tuition fee and user's charges particularly from those categories of beneficiary of education whose ability to pay is higher. Such a shift in emphasis on the mode of collection of revenues from the potential sources would very much be in tune with the principle of equity and efficiency in resource mobilization. We shall return to this issue in Chapter 7.

3.2.3 *Pattern of Public Expenditure and the Place of Education*

As regards the deployment of resources on various developmental and non-developmental programmes, the data reveal that the share of non-developmental expenditure has substantially declined from 68.8 per cent in 1950-51 to 49.2 per cent in 1988-89, whereas the corresponding share of development expenditure has increased from 28.7 per cent to 48.5 per cent over the respective years (Table 3.5). The share of other expenditure has, however, remained around 2.5 per cent or so over the last three and a half decades.

The breakup of expenditure for the Centre and the States reveal that while the Centre spends more on non-developmental activities, the States incur a relatively high proportion of expenditure on developmental activities. The shares of the Centre in developmental expenditures has, however, been rising overtime and has increased from 9.4 per cent in 1950-51 to 36.9 per cent in 1988-89. Thus, it emerges that while the focus of the States' efforts has largely been on the developmental programmes, the Centre's role in developmental activities has been steadily increasing.

TABLE 3.5: Pattern of Revenue Expenditure — The Centre and States*

(*Rs. in Crores*)

Year	Heads of Expenditure	Non-Developmental Expenditure	Development Total	Expenditure of which Education	Others	Total
	1	2	3	4	5	6=(2+3+5)
1950-51	(a) Centre	334 (86.8)	36 (9.4)	32 (8.3)	15 (3.8)	385 (100.0)
	(b) States	188 (50.3)	182 (48.7)	58 (15.5)	4 (1.0)	374 (100.0)
	(c) Total (a+b)	522 (68.8)	218 (28.7)	90 (11.9)	19 (2.5)	759 (100.0)
1960-61	(a) Centre	596 (62.5)	240 (25.2)	44 (4.6)	117 (12.3)	953 (100.0)
	(b) States	439 (43.2)	566 (55.7)	195 (19.2)	11 (1.1)	1016 (100.0)
	(c) Total (a+b)	1035 (52.6)	806 (40.9)	239 (12.1)	128 (6.5)	1969 (100.0)

(*Contd.*)

TABLE 3.5 (*Contd.*)

	1	2	3	4	5	6=(2+3+5)
1970-71	(a) Centre	2179	814	102	160	3153
		(16.9)	(25.8)	(3.2)	(5.1)	(100.0)
	(b) States	1572	1887	797	26	3440
		(44.4)	(54.9)	(23.2)	(0.7)	(100.0)
	(c) Total	3706	2701	899	186	6593
	(a+b)	(56.2)	(41.0)	(13.6)	(2.8)	(100.0)
1980-81	(a) Centre	8424	4499	293	338	13261
		(63.5)	(33.9)	(2.2)	(2.6)	(100.0)
	(b) States	4699	9088	3143	349	14136
		(33.2)	(64.3)	(22.2)	(2.5)	(100.0)
	(c) Total	13123	13587	3436	687	27397
	(a+b)	(47.9)	(49.6)	(12.5)	(2.5)	(100.0)
1988-89	(a) Centre	32771	19971	1922	1365	54107
		(60.6)	(36.9)	(3.6)	(2.5)	(100.0)
	(b) States	18186	30357	10860	1048	49591
		(36.7)	(61.2)	(21.9)	(2.1)	(100.0)
	(c) Total	50957	50328	12782	2413	103698
	(a+b)	(49.2)	(48.5)	(12.3)	(2.3)	(100.0)

Note: Includes Union Territories

* Figures within parantheses indicate percentages

Source: *Indian Economic Statistics* (Public Finance), Ministry of finance, Govt. of India. December 1991.

It is worthwhile to note that of the total developmental expenditure, the share of education sector has been about 12 per cent since 1950-51. While the educational expenditure by the Centre has declined from 8.3 per cent of the total expenditure in 1950-51 to 3.2 per cent in 1988-89, the corresponding share of the States has increased from 15.5 per cent to 21.9 per cent in the respective years. Obviously, the educational efforts, as measured by the extent of expenditure, by the Centre has declined even though the task of promoting education is a joint responsibility of the Centre and the States especially since 1976 when education was included in the concurrent list of the Constitution.

An assessment of long-term growth rates reveals that the Government revenue buoyancy has generally been much lower than the expenditure buoyancy; as a result of which, there has generally been paucity of resources. Much of the expenditure incurred on various developmental and non-developmental programmes have, therefore, been met out of foreign loans and by printing additional currency notes. While the former has invariably increased the debt servicing liability, the latter approach of financing the economy, widely known as deficit financing, has largely been responsible for fueling the rise in prices of goods and services; which, in turn, has eroded the real value of expenditure that has been made for expediting the process of development. For instance, of the total outlays during the various five year plans, the contribution of external financial assistance has ranged between 12 to 15 per cent. Likewise, over the last one decade, the Central Government's deficits have tended to rise from 5 per cent of GDP in the beginning of Sixth Plan to 8.5 per cent in the Seventh Plan. In the recent past it has marginally declined to about 6 per cent of GDP which is attributable to the drastic changes in economic policy of the Government. The fiscal behaviour of most of the States is almost similar as they too meet their budgetary deficits through the provision of overdrafts. This, therefore, demonstrate that the fiscal crisis in the country has perpetuated and, therefore, some revolutionary steps have to be taken for augmenting adequate finances for educational development.

It follows that whenever there is paucity of resources, especially in the regime of competing claims on funds by various sectors of development, the poverty alleviation programmes duly get top priority over others as about 40 per cent of the Indian population falls below the poverty line. The services like education particularly at territory level and other welfare programmes obviously receive somewhat lower priority in the process of policy planning which is guided by a mix of socio-economic and political considerations especially because India has committed itself to adopt federal set up and democratic polity in all the decision-making processes. It emerges from the foregoing that the entire gamut of educational finances should be examined against the backdrop of overall fiscal scene in the country. Because, on the *a priori* it can be said that the availability of funds for the promotion of educational and training programmes depends on the strength and vitality of the fiscal system which, in turn, is dependent on the health of the country's economy. A comparison of the patterns of expenditure across various developed and developing countries duly prove the point. For instance, while the share of educational expenditure in the GNP for India compares favourably with the developing countries, this share is much lower when it is compared to the developed countries. Table 3.6 presents the relevant ratios for different developed and developing countries. Likewise, the proportion of educational expenditure to the total Government expenditure has generally been lower for developing countries as compared to the developed countries. In the context of resource allocation for the development of various socio-economic sectors of the country including the promotion of education and training, the availability of funds, it may be noted, is crucially dependent on the soundness of the fiscal system in general, and the economy, in particular.

To sum up this part of discussion, it may be reiterated that the determinants of education budget are more complex. The major factors which determine the availability of funds for education are (i) competing claims or demands of other public services like health and the requirements for alleviating nutritional poverty; (ii) the rate of growth of the national economy; (iii) the system and structure of taxation including various other forms of revenue collection; (iv) the elasticity and buoyancy of educational revenues; (v) the rate of inflation; and (vi) the extent of foreign assistance either to offset the resource deficiency of the country or to directly finance the educational programmes. The impact of all these factors are, however, reflected, as discussed above, in the overall performance of the economy and its ability to finance human development through programmes of HEIs. This ought to be borne in mind throughout the discussion on educational finances.

3.3. Financing Higher Education System: The Centre-States Partnership

In view of the perceived need to enrich human resources especially by way of promoting education and training, the network of educational facilities are planned such that equity in the provision of such facilities and efficiency in delivery of services are duly ensured for various sections of the society. As we know, with a view to pursuing the social and economic goals of the country within the Constitutional framework, India has adopted a mixed economic system whereby public sector has largely assumed the responsibility of providing infrastructural facilities, whereas the private sector is to concentrate more on the mainstream of economic activities such as manufacturing and production of goods and services. In this mixed system, like the other sphere of development, the private and public sectors participate

TABLE 3.6: Educational Expenditure in Different Countries: A Comparison

Sl. No.	Countries	As % of GNP			As % of Total Govt. Expenditure		
		1975	1986	1989	1975	1986	1989
1.	Argentina	2.5	1.8	1.5	8.5	7.5	8.0
2.	Australia	6.50	5.6	5.5	14.8	(12.6)	12.5
3.	Brazil	3.0	(4.6)	37+++	N.A.	(17.7)	N.A.
4.	Canada	7.6	7.4	7.0	17.8	15.5	15.3
5.	China	1.8	27*	2.4	4.2	N.A.	12.4
6.	Egypt	5.1	55*	6.8	9.4$	11.5*	N.A.
7.	France	5.2	6.1++	53+++	N.A.	18.5	N.A.
8.	Ghana	5.9	3.4	3.4	21.5	(24.3)	N.A.
9.	India	2.8	3.6*	3.2	8.6	9.4*	10.5
10.	Indonesia	2.7	2.0+	0.9	13.1	9.3+	4.3
11.	Italy	(4.1)	(5.0)	-	9.4	(8.3)	-
12.	Japan	5.5	(5.0)	48+++	22.4	(17.7)	16.2+++
13.	Kenya	6.3	6.4++	65+++	(19.4)	N.A.	27.0+++
14.	Korea	2.2	4.5	3.6	13.9	27.3	23.3
15.	Malaysia	6.0	7.8	5.6	19.3	(16.9)	-
16.	Mexico	3.8	(3.8*)	3.8	11.9	(13.2)	7.6+++
17.	Pakistan	2.2	(2)*	2.6	5.2	-5.0	-
18.	Philippines	1.9	1.3*	2.9	11.4	-7.0	-
19.	Spain	1.8	3.2	43+++	13.6	13.3	121+++
20.	Sri Lanka	2.8	3.5	30+++	10.1	9.4	7.8+++
21.	U.K.	6.7	5.2++	47+++	14.3	11.3++	-
22.	USA	7.4	6.8	6.8	(21.3)	(21.0)	-
23.	USSR	7.6	7.0*	7.9	12.9	(11.2)	-
24.	W. Germany	5.1	(4.4)	42+++	10.7	9.2	8.8

Source: Statistical Year Book 1991, UNESCO, Paris.

Note: * 1985, + 1981, ++1984, $1981, +++1988, ** 1987

in extending the educational services at almost all levels and areas of specialisations. The responsibility for making adequate provision for educational facilities, however, devolves mainly on the Government as even the private recognised institutions receive a considerably large proportion funds (about 55 per cent or so) from its different agencies. The maintenance of standards of education, however, falls under the domain of the Government. Further, the responsibility of providing education is shared by various federating units of the Government – the Centre, the States and the local bodies. Till 1976, education was included in the States list of the Constitution and, therefore, the States were largely responsible for the development of education while the Centre assumed a limited role in this regard. After the inclusion of education in the concurrent list of the Constitution, education has become a joint responsibility of the Centre and the States; and, therefore, both the levels of governments are equally responsible for expediting the process of educational development by way of extending infrastructural facilities, providing necessary finance, monitoring of programmes through mutual cooperation and coordination of educational activities and maintenance of the standards of education. The costs of education are, thus, largely borne by both levels of the Government – the Centre and the States – and partly by the individuals who benefit from education or buy education for their wards. As we shall examine below, the burden of financing education at all levels largely devolves on the States. Throughout the discussion in this study, it may be noted, we shall confine to Government expenditure on education as the private expenditure is out of purview of the study. Moreover, as the focus of our discussions would be on fiscal aspects of HEIs, we may describe the nature and types of HEIs and the methods of resource allocation for the promotion of higher education and research.

There are different types of HEIs. These include the Central, the State, Agricultural and 'deemed to be' universities and the Institutions of National Importance (INI). While the Central universities and the INIs are established by the Central government, the State and agricultural universities are established by the state governments. The institutions 'deemed to be' universities are given recognition under the Article 17 of the University Grants Commission Act 1956.

The universities and colleges are largely financed by the Central and the State Governments (about three-fourths) and the remaining portion is financed from fees, endowments and philanthropic contributions. The burden of financing higher education largely devolves on the States which contribute more than 80 per cent of the total expenditure. In addition, the Central Ministries like Agriculture, Industry and Human Resource Development, etc., directly extend financial assistance to HEIs which cater to their specific teaching and research requirements. The UGC which is mainly responsible for maintenance of standards of higher education and co-ordination of university activities provide funds for the maintenance and development of all the ten Central universities, all the 54 colleges of Union Territory of Delhi and ten of the 31 'deemed to be' universities also. The sources of finance of the later category of universities widely differ. There are those like Gujarat Vidyapith which are funded on the pattern of the Central universities which receive plan and non-plan grants from the UGC whereas some others are given almost the same treatment as State universities which receive non-plan grants from the States while the plan grants are shared on matching basis between the States and the UGC. There is still another category of 'deemed to be' universities like Jamia Hamdard which do not receive plan and non-plan grants from the Government as they are fully dependent on private sources of financing. The INIs are directly funded by the Department of Education of the Ministry of Human Resource Development. The States are responsible for meeting the entire non-plan expenditure of the institutions created by them while the UGC provides merely plan grants on matching basis to the State universities and colleges. As most of the institutions fall under the purview of the States, the finances for the development of higher education are largely provided by them from their own resources and partly from devolution of resources by the Centre through different channels of the Central Government especially the Planning and Finance Commissions. The Central and the State governments have thus entered into a meaningful partnership in providing financial sustenance to education system and their collective role determines the pace of development in the field of education. The pattern of plan and non-plan expenditure by the Centre and the States shall be discussed in Chapter 4.

A major portion of expenditure on universities (about 80 per cent) comprises of non-plan expenditure, which is fully borne by the States in respect of the institutions created by them while some universities are provided funds on incremental basis in the form of block grants mainly in the range of 5 to 7 per cent over the previous level of expenditure, others receive funds on deficit basis, in the case of which entire expenditure on approved items are fully provided by the States. The method of assessment of financial requirement and the level of funding differ a great deal across the universities. Moreover, as a measure of economy in expenditure, there have been frequent cuts to the extent of 5 to 10 per cent or so by both the Central and the State governments in the non-plan expenditure. The persistence of inflationary pressure further erodes the financial base of HEIs. Since education budget constitutes about one fifth of the overall States' budget and a large part of it is on account of non-plan expenditure, education sector including higher education obviously suffers a great deal. As a result, the ongoing programmes get hampered; affecting thereby, the quality and relevance of education. In view of this, the question of resource allocation for higher education is a vital issue which we seek to examine in the following analysis.

3.3.1 *Sources of Income of Educational System*

An examination of sources of finance, reveal that educational programmes of all types and levels are largely financed by the Government – the Centre and the States. In 1950-51, 68.0 per cent of the entire educational expenditure was met by the Government including local bodies which contributed 10.9 per cent while the remaining proportion was financed by the incomes from fees (20.4 per cent), endowments and others (11.6 per cent) (Table 3.7). Over the successive years, the Government contribution has gradually increased to about 87 per cent of the total expenditure in 1983-84. Obviously, in financing education, the relative importance of such sources of income as fees, endowments and donations, and other community resources have declined. The break up for the Centre and the States shows that roughly about 90 per cent of the Government funds is provided by the States which is attributable to the arrangements as envisaged in the Constitution of India about the sharing of responsibilities between the two levels of Governments for planning and management of education. After the inclusion of education in the Concurrent List of the Constitution, the financial contribution of the Centre has marginally increased especially for the promotion of such programmes as vocational, technical and elementary education particularly in the backward States.

TABLE 3.7: Educational Expenditure in India by Source

(*Percentage*)

Years	Govt. Funds	Local Body	University Funds	Fees	Endowment & Other Sources	Total
1950-51	57.1	10.9	-	20.4	11.6	100.0
1960-61	68.0	6.5	-	17.1	8.4	100.0
1970-71	76.2	3.6	1.4	12.9	5.9	100.0
1979-80	80.8	5.0	1.3	8.7	4.2	100.0
1980-81	81.7	4.7	1.4	8.2	4.0	100.0
1981-82	81.3	5.1	1.6	8.0	4.1	100.0
1982-83	81.3	5.4	1.7	7.7	4.0	100.0
1983-84	81.5	5.6	1.6	7.5	3.8	100.0

Note: Latest published data

Source: Computed on the basis of data collected from *Education in India* Vol.II (various issues), Ministry of Human Resource Development, Government of India, New Delhi, 1987.

3.3.2 *Sources of Income of Higher Education Institutions : A Disagregative Analysis*

As regards higher education finances, the relative financial dependence of HEIs on the Government shows a great deal of variation. On an average, they receive more than 70 per cent of their total incomes from the Governmental sources (Table 3.8). Though there are differences in the extent of funding by the Central and the State Governments to the HEIs under their purview, the Central universities which are largely funded by the UGC, an agency of the Centre, receive a higher proportion of their incomes as compared to the universities funded by the States. Moreover, the Government share in the total income of universities show a rising trend over the period 1975-85. Tables 3.9, 3.10 and Table 3.11 indicate the patterns of incomes of various Central, 'deemed to be' as well as the State universities. For the year 1985-86, the data demonstrate that as high as 90,75 and 60 per cent of the total incomes, respectively, accrued to the above category of universities from the Government sources – the Centre and the States.

There are wide variations in the extent of funding of HEIs by the agencies of the Centre and the States. Whereas the co-efficient of variations (CV) for the year 1985-86 has been merely 10.3 per cent for the Central universities, the same was 42.6 per cent and 94.1 per cent, respectively, for the institutions 'deemed to be' and the state universities. The inequity in funding is attributable to the lack of uniformity or objectivity in assessing the resource requirements of the universities by the UGC and the States. The CVs in respect of other sources of income are generally high, thereby indicating differences in the efforts and abilities of the universities to raise funds from tuition fees, donations and endowments and other user's charges like hostel, examination fees, etc. In 1985-86, for instance, the Central universities, on an average, mobilised only 5.9 per cent of the total income from fees whereas the 'deemed to be' universities and the State universities raised 12.3 and 30.0 per cent respectively. The revenue from this source has, however, declined in varying proportions over the period 1975 to 1986 for both the Central and the State universities as may be observed from Tables referred to above. In brief, the evidences indicate the following:

(i) While the universities are largely dependent on the Government support for financing their programmes, the Central universities are relatively more dependent than other types of institutions of higher learning. The financial dependence in respect of all types of institutions has tended to rise over the past decade.

(ii) Inter-university differences in allocation of funds by the UGC are much higher in respect of the State and 'deemed to be' universities whereas the same are very low for the Central universities. The UGC has seemingly not tried to evolve an acceptable method of resource allocation whereby the institutions under its purview could be treated equitably in respects of comparable programmes of teaching, research and training.

(iii) The extent of funds mobilised by different types of universities from non-government sources indicate large variations. And in this respect, the State universities are able to augment relatively more funds from non-government sources, such as, fees, endowments, etc., than other types of institutions. Obviously, higher education in Central universities is relatively more subsidised than others. It has also been observed that most of the State universities mainly of affiliating type, are able to generate resources from activities like conduct of examinations. Similarly, the conventional universities offering distance education programmes are also able to raise considerable amount of funds through various charges from distance learners. The amount thus raised are utilized for meeting the maintenance expenditure of universities.

(iv) The share of income from tuition fees and utility charges on account of lab, hostel, examination, etc., has generally declined; thereby indicating the lack of concerted efforts to augment resources from the beneficiary groups of higher education.

(v) In financing higher education, the contributions of the Centre have declined from 31 per cent in 1970-71 to 24 per cent in 1983-84 even though education has been included in the Concurrent List of the Constitution. In respect of technical higher education, its share has, however marginally increased to 38 per cent in 1984-85 as against 35 per cent in 1970-71. In all, at least three-fourths of financial burden of meeting the requirements of universities and other higher education falls on the State Governments, which also means that health and vitality of higher education in India is heavily dependent on fiscal capacity of the States as well as their perception about the relative role of higher education in promoting economic and social development.

TABLE 3.8: Recurring Income of Universities in India by Source

Year	Central Govt.	State Govt.	U.G.C.	Universities	Local Board	Fees	Endowments	Other Sources	Total
1976-77	5.1	48.2	13.9	6.1	1.2	15.0	0.8	9.7	100.0
1977-78	5.7	46.5	18.3	4.8	2.0	14.0	0.8	7.9	100.0
1978-79	4.4	47.9	17.7	2.8	0.1	15.9	0.5	10.7	100.0
1979-80	3.4	47.0	19.8	3.4	0.1	16.5	0.4	9.4	100.0
1980-81	7.8	44.7	20.2	4.2	0.1	14.3	0.5	8.2	100.0
1981-82	8.5	45.9	13.7	7.5	0.4	14.2	0.6	9.2	100.0
1982-83	7.5	46.8	14.2	7.9	0.3	14.2	0.3	8.8	100.0
1983-84	9.1	46.6	15.1	7.3	0.1	13.5	0.3	8.0	100.0

Source: Computed on the basis of data available in the various issues of Education in India, Ministry of Human Resource Development, Government of India.

TABLE 3.9: Pattern of Recurring Income in Selected Central Universities 1985-86

Universities	Central Govt.	U.G.C.	State Govt.	Local Boards	Fees (including Lab.Hostel Exam. etc.)	Endowments	Other Sources	Total Income
Hyderabad	N.A.	95.7	-	-	1.9	-	2.4	100.0
N.E. Hill	-	95.3	-	-	4.4	0.3	-	100.0
		(74.0)			(17.9)	(5.6)	(2.6)	(100.0)
Aligarh	0.3	92.7	0.7	-	1.9	0.3	4.1	100.0
	-	(95.8)		(0.1)	(3.4)	(0.3)	-	(100.0)
Banaras	-	83.6	-	-	1.2	0.3	14.9	100.0
	(4.3)	(81.5)	(1.0)		(5.9)	(0.1)	(7.2)	(100.0)
Visva Bharati	-	75.9	0.2	-	19.9	4.0	-	100.0
		(75.3)	(0.3)		(10.0)	-	(14.4)	(100.0)
Delhi	-	89.0	-	-	11.0	-	-	100.0
	(78.1)				(20.1)	(1.2)	(0.6)	(100.0)
J. Nehru	-	94.8	-	-	1.1	-	4.1	100.0
	(0.1)	(93.6)	-	-	(6.3)			(100.0)
Average	-	89.5	0.1	-	5.9	0.7	3.6	-
	(0.7)	(83.1)	(0.2)		(10.6)	(1.2)	(4.1)	
Coefficient of	-	7.7	200.0	-	111.9	200.0	136.1	-
Variation	(228.6)	(10.3)	(200.0)		(59.4)	(166.71)	(126.8)	

Note: Figures in paranthesis pertain to 1975-76

@ For the reasons of comparability of data, new universities like Pondicherry University and IGNOU have been excluded.

Source: Computed on the basis of data compiled by the University Grants Commission, New Delhi.

TABLE 3.10: Pattern of Recurring Income in Selected Institutions Deemed to be Universities 1985-86

(*In percentage*)

Deemed Universities	Central Govt.	U.G.C.	State Govt.	Local Boards	Fees (Including Lab, Hostel exam. etc.)	Endlwments	Other Sources	Total Income
C.I.E.F.L.	-	88.3	-	-	5.4	-	6.3	100.0
		(85.7)			(4.7)		(9.6)	(100.0)
School of Mines	-	88.5	-	-	11.5	-	-	100.0
		(32.9)	(58.3)		(3.0)		(5.8)	(100.0)
Gujarat Vidyapeeth	-	90.2	4.9	-	2.0	-	2.9	100.0
		(74.5)	(18.5)		(7.5)			(100.0)
Tata Instt. of	-	91.6	1.1	2.1	1.8	-	3.4	100.0
Social Sciences		(74.5)	(4.9)		(5.8)		(14.8)	(100.0)
B.I.T.S.	-	0.3	-	-	55.2	44.5	-	100.0
					(14.2)	(82.2)	(3.6)	(100.0)
Gurukul Kangri	-	96.9	-	-	3.0	-	0.1	100.0
		(93.4)	(0.2)		(5.2)	(0.8)	(0.4)	(100.0)
Jamia Millia	222.3	65.5	-	0.2	7.1	-	4.9	100.0
Islamia		(94.7)	(0.1)		(3.7)		(1.6)	(100.0)
Average	3.2	74.5	0.9	0.7	12.3	6.4	2.5	-
		(65.1)	(11.6)		(6.3)	(11.9)	(5.1)	
Coefficient of	243.8	42.6	188.9	100.0	144.7	243.8	96.0	-
Variation	-	(50.4)	(172.4)	-	55.6	(241.2)	(98.0)	

Note: Figures in paranthesis pertain to 1975-76

S[illegible] As in Table 3.7

TABLE 3.11 Pattern of Recurring Income in Selected Teaching and Affiliating Universities 1985-86

(In percentage)

Universities	Central Govt.	U.G.C.	State Govt.	Local Boards	Fees (Including Labs Hostel, Exam. Etc.)	Endowment	Other Sources	Total
	1	2	3	4	5	6	7	8
Andhra	-	-	68.7	-	17.6	0.2	13.5	100.0
			(54.6)		(44.5)	(0.1)	(0.8)	(100.0)
Gauhati	0.3	0.7	59.4	-	28.2	-	11.4	100.0
	-	-	(52.0)		(33.0)		(15.0)	(100.0)
Sardar Patel	-	5.5	79.0	-	7.9	0.6	7.0	100.0
	(0.1)	(2.4)	(61.1)		(25.9)	(2.5)	(8.0)	(100.0)
Kurukshetra	0.1	6.2	67.5	-	14.6	0.2	11.4	100.0
	(0.1)	(3.8)	(40.7)		(52.5)	(0.4)	(2.5)	(100.0)
Karnatak	-	-	77.0	-	13.5	-	9.5	100.0
		(6.9)	(58.8)	-	(26.7)		(7.6)	(100.0)
Kerala	-	4.8	47.3	-	39.7	0.9	7.3	100.0
	(1.2)	(0.5)	(31.8)		(58.7)		(7.8)	(100.0)
Dr. H.S. Gaur	-	9.7	44.6	6.1	39.6	-	-	100.0
			(31.9)	-	(56.4)	(4.0)	(7.7)	(100.0)
Vikram	-	-	55.7	-	39.3	-	5.0	100.0
		(0.1)	(36.9)		(50.0)		(13.0)	(100.0)
Bombay	0.1	5.6	30.5	-	46.4	7.7	9.7	100.0
		(1.0)	(30.9)		(60.9)	(2.9)	(4.3)	(100.0)

(Contd.)

TABLE 3.11 (*Contd.*)

Universities	Central Govt.	U.G.C.	State Govt.	Local Boards	Fees (Including Labs Hostel, Exam. Etc.)	Endowment	Other Sources	Total
	1	2	3	4	5	6	7	8
Poona	-	1.5 (3.8)	41.8 (30.8)		53.0 (52.2)	3.7	- (13.2)	100.0 (100.0)
Average	0.1 (0.1)	3.4 (1.9)	57.2 (43.0)	0.6 -	30.0 (46.1)	1.3 (1.0)	7.5 (8.0)	
Coefficient of Variation	100.0 (400.0)	94.1 (115.8)	26.6 (27.2)	300.0 -	49.7 (26.9)	184.6 (150.0)	58.7 (55.0)	

TABLE 3.12: Distribution of Universities According to the Status of Budget i.e. Deficit/Surplus/Balance Budget During the Period of 1984-89

Type of Universities	Deficit/Surplus/ Balance Budget Budget	Number of Universities 1984-85	1985-86	1986-87	1987-88	1988-89	Total for ** five years
Central Universities (7)	Deficit	4	4	2	4	4	3
	Surplus	3	3	5	3	3	4
	Balance	NIL	NIL	NIL	NIL	NIL	NIL
State Universities (49)	Deficit	31	24	29	29	25	30
	Surplus	17	25	19	20	24	19
	Balance	1	NIL	NIL	NIL	NIL	NIL
Agricultural Universities (16)	Deficit	10	5	7	8	8	8
	Surplus	5	11	9	8	8	8
	Balance	1	NIL	NIL	NIL	NIL	NIL
Deemed to be Universities (8)	Deficit	5	4	6	6	4	4
	Surplus	1	2	2	2	3	4
	Balance	2	2	NIL	NIL	1	NIL
Total All Universities (80)	Deficit	50	37	44	47	42	45
	Surplus	26	41	35	33	37	35
	Balance	4	2	1	NIL	1	NIL

Note: * Figures below the type of universities indicate the number of responding universities in the respective groups.

** Computed on the basis of aggregate income and expenditure for five year.

Source: Adopted from 'Financial Deficit in Universities', AIU, 1991, P.9.

TABLE 3.13: Magnitude of Deficit/Surplus as Proportion of the Total Expenditure in Five Years 1984-88

Sl. No.	Ranges of Deficit/Surplus, as Proportion of of Total Exp.(%)	Number of Universities									
		Central		State Agriculture			Deemed		Total		
		Deficit	Surplus	Deficit-Surplus	Deficit	Deficit	Surplus	Deficit	Surplus	Deficit	Surplus
(1)	(2)	(3)	(4)	(5)	(6)	(7)	(8)	(9)	(10)	(11)	(12)
1.	0-1.9	1	1	3	6	3	3	1	3	8	13
2.	2-4.9	2	3	15	3	2	4	1	1	20	11
3.	5-9.9	--	--	5	7	2	--	--	--	7	7
4.	10>	--	--	7	3	1	1	2	--	10	4
	Total	3	4	30	19	8	8	4	4	45	35

Source: Adopted from 'Financial Deficit in Universities', AIU, 1991, p.9.

3.4 Concluding Observations

In spite of the substantial contributions which the Central and the State governments are making towards the financing of higher education and research, the finances of universities and colleges are inadequate as they have not increased commensurate with the rise in enrolment, rate of inflation and increased requirements for modernisation and diversification of tertiary education. The absence of valid criteria or scientific norms is the main reason for underestimation resource requirements. The existing arrangements under which the Centre and the State are financing universities have quite often given rise to diverse and dilutory practices and procedures between the two levels of governments, so much so that the attention of the government's gets diverted from ensuring a sound financial base for HEIs. The fact that development schemes of a majority of the State universities are financed on matching basis by the UGC and the States, and the implementation of most of the schemes suffer because of the lack of adequate support from the States. The States do not provide matching shares because of either paucity of resources or low priority for general higher education or the fear of impending financial burden which devolves on the States after the plan period is over. Also, a number of State universities are observed to have been resorting to financial and accounting gimmick whereby the plan outlays are being utilized for non-plan purposes, mainly the payment of salaries to the teaching and non-teaching staff. Thus, the developmental activities pertaining to the relevance and quality of educational and training schemes get hampered.

As pointed out above, the main source of distortion in the allocation of funds is lack of objectivity in determination of requirements of HEIs.[4] An analysis of budgetary positions of 80 universities for the last 5 years has revealed that as many as 45 universities suffered from deficits while 35 of them experienced surpluses. As many as 78 of these 80 universities had deficit budgets for varying years during the periods of analysis (Table 3.12); and at least 10 universities suffered from perpetual deficit for all the five years.[5] The magnitude of deficits also varied a great deal across the universities (Table 3.13). Of the 45 universities, as many as 20 of them had deficits between 2 to 5 per cent of the total expenditure. The second highest (10) universities recorded more than 10 per cent deficits. Likewise, out of 35 universities having surpluses, 13 of them emerged with surpluses of less than 2 per cent of the total expenditure whereas 4 universities had surpluses of more than

10 per cent of the total expenditure. In the ranges of 2 to 5 per cent and 5 to 10 per cent of surpluses, there were 11 and 7 universities, respectively. These evidences demonstrate the lack of planning and management of financial resources either by the funding agencies or by the universities themselves. This, therefore, calls for modification in the existing mechanisms of distribution of funds while taking duly into account the aspects of utilization of funds by HEIs. In the following Chapter 4, an attempt is made to make a thorough analysis of the patterns of expenditures on higher education.

REFERENCES

1. Psacharopoulos, G. (1981) 'Returns to Education: An updated International Comparison', *Comparative Education,* vol.17, No.3.
2. Gupta, S. (1987) Indian Plans: Retrospects and Prospects, *The Indian Economic Journal,* Vol. 34, No.4, pp. 89.
3. Gupta, S. *ibid.*
4. *Financial Deficits in Universities*, AIU, 1991.
5. *Financial Deficits. . . , ibid.*

4

GROWTH OF EXPENDITURE ON HIGHER EDUCATION

An Analysis of the Pattern of Utilization of Funds

This chapter seeks to discern the trend in growth of expenditure as well as to examine the pattern of utilisation of funds especially in the context of universities. The study of pattern of growth of educational expenditure and its composition lend desirable perspective for designing appropriate policy for allocation of resources for various educational purposes. Such analyses assist in identifying the areas which either suffer from deficiency in resources and, thus, impinge upon the qualitative and quantitative development of educational programmes or require close scrutiny with a view to ensuring efficiency in the use of resources or minimising diseconomies. Therefore, an attempt is made below to delineate the trend in growth of educational expenditure in general, and the expenditure on higher education in particular. The analysis would be carried out at aggregated as well as disaggregated levels. In the first instance, the data at all India level as well as State-wise would be examined and, subsequently, the spending behaviour of different HEIs would be studied in detail. The relevant comparisons in respect of expenditure on comparable programmes would also be made so as to gauge the performance of one institution against the other especially in respect of fiscal prudence observed by them.

4.1 Determinants of Educational Expenditure

A number of factors are attributable to the growth of educational expenditure. The identification of such factors and the quantification of the extent to which each of them exert pressure on budgetary outlays are crucial to the tasks of planning and management of education system. The most important determinants of expenditure may be broadly classified into two categories, viz. exogeneous and endogeneous.

4.1.1 *Exogeneous Factors*

The major exogeneous factors are: (i) the growth of educational demand ; and (ii) the market forces influenced by the general economic conditions under which various educational inputs are purchased by the institutions. These factors lie outside the education system and are, therefore, beyond the control of educational planners and decision-makers. The cause and effect process in respects of these external factors may be briefly described below.

(i) *Educational Demand*

The increase in population pressure and widening base of elementary and secondary education due to the national policy of democratising education have led to significant increase in demand for education at all levels and types of education. The growing realization among the people about the role of education in raising the social status and improving the quality of life have spurt the demand further. The increasing trend in educational demand is most likely to continue and even escalate further in the future as each generation of parents want their children to have more education that they had and the manpower requirements of the economy in all the categories are rising due to various factors including technology induced economic growth. Thus, the pressure of educational demand is the single important factor responsible for the growth of educational expenditure. An idea of extent of increase in educational parameters has already been provided in Chapter 2.

(ii) *Market Forces*

The education sector operates within the overall frame of the national economy and is, therefore, exposed to the general market conditions in which much of what is used as educational inputs are acquired by paying a price at the market rates. The HEIs programmes of teaching and research which results in production of skilled manpower, trained graduates and research services are, however, not sold at market prices due to the policy of regulation of educational services. As a result, HEIs are unable to recover the full costs from their outputs. Even though such factors, as above, are duly taken into account while determining budgetary allocations by the Government, the fluctuations in prices of inputs like stationery, furniture, consumable items, construction materials, etc., greatly influence the growth of expenditure. Also, the revision in salaries and wages of teaching and non-teaching staff due to general shift in economic structure or market forces have significant bearing on educational expenditure.

4.1.2 *Endogeneous Factors*

Of the various factors that are internal to the system and are responsible for determining the size of expenditure are: (i) the nature and the extent of use of educational technologies; (ii) structure and level of salaries of teaching and supporting staff; (iii) the degree of wastage and stagnation i.e. the rates of drop out and repeaters; and (iv) the extent of utilization of infrastructural facilities. All these factors are influenced by the forces that are within the control of the education system and have significant bearing on the growth of expenditure. The nature of impact of these factors on the budgetary outlays may be briefly described below.

(i) *Educational Technologies*

Education system is largely labour intensive sector as more than two-thirds of education budget is accounted for by the salaries and wages of teaching and non-teaching staff. HEIs are somewhat less labour intensive as compared to other lower levels of education. Whereas salaries and wages account for more than 90 per cent of the total expenses at lower levels, the corresponding shares for post-secondary education at colleges and university levels are 75 and 60 per cent respectively. In marked contrast to other sectors of development such as agriculture, manufacturing, transportation, communication and health, whose technologies have made spectacular advances in the recent times, the technologies of education system have not changed significantly; and, they, therefore, remain largely labour intensive. The system has, therefore, not taken advantage of the advances in technologies for reducing the costs of education or for improving the quality of education. Due to the large share of salaries in the total educational expenditure and general upward revision of salaries from time to time and its indexation with the rise in prices, the use of traditional labour intensive technologies escalate the budgetary costs of education.

(ii) *Salary Structure of Teaching and Non-teaching Staff*

Expenditures on account of salaries and wages are rising due to both automatic increase in salaries on the basis of number of years of service and other pressures mounted from time to time by the organisation of teaching and non-teaching staff. Even though most staff of the universities perform comparable level and nature of services, they are at different levels and in different scales of pay. This is evident from the lack of uniformity in the ratio of Professors to Readers to Lectures in various teaching departments of universities. There are those university departments where the majority of teachers are at the Professor level whereas as in some others they are at Reader level. Similarly, in a large number of HEIs expenditure on the salaries of non-teaching staff is more than the expenditures on salary of teaching staff. This, therefore, reveal that *ad hoc* method of recruitment and promotional policy in respect of both teaching and non-teaching staff, generally escalate the volume of expenditure.

(iii) *Wastage and Stagnation*

Most educational systems especially in developing countries like India are characterised by high dropout and repeater rates. These rates denote wastages of resources. Such wastages vary across the institutions, levels and areas of studies as well as regions. Higher drop out rate constitute the loss of resources while the higher repeater rate increases the actual time and resources consumed for completing the specific programme within the stipulated period. As pointed out in Chapter 2, of the total number of students in higher education merely 60 per cent pass out and those who do so merely 25 per cent or so score more than 50 per cent marks. This, therefore, reduces the cost effectiveness of education and increases the actual costs of higher education per completer. In effect, thus, high dropout and repeater rates increase the costs of education, hence, the budgetary requirements.

(iv) *Facility Utilization Rates*

Cost-effectiveness of educational programmes and the unit costs per student are also substantially influenced by the rates of utilization of infrastructure facilities. A study by the author revealed for the selected number of HEIs that rates of utilization of facilities like class rooms, laboratories and libraries were merely about 60 per cent of the total capacity. It also emerged that for one teacher there were 3 to 5 non-teaching supporting staff which indicated a high proportion of non-academic expenditure. Moreover, the effective teaching hours are estimated to be much less than that stipulated by the UGC. The degree of utilization of facilities is thus a major factor influencing the expenditure on education.

In the following discussions, an attempt is made to examine the extent to which various factors are responsible for the growth of expenditure at the national, states and institutional levels. The impact of various factors discussed above would be duly reflected in the following analyses, though at this stage no attempt is made to carry out decomposition analysis to separate out the influence of each of the above factors.

4.1.3 *Long-term Growth Rates*

Using the semi-log function with respect to time, the growth rates of educational expenditure by the two levels of Governments – the Central and the States - were estimated for the period 1970-71 to 1984-85.

The following type of equation was filled to the data:

$$\text{Log E} = \text{Log a+bT} \text{ ....} \quad (1)$$

where:

E = Educational Expenditure

T = Time; and

b = Regression coefficient which indicate annual average growth rate.

The results showed that the rates of growth in expenditure by both the levels of governments on education as a whole as well as higher education were generally higher as compared to the growth rate of national income. Table 4.1 presents the relevant growth rates. It may be observed that during the above period, national income rose at the rate of 5 per cent per annum while the educational expenditure grow at the rate of 6.3 per cent per annum. A breakup of expenditure for the

Central and the State Governments indicated that the expenditure by the former rose marginally above (7 per cent) the rate of the latter (6.2 per cent). The total expenditure on higher education grew at the rate of 6.7 per cent per annum. The corresponding rates for the centre and States separately emerged out to be 5.2 and 7.1 per cent per annum, respectively.

TABLE 4.1: Annual Average Growth Rates of Different Indicators of Educational Expenditure, 1970-71 to 1984-85

Variables	Annual Average Growth Rates
1. Gross National Product at Current Prices	5.0
2. Gross National Product at Constant (1970-71) Prices	1.7
3. Wholesale Price Index	3.7
4. Total Expenditure on Education by All Departments — Centre, States & Union Territories	6.3
5. Total Expenditure on Education by all Departments — Central Government	7.0
6. Total Expenditure on Education by all Departments — States & Union Territories	6.2
7. Total Expenditure on Univ. & other Higher Education — (Non-technical) by Education Departments — Centre + State & Union Territories	6.7
8. Total Expenditure on Univ. & other Higher Education (non-technical) by Education Departments — Central Government	5.2
9. Total Expenditure on University & other Higher Education (Non-technical) by Education Departments — States & Union Territories	7.1

Note: Growth rates were estimated using by semi-log function of the type Log $(Y) = a + bt$; where Y = Values of the respective variables; and t = time.

Source: (i) *Economic Survey* 1986-87, Ministry of Finance, Govt. of India.
(ii) *Analysis of Budgeted Expenditure on Education in India.* (Various issues) Ministry of Human Resource Development, Govt. of India.

Thus, the rates of growth of expenditure by the Centre and the States at the different levels of education have generally been higher than the rate of increase in income.

4.1.4 *Income Elasticity of Expenditure*

As the educational expenditure is largely financed out of the national income, an attempt was made to establish relationship between these two factors by employing the functional form of the following type:

$$\text{Log } E = \text{Log } a + b \log y \; \ldots\ldots\ldots\ldots \qquad (2)$$

where:

E, a, b are as before and *y* is income i.e. GNP

A long term trend in the allocation of financial resources for the development of education revealed that the increase in educational expenditure was more than proportionate as compared to the growth in national income. The econometric results for a period of 15 years beginning from 1970-71 demonstrated that, on an average, 4.7 per cent of Gross National Product (GNP) was spent on education; and, the coefficient of income elasticity of expenditure emerged out to be 1.25 which may be interpreted to mean that one per cent increase in GNP led to an increase of 1.25 per cent in educational expenditure; thereby indicating more than proportionate increase in expenditure (Table 4.2, equation-1). In other words, the growth in educational expenditure due to the corresponding increase in national income for the above period was more than proportionate which demonstrated that, given the income constraint, allocation of funds to education sector vis-a-vis other sectors of economy was duly high.

On the *a priori* grounds it may be argued that the national income is the major indicator of a country's ability to finance *inter-alia* its educational system and, therefore, it should be treated as a major determining factor to finance education. The phenomenon of rise in prices, however, reduce the real value of expenditure on education. Thus, while the income variable is expected to exert positive influence on the magnitude of allocation of funds for education, the impact of inflation on such allocation may be negative to cause reduction in the real value of money. In view of this, an attempt was made to study the strength and degree of relationship between educational expenditure, on the one hand, and national income as well as rises in price on the other. The following type of functional form was fitted to the data :

$$\text{Log } E = \text{Log } a + \text{Log } y + C \text{ Log } Y \text{def} \quad ....(3)$$

where:
Y def is income deflator and C is regression coefficient, *E, Y, A,* and *b* are as before.

The estimates of econometric results emerged out to be very interesting and lend a sound perspective on the following aspects: (i) the strength of relationship between expenditure, income and inflation, and (ii) the extent of automatic response by the Indian economy to meet the challenge of education by way of meeting its expenditure requirements. The results of our various exercises pertaining to different types and levels of expenditure are presented in Table 4.2. The results for other levels are interpreted and discussed below.

As judged from the goodness of the fit of above econometric formulation, the results demonstrate that the two explanationary variables namely income and index of inflation are able to explain considerable variations in the growth of educational expenditure and have thus emerged out to be major determinants of expenditure which is consistent with our *a priori* reasoning. As expected, while income variable has strong and positive impact on expenditure, the index of rise in prices namely GNP deflator in negatively associated, meaning thereby reduction in the real value of expenditure due to inflationary pressure. It is, however, interesting to note that almost all the formulations demonstrate that even though inflationary conditions have had adverse effect on the growth of expenditure, the increase in real terms have generally been above unity or more than the rate of increase required for off-setting the negative impact of prices.

The relevant coefficients with respect to higher education demonstrated as under:

The income elasticity of expenditure on higher education emerged out to be above unity; thereby indicating more than proportionate increase in expenditure due to rise in income. Over the period under study, one per cent increase in income induced the growth in expenditure by 1.32 per cent per annum (equation-7). When an attempt was made to decompose this coefficient to show the break up for the Centre and the states separately, the relevant income elasticity coefficients emerged out to be higher for the States (1.40) (equation-11) as compared to the Centre (1.03) (equation-9); thereby indicating a relatively higher efforts by the former in promoting tertiary education.

TABLE 4.2: Determinants of Educational Expenditure : A Time Series Analysis, 1970-84

Educational Expenditure by Various Types and Levels	Intercept	Gross national	GNP Products (GNP) at current prices	R Deflator
	1	2	3	4
1. Total Govt. (Centre + States & U.Ts.) Exp. on Education by all Deptts.	-2.6976	1.2549 (42.7855)	-	0.9930
2. - do -	-4.9799	1.7611 * (6.4415)	-0.7578 (1.8605)	0.9945
3. Total Govt. (Centre) Exp. on Education by all Deptts.	-4.3643	1.3785 * (23.2617)	- -	0.9765
4. - do -	-7.2665	2.0223 * (3.3789)	-0.9637 (1.0809)	0.9786
5. Total Govt. (States & U.Ts) Exp. on Education by all Deptts.	-2.6658	1.2402 * (44.9348)	-	0.9936
6. - do -	-4.8288	1.7199 * (6.6974)	-0.7181 (-1.8774)	0.9950
7. Total Govt. (Centre+States & U.Ts) Exp. on Univ. and Other Higher Education (Non-technical) by Edn. Deptts.	-3.9094 -	1.3150 * (27.0576)	-	0.9826
8. - do -	-7.3909	2.0873 * (4.5102)	-1.1560 (1.6766)	0.9850
9. Total Govt. (Centre) Exp. on University & Other Higher Education (Non-technical) by all Edn. Deptts.	-3.1673	1.0313 * (14.6284)	-	0.9427

(*Contd.*)

TABLE 4.2 (*Contd.*)

	1	2	3	4
10. - do -	-9.9632	2.5388 * (4.1978)	-2.2567 (2.5049)	0.9624
11. Total Govt. (States & U.Ts) Exp. on Univ. & Other Higher Education (Non-technical) by Edn. Deptts.	-4.4262	1.3968 * (34.3194)	-	0.9891
12. - do -	-6.6005	1.8792 * (4.6081)	-0.7220 (1.1885)	0.9902

Note:(i) The figures used in regression equations are in crores of rupees.
(ii) Figures within parenthesis indicate respective T-values.
(iii) à E = Educational Expenditures of various types and levels.
Y = Gross National Product at Current Prices.
Y Def. = G N P Deflator
(iv) * = The results are significant at 1 per cent level.

Source: (a) *Economic Survey 1986-87*, Ministry of Finance, Government of India.
(b) *Analysis of Budgeted Expenditure on Education* (various issues) Ministry of Human Resource Development, Government of India.

(Results for Log Linear Function of the type :
1. Log E = Log a + b Log Y
2. Log E = Log a + b Log Y + c Log Y def.) à

Interestingly, the elasticity co-efficient for higher education (1.32) emerged out to be marginally higher as compared to the corresponding figure for the entire expenditure on education (i.e. 1.25). On an average, 0.57 per cent of GNP was spent on higher education during the above period as against 4.7 per cent for the entire education system. As may be expected, the increase in national income is the major determining factor of the growth in educational expenditure including higher education which has duly risen at a higher rate as compared to income

4.1.5 *Impact of Prices*

As pointed out before, the phenomenon of rise in prices increases the nominal value of expenditure but it reduces the real value. In order to get an idea of the impact of rise in prices, income deflator was incorporated as an additional explanatory variable in the econometric function characterising the relationship between income and educational expenditure. The results showed that the rise in prices has tended to reduce the value of the total expenditure in real terms.

Table 4.2 reveals that while one per cent increase in GNP led to rise in expenditure by 2.09 per cent, the rise in prices reduced it by more than the proportionate rate of 1.16 per cent. Thus, the real value of expenditure got adversely affected (equation-8). In other words, the growth in expenditure on higher education due to one per cent increase in real income was less than unity. But, the *t* - statistics of 1.67 being less than normal (2.0) reduces the statistical reliability of the above price coefficient.

A decomposition analysis of expenditure for the Centre and the States showed that the impact of prices on the expenditure was much higher in the Central sector than the States as, after netting out the effects of prices, the growth of expenditure in real terms emerged out to be above unity for the latter and below unity for the former. It therefore, recommends adoption of a set of suitable measures so as to nullify the influence of the rise in prices on expenditure.

4.2 **Inter-State Variations in Educational Efforts**

As the macro-level aggregates hide a number of characteristics especially relating to the extent of variations in the magnitude of educational expenditure, an attempt was made to work out the relevant ratios, for various states for the year 1970-71 and 1984-85. The results are presented in Table 4.3.

TABLE 4.3: Share of Educational Expenditure in Income and the Gross Expenditure by States

(*In Percentage*)

States	Total Exp. on Edn. by all Deptts. as percentage of Net Domestice Product		Total Exp. on Univ. & other Higher Edn. (including Tech. Edn.) by Edn. Deptts. as percentage of Net Domestic Product		Total Exp. on Univ. & Other Higher Edn. (including Tech Edn.) by Edn. Deptts. as percentage of Total Exp. on Edn. by all Deptts.	
	1970-71	1984-85	1970-71	1984-85	1970-71	1984-85
Andhra Pradesh	2.8	5.2	0.4	0.9	14.6	17.4
Assam	3.6	4.8	0.4	0.4	12.3	9.2
Bihar	2.3	4.2	0.3	0.5	12.1	11.0
Gujarat	2.2	4.3	0.2	0.5	11.0	10.5
Haryana	2.2	3.7	0.3	0.4	14.7	11.8
H.P.	1.8	7.0	0.1	0.7	4.9	9.5
J & K	3.9	5.8	0.8	N.A.	19.4	N.A.
Karnataka	3.1	4.6	0.4	0.8	12.0	17.9
Kerala	5.2	6.5	0.6	1.0	10.0	15.6
M.P.	3.0	4.0	0.4	0.5	12.1	11.3
Maharashtra	2.7	3.8	0.3	0.5	10.4	12.8
Manipur	11.4	10.2	0.7	1.4	6.4	14.3
Meghalaya	N.A.	N.A.	N.A.	N.A.	N.A.	N.A.
Nagaland	N.A.	N.A.	N.A.	N.A.	N.A.	N.A.
Orissa	2.7	4.6	0.4	0.6	14.7	14.1
Punjab	2.2	3.5	0.3	0.5	15.2	13.1
Rajasthan	2.6	4.3	0.4	0.5	14.7	11.1
Sikkim	N.A.	N.A.	N.A.	N.A.	N.A.	N.A.
Tamil Nadu	3.5	5.0	0.3	0.9	10.0	17.4
Tripura	7.4	N.A.	1.3	N.A.	8.6	6.7
Uttar Pradesh	1.9	3.7	0.2	0.4	11.4	10.4
West Bengal	2.3	3.3	0.4	0.5	14.2	14.0
India	2.8	4.4	0.5	0.5	16.3	15.6
Coefficient of Variation (%)	63.51	32.11	59.09	40.63	27.10	23.38

Source: (i) *Estimates of State Domestic Product 1970-71 - 1984-85* Central Statistical Organisation, New Delhi, 1986.

(ii) Various Issues of *Analysis of Budgeted Expenditure on Education*, Ministry of Human Resource Development, New Delhi.

(i) The educational expenditure as proportion of the State Domestic Product (SDP) has increased in respect of almost every State. On an average, this share has increased from 2.8 per cent of national income in 1970-71 to 4.4 per cent in 1984-85. The States, however, differ a great deal in making resources available, out of their incomes, for the development of education. In 1984-85, for instance, whereas Manipur, Himachal Pradesh and Kerala spent as high as 10.2, 7.0 and 6.5 per cent of their respective SDPs on education, the corresponding figures for the States of West Bengal, Punjab, Haryana, Uttar Pradesh and Maharashtra were as low as 3.3, 3.5, 3.7 and 3.8 per cent respectively.

(ii) The expenditure on higher education as proportion of SDP considerably vary across the States, though on an average this proportion is sticky at 0.5 per cent of the national income. In 1984-85, the States which spent more than the national average were Manipur (1.4%), Kerala (1.0%) Andhra Pradesh and Tamil Nadu (0.9% each). Among the States which spent less than the average were Assam, Haryana and Uttar Pradesh (0.4% each)

(iii) Of the total expenditure on education, about 16 per cent was spent on higher education. In this respect also, the variations in allocation of resources for higher education across the States are pronounced. The inter-state differences can be gauged from the highest category of the States of Andhra Pradesh (17.4%), Karnataka (17.9%) and Tamil Nadu (17.4%) *vis-a-vis* the lowest category of the States like Tripura (6.7%), Assam (9.2%), Himachal Pradesh (9.5%) and Uttar Pradesh (10.4%).

(iv) Though there are State to State differences in educational efforts as revealed from the relative share of expenditure on education, the advanced States, in general, are spending more than other States as may also be expected on theoretical grounds. The reasons for variations in spending behaviour of the States may be attributed to both the historical factors as well as the political predilections or the perceptions of the States with regard to relative contribution of education in economic and social development.

4.3 Distributional Pattern of Expenditure on Higher Education by Major Categories

An analysis of the composition of different types of expenditure for the period 1969-70 to 1983-84, for which actual data are available, demonstrated the following:

(i) The patterns of recurring expenditure on higher education including universities, deemed to be universities, institutions of national importance, research institutes and other institutions awarding degrees, indicated that the payment of salaries constitute about 70 per cent in 1983-84 of the total expenditure on higher education (Table 4.4). This share moreover has marginally increased over the period last two decades. Of the total expenditure on salaries, the share of teaching and non-teaching staff has been 48 and 22 per cent respectively. The expenditure on non-salary items has been almost sticky at about 30 per cent. The relative share of expenditure on equipment and other appliances, miscellaneous expenses, etc., however, showed a downward trend as may be observed in the Table referred to above.

(ii) When the relevant data pertaining to universities were examined separately, the patterns of expenditure indicated a rising trend in respect of payments of salaries to academic and non-academic staff for the period 1969-70 to 1983-84. The share of salaries constitute about 56 per cent in 1983-84, of the total expenditure of universities (Table 4.5). The relative increase in expenditure overtime is fully captured by the salaries of academic and non-academic staff. As a result of which, the share of expenditure on non-salary items like equipment, library and other support services has declined. As may be observed in Table 4.5 (column 7), the share of expenditure on non-salary items has declined from 54 per cent in 1969-70 to 43 per cent in 1984-85. It may be mentioned, in passing, that a similar analysis for colleges separately indicated that salaries constitute about 75 per cent of the total expenditure and this share has remained almost constant since the year 1969-70 for which data was available.

TABLE 4.4: Pattern of Recurring Expenditure of Higher Education in India 1969-70 to 1984-85

(*Rs. in crores*)

Years	Salaries & allowances to teaching staff	Salaries & allowances to non-teaching staff	Total	Equipment & other appliances	Miscellaneous Expenses	Total on non-salary items	Grand Total expenditure
1	2	3	4	5	6	7	8
1969-70	109.89	44.67	154.56	16.88	50.50	75.47	230.03
	(47.77)	(19.42)	(67.19)	(7.34)	(25.47)	(32.81)	(100.00)
1970-71	126.17	50.43	176.60	19.61	63.39	83.00	259.60
	(48.60)	(19.43)	(68.03)	(7.55)	(24.42)	(31.97)	(100.00)
1971-72	143.01	59.16	202.17	22.53	70.38	92.91	295.08
	(48.46)	(20.05)	(68.51)	(7.64)	(23.85)	(31.49)	(100.00)
1972-73	158.35	67.18	225.53	26.78	75.45	102.23	327.76
	(48.31)	(20.50)	(68.81)	(8.17)	(23.02)	(31.19)	(100.00)
1973-74	180.52	78.16	258.68	29.31	83.97	113.28	371.96
	(48.53)	(21.01)	(69.54)	(7.83)	(22.58)	(30.46)	(100.00)
1974-75	206.01	90.86	296.87	30.78	93.17	123.95	420.82
	(48.95)	(21.54)	(70.54)	(7.31)	(22.10)	(29.45)	(100.00)
1975-76	231.30	104.02	335.32	31.85	100.28	132.13	467.45
	(49.48)	(22.25)	(71.73)	(6.81)	(21.46)	(28.27)	(100.00)
1976-77	278.76	111.67	390.43	31.65	150.98	182.63	573.06
	(48.64)	(19.49)	(68.13)	(5.52)	(26.35)	(31.87)	(100.00)
1977-78	299.91	122.90	422.81	35.03	157.38	192.41	615.22
	(48.75)	(19.98)	(68.73)	(5.69)	(25.58)	(31.27)	(100.00)
1978-79	357.75	138.87	496.62	35.48	193.97	229.45	726.07
	(49.27)	(19.13)	(68.40)	(4.89)	(26.71)	(31.60)	(100.00)

(*Contd.*)

TABLE 4.4 (*Contd.*)

1	2	3	4	5	6	7	8
1979-80	381.24	154.67	535.91	41.56	203.42	244.98	780.89
	(48.82)	(19.81)	(68.63)	(5.32)	(26.05)	(31.37)	(100.00)
1980-81	434.88	186.40	621.28	50.26	359.02	409.28	1030.56
	(42.20)	(18.09)	(60.29)	(4.87)	(34.84)	(39.71)	(100.00)
1981-82	504.75	215.09	719.84	55.50	270.09	325.59	1045.43
	(48.28)	(20.57)	(68.85)	(5.31)	(25.84)	(31.15)	(100.00)
1982-83	578.22	254.58	832.80	63.42	307.60	371.02	1203.82
	(48.03)	(21.15)	(69.18)	(5.27)	(25.55)	(30.82)	(100.00)
1983-84	623.03	284.07	907.10	70.48	324.84	395.32	1302.42
	(47.84)	(21.81)	(69.65)	(5.41)	(24.94)	(30.35)	(100.00)

Note: *(i) Include Universities, Deemed Universities, Institutions of National Importance, Research Institutions, and all Institutions of Higher Education (Degree Standard and above and below degree standard).

(ii) Figures within parantheses indicate percentages to total.

Source: Calculated on the basis of data collected from various issues of *Education in India*, Vol. II, Ministry of Human Resource Development, Govt. of India.

TABLE 4.5: Pattern of Recurring Expenditure in Universities — All India 1969-70 to 1984-85

(Rs. in crores)

Years	Salaries & allowances to teaching & academic staff	Salaries & allowances to non-teaching staff	Total on salaries & allowances	Equipment & other appliances	Miscellaneous expenses	Total Expenditure on non-salary items	Grand Total expenditure
1	2	3	4(2+3)	5	6	7(5+6)	8
1969-70	13.52	10.74	24.26	2.72	26.06	28.78	53.04
	(25.49)	(20.25)	(45.74)	(5.13)	(49.13)	(54.26)	(100.00)
1970-71	15.74	11.25	24.99	3.13	24.80	27.93	92.92
	(25.96)	(21.26)	(47.22)	(5.91)	(46.87)	(52.78)	(100.00)
1971-72	15.27	13.14	28.41	3.39	27.14	30.53	58.94
	(25.91)	(22.29)	(48.20)	(5.75)	(46.05)	(51.80)	(100.00)
1972-73	17.73	15.98	33.71	5.85	28.18	34.03	67.74
	(26.17)	(23.59)	(49.76)	(8.64)	(41.60)	(50.24)	(100.00)
1973-74*	19.82	19.62	39.44	6.31	32.89	39.20	78.64
	(25.20)	(24.95)	(50.15)	(8.02)	(41.83)	(49.85)	(100.00)
1974-75	22.63	23.16	45.79	5.81	38.23	44.04	80.83
	(25.19)	(25.78)	(50.97)	(6.47)	(42.56)	(49.03)	(100.00)
1975-76	27.28	25.70	52.98	5.39	41.19	46.58	99.56
	(27.40)	(25.81)	(53.21)	(5.41)	(41.37)	(46.78)	(100.00)
1976-77	39.84	27.16	67.00	6.42	50.78	57.20	124.20
	(32.08)	(21.87)	(53.95)	(5.17)	(40.88)	(46.05)	(100.00)
1977-78	45.99	32.66	78.65	6.72	50.60	57.32	135.97
	(33.82)	(24.02)	(57.84)	(4.94)	(37.22)	(42.16)	(100.00)

(Contd.)

TABLE 4.5 (*Contd.*)

1	2	3	4(2+3)	5	6	7(5+6)	8
1978-79	57.11	36.77	93.88	5.41	64.69	70.10	163.98
	(34.83)	(22.42)	(57.25)	(3.30)	(39.45)	(42.75)	(100.00)
1979-80	61.59	42.38	103.97	8.75	77.46	86.21	190.18
	(32.39)	(22.28)	(54.67)	(4.60)	(40.73)	(45.33)	(100.00)
1980-81	73.56	53.23	126.79	11.90	221.97	233.87	360.66
	(20.40)	(14.76)	(35.16)	(3.30)	(61.54)	(64.84)	(100.00)
1981-82	89.48	65.93	154.91	13.32	106.22	119.54	274.45
	(32.60)	(23.84)	(56.44)	(4.86)	(38.70)	(43.56)	(100.00)
1982-83	102.70	79.40	182.10	16.15	125.87	142.02	324.12
	(31.69)	(24.49)	(56.18)	(4.98)	(38.84)	(43.82)	(100.00)
1983-84	106.94	82.75	189.69	18.50	128.60	147.10	336.79
	(31.75)	(24.57)	(56.32)	(5.49)	(38.19)	(43.68)	(100.00)

Notes: * (i) As *Education in India* was not published in 1973-74, data for this year were worked out through interpolation method.
(ii) Figures within parantheses indicate percentages to total.

Source: Compiled on the basis of data available in various issues of *Education in India*, Ministry of Human Resource Development, Govt. of India, New Delhi.

TABLE 4.6: Pattern of Recurring Expenditure on Higher Education — By States, 1983-84

(*In percentages*)

States/Union Territories	Salaries & allowances			Equipment & other appliances	Miscellaneous expenditure	Total exp. on non-salary items	Grand total expenditure
	Teaching staff	Non-teaching staff	total				
(1)	(2)	(3)	(4)	(5)	(6)	(7)	(8)
A.P.	48.5	22.4	70.9	4.2	24.9	29.1	100.0
Assam	48.1	23.1	71.2	6.0	22.8	28.8	100.0
Bihar	58.7	19.1	77.8	5.1	17.1	22.2	100.0
Gujarat	42.8	25.1	67.9	2.9	29.2	32.1	100.0
Haryana	54.8	26.6	81.4	4.0	14.6	18.6	100.0
H.P.	44.5	30.5	75.0	4.0	21.0	25.0	100.0
J & K	48.5	23.5	72.0	6.6	21.4	28.0	100.0
Karnataka	53.8	11.7	73.5	6.2	20.3	26.5	100.0
Kerala	52.0	17.7	69.7	2.8	27.5	30.3	100.0
M.P.	51.0	22.1	73.1	2.7	24.2	26.9	100.0
Maharashtra	56.1	22.3	78.4	4.0	19.6	23.6	100.0
Manipur	56.8	20.7	77.5	2.9	19.6	22.5	100.0
Maghalaya	35.8	18.8	54.6	0.8	44.6	45.4	100.0
Orissa	53.2	18.6	71.8	5.1	23.1	28.2	100.0
Punjab	52.3	20.2	72.5	3.9	23.6	27.5	100.0
Rajasthan	51.4	26.1	77.5	4.2	18.3	22.5	100.0
T.N.	44.1	17.5	61.6	6.1	32.3	38.4	100.0
Tripura	42.2	26.5	68.7	2.6	28.7	31.3	100.0

(*Contd.*)

TABLE 4.6 (*Contd.*)

(1)	(2)	(3)	(4)	(5)	(6)	(7)	(8)
U.P.	44.8	21.9	66.7	7.3	26.0	33.3	100.0
W.B.	42.0	24.2	66.2	3.3	30.5	33.8	100.0
Chandigarh	43.3	16.9	60.2	14.8	25.0	39.8	100.0
Delhi	37.0	22.1	59.1	10.8	30.1	40.9	100.0
Goa, Daman & Diu	32.8	38.2	71.0	16.5	12.5	29.0	100.0
Average	47.6	22.8	70.3	5.5	24.2	29.7	100.0
	à	à	à	à	à	à	
	(28.2)	(26.9)	(55.1)	(6.2)	(38.7)	(44.9)	(100.0)
C.V. (%)	14.3	20.6	9.4	67.3	27.3	21.9	0

Note: * Includes Universities, Deemed Universities, Institutions of National Importance, Research Institutions, Colleges for General and Professional Education (including institutions below degree level).

à Pertain to 1979.

Source: Education in India, Vol.11 (various issues), Ministry of Human Resource Development, Govt. of India, New Delhi.

TABLE 4.7: Pattern of Recurring Expenditure in the Indian Universities, 1983-84

(*In percentages*)

States/Union Territory	Salary & allowances			Equipment & Other appliances	Miscellaneous expenditure	Total expen. on non-salary items	Grand total expenditure
	Teaching staff	Non-teaching staff	Total				
A.P.	32.4	28.3	60.7	3.8	35.5	39.3	100.0
Assam	23.0	37.2	60.2	5.2	34.6	39.8	100.0
Bihar	53.2	8.2	61.4	6.7	31.9	38.6	100.0
Gujarat	13.8	28.4	42.2	-	57.8	57.8	100.0
Haryana	40.3	26.6	66.9	3.7	29.4	33.1	100.0
H.P.	22.2	40.6	62.8	2.8	34.4	37.2	100.0
J & K	32.3	29.2	61.5	7.6	30.9	38.5	100.0
Karnataka	43.6	13.9	57.5	9.1	33.4	42.5	100.0
Kerala	18.0	29.2	47.2	3.2	49.6	52.8	100.0
M.P.	18.4	29.8	48.2	1.5	50.3	51.8	100.0
Maharashtra	19.2	27.1	46.3	3.0	50.7	53.7	100.0
Manipur	35.7	15.7	51.4	5.1	43.5	48.6	100.0
Meghalaya	22.6	23.8	46.4	-	53.6	53.6	100.0
Orissa	24.9	16.8	41.7	10.9	47.4	58.3	100.0
Punjab	35.7	22.0	57.7	2.4	39.9	42.3	100.0

(*Contd.*)

TABLE 4.7 (*Contd.*)

States/Union Territory	Salary & allowances			Equipment & Other appliances	Miscellaneous expenditure	Total expen. on non-salary items	Grand total expenditure
	Teaching staff	Non-teaching staff	Total				
Rajasthan	39.9	32.1	72.0	3.0	25.0	28.0	100.0
T.N.	11.9	15.0	26.9	-	73.1	73.1	100.0
Tripura	43.9	34.0	77.9	7.7	14.4	22.1	100.0
U.P.	30.7	22.7	53.4	9.8	36.8	46.6	100.0
W.B.	38.2	29.0	67.2	2.6	30.2	32.8	100.0
Chandigarh	35.6	27.3	60.9	1.5	37.6	39.1	100.0
Delhi	22.6	27.0	49.6	3.4	47.0	50.4	100.0
Goa, Damam & Diu	40.6	24.4	65.1	5.6	29.3	34.9	100.0
Average	30.3	25.6	55.9	4.3	39.8	44.1	100.0
C.V.(%)	35.2	29.5	20.0	71.2	31.0	25.3	0

Note: * Including Institutions Deemed to be Universities.
Source: Education in India, Vol.II, 1983-84, Ministry of HRD, GOI, New Delhi.

(iii) A cross-section analysis of data pertaining to expenditure incurred by various States on overall the higher education and universities, separately, revealed considerable variations, as may be seen from Tables 4.6 and 4.7. As the relevant data are self-evident, the results are not discussed here. The relevant coefficients of variations (CVs) indicate the extent to which different States vary with respect each item of expenditure presented in the Table 4.6 and 4.7.

(iv) A major conclusion that has emerged from the foregoing is that the staff salaries are the major determinant of expenditure on higher education as it accounts for 55 to 70 per cent of the total expenditure. The share of payments to non-teaching staff is very significant. Further, the expenditure on non-salary items especially student support services is declining.

4.4 **Analysis of Expenditure by Types of Universities**

As against the macro, i.e. all India level scene of university finances, as discussed above, an attempt is made below to analyse the distributional pattern of expenditure among the Central Universities (CUs), the Deemed to be Universities (DUs), and the State Universities (SUs) especially in respect of such items of expenditure as salaries of teaching and non-teaching staff, apparatus and chemicals, furniture, library, etc. The data examined here relate to two points of time, i.e. 1975-76 and 1985-86 which provide a perspective on growth for a period of 10 years. Table 4.8, presents the summary statistics in respects of CUs, DUs, and SUs. The detailed break-up of expenditure for different universities by type may be seen in Tables 4.9 through 4.11, on the basis of which the following observations may be made.

4.4.1 *Payments of Salaries*

The expenditure on salaries of teaching and non-teaching staff has generally declined for all the CUs and DUs over the period of 1975-76 and 1985-86, whereas the same has risen for SUs. The expenditure on salaries of teaching staff has declined more steeply than the payment of salaries to non-teaching staff. The inter-university differences in the proportions of expenditure incurred on the above items are even more pronounced than those for different types of universities.

TABLE 4.8: Pattern of Expenditure Across Various Types of Universities — A Summary Statement

(In percentage)

Items of Expenditure / Types of Universities	Central Universities		Deemed Universities		State Universities	
	1975-76	1985-86	1975-76	1985-86	1975-76	1985-86
1. Salaries & Allowances to	30.2	22.4	39.7	31.4	23.9	24.0
Teaching Staff	(28.5)	(19.6)	(32.7)	(32.5)	(28.5)	(37.9)
2. Salaries & Allowances to	29.8	27.9	26.2	24.8	23.6	35.4
Non-teaching staff	(20.8)	(27.9)	(20.2)	(30.6)	(30.5)	(21.2)
3. Total on Salaries (1+2)	58.3	50.3	65.9	56.1	47.5	59.4
	(22.8)	(17.7)	(17.5)	(8.9)	(16.0)	(9.8)
4. Grants to Colleges	0.2	0.1	-	2.0	2.0	0.1
	(250.0)	(100.0)	(165.0)	(275.0)	(200.0)	
5. Apparatus, Chemicals &	2.6	2.8	2.4	3.3	5.8	2.2
Consumable Stores	(96.2)	(128.6)	(116.7)	(184.8)	(122.4)	(104.5)
6. Furniture	1.0	0.8	0.6	2.6	0.5	0.2
	(90.0)	(150.0)	(216.7)	(161.5)	(10.0)	(100.0)
7. Library	1.8	4.0	2.5	4.5	4.2	2.9
	(94.4)	(97.5)	(92.0)	(80.0)	(40.5)	(65.5)
8. Other Miscellaneous Exp.	28.7	42.0	28.6	31.6	40.0	35.2
	(57.5)	(17.4)	(57.7)	(35.1)	(21.0)	(20.5)
9. Total on Non - Salary Items (4 to 8)	41.7	48.3	34.1	43.9	52.5	40.6
	(31.9)	(17.0)	(51.3)	(20.3)	(14.5)	(14.3)
10. Grand Total (3+9)	100.0	100.0	100.0	100.0	100.0	100.0

Note: Figures within parenthesis indicate Coefficient of Variations.
Source: Compiled from the Tables 4.8, 4.9 and 4.10.

TABLE 4.9: Recurring (Plan + Non-Plan) Expenditure in the Central Universities 1975-76 and 1985-86

(*Rs. in Lakhs*)

Items of Expenditure	Salaries to Teaching Staff		Salaries to Non-Teaching Staff		Total on Salary Items		Grants to Colleges		Apparatus, Chemicals etc.	
Universities	1975-76	1985-86	1975-76	1985-86	1975-76	1985-86	1975-76	1985-86	1975-76	1985-86
	1		2		3 = (1+2)		4		5	
Hyderabad	N.A.	44.4	N.A.	79.3	N.A.	123.7	N.A.	-	N.A.	34
	(14.8)	(26.4)	(41.2)	(11)						
NEHU	9.5	106.0	13.5	107.0	23	213.0	-	1.9	0.9	5
	(23.1)	(21.8)	(23.0)	(22.0)	(46.1)	(43.8)		(0.4)	(2.2)	(1)
à Aligarh	220.5	434.9	184.9	701.3	405.4	1136.2	-	-	17.5	13
	(36.5)	(25.3)	(30.6)	(40.8)	(67.1)	(66.1)			(2.9)	(0)
à Banaras	270.8	517.7	385.7	867.6	656.5	1385.3	-	-	80.9	8
	(27.1)	(17.0)	(38.6)	(30.0)	(65.7)	(47.9)			(8.1)	(0)
Visva Bharati	87.9	186.1	61.7	153.3	149.6	339.4	-	-	4.0	12
	(45.7)	(29.0)	(32.1)	(23.9)	(77.8)	(52.9)			(2.1)	(2)
Delhi	137.8	287.5	130.8	437.3	268.6	724.8	10.4	-	2.8	13
	(19.9)	(23.6)	(18.9)	(35.9)	(38.8)	(59.5)	(1.5)		(0.4)	(1)
J. Nehru	52.2	155.3	46.9	101.6	99.1	256.9	-	-	4.7	18
	(28.7)	(24.6)	(25.8)	(16.1)	(54.5)	(40.7)			(2.6)	(3)
Average	129.8	247.4	137.3	349.6	267.0	597.0	1.5	0.3	15.8	15
	(30.2)	(22.4)	(29.8)	(27.9)	(58.3)	(50.3)	(0.2)	(0.1)	(2.6)	(0)
Standard Deviation	91.7	161.8	124.6	300.4			3.6	0.7	27.1	8
	(8.6)	(4.4)	(6.2)	(7.8)			(0.5)	(0.1)	(2.5)	(3)
Coefficient of Variation %	70.6	65.4	90.8	85.9	79.8	77.1	240.0	233.3	171.5	56.0
	(28.5)	(19.6)	(20.8)	(27.9)	(22.8)	(17.7)	(250.0)	(100.0)	(96.2)	(128.0)

(*Contd.*)

TABLE 4.9 (*contd.*)

Items of Expenditure	Furniture		Library		Other Misc. Items		Total on Non-Salary Items		Total Recurring Expenditure	
Universities	1975-76	1985-86	1975-76	1985-86	1975-76	1985-86	1975-76	1985-86	1975-76	1985-86
	6		7		8		9 = (4+5+6+7+8)		10	(3+9)
Hyderabad	N.A.	2.1 (0.7)	N.A.	37.2 (12.4)	N.A.	103.0 (34.3)	N.A.	176.5 (48.8)	N.A.	300.2 (100.0)
N.E.H.U.	-	18.5 (3.8)	-	29.7 (6.1)	17.1 (41.7)	217.8 (44.8)	18 (53.9)	273.2 (56.2)	41.0 (100.0)	486.2 (100.0)
à Aligarh	3.6 (0.6)	5.2 (0.3)	8.5 (1.4)	30.9 (1.8)	169.1 (28.0)	532.9 (31.0)	198.7 (32.9)	582.8 (33.9)	604.1 (100.0)	1719.0 (100.0)
à Banaras	8.0 (0.8)	5.8 (0.2)	7.0 (0.7)	34.7 (1.2)	246.8 (24.7)	1457.6 (50.7)	342.7 (34.3)	1506.8 (52.1)	999.2 (100.0)	2892.1 (100.0)
Visva Bharati	4.0 (0.1)	1.9 (0.3)	4.2 (2.2)	8.3 (1.3)	30.4 (15.8)	279.1 (43.5)	42.6 (22.2)	302.1 (47.1)	192.2 (100.0)	641.5 (100.0)
Delhi	4.8 (0.7)	7.3 (0.6)	24.9 (3.6)	7.3 (0.6)	380.8 (55.0)	465.3 (38.2)	423.7 (61.7)	493.3 (40.5)	692.3 (100.0)	1218.1 (100.0)
J.Nehru	4.7 (2.6)	-	8.9 (4.9)	28.4 (4.5)	64.3 (35.4)	327.0 (51.8)	82.6 (45.5)	374.3 (59.3)	181.7 (100.0)	631.2 (100.0)
Average	3.5 (1.0)	5.8 (0.8)	7.6 (1.8)	25.2 (4.0)	129.8 (28.7)	483.2 (42.0)	184.7 (41.7)	529.9 (48.3)	387.2 -	1126.9 -
Standard Deviation	2.6 (3.6)	5.7 (1.2)	7.8 (1.7)	11.4 (3.9)	132.0 (16.5)	419.7 (7.3)	-	-	351.5 -	849.4 -
Coefficient of Variation %	74.3 (90.0)	98.3 (150.0)	102.6 (94.4)	45.2 (97.5)	101.7 (57.5)	86.9 (17.4)	82.9 (31.9)	79.0 (17.0)	90.8 -	75.4 -

Note: Figures within parenthesis indicate percentages to total

à Figures relate to 1976-77, instead of 1975-76

Source: Calculated on the basis of unpublished data obtained from the University Grants Commission, New Delhi.

TABLE 4.10: Recurring (Plan + Non Plan) Expenditure in the Institutions Deemed to be Universities 1975-76 and 1985-86

(*Rs. in Lakhs*)

Items of Expenditure	Salaries of Research Guiding & Teaching Staff		Salaries of Administrative and other staff		Total on Salary		Grants to Colleges		Apparatus, Chemicals	
Institutions	1975-76	1985-86	1975-76	1985-86	1975-76	1985-86	1975-76	1985-86	1975-76	1985-86
	1		2		3		4		5	
C.I.E.F.L.	9.7	22.6	7.6	33.6	17.3	56.2	-	7.8	0.1	1.0
	(30.7)	(26.0)	(23.6)	(38.6)	(54.3)	(64.6)		(9.0)	(0.3)	(2.0)
School of Mines	11.5	40.1	9.7	78.1	21.2	118.2	-	-	4.5	-
	(17.1)	(16.6)	(14.3)	(32.3)	(31.4)	(48.9)			(6.7)	
Gujarat Vidyapeeth	9.0	24.2	4.8	13.6	13.8	37.8	-	-	-	
	(56.7)	(27.0)	(30.2)	(15.2)	(86.9)	(42.2)				
Tata Instt. of	5.9	28.3	4.7	20.8	10.6	49.1	-	-	-	-
Social Sciences	(37.5)	(34.4)	(30.3)	(25.3)	(67.8)	(59.7)				
B.I.T.S.	29.0	50.5	24.8	41.6	53.8	92.1	-	-	5.8	33
	(33.9)	(27.7)	(28.9)	(22.8)	(62.8)	(50.5)			(6.8)	(18.0)
Gurukul Kangri	5.7	25.4	3.1	8.8	8.8	34.2	-	2.3	0.2	1
	(51.1)	(51.8)	(27.9)	(18.0)	(79.0)	(69.8)		(4.7)	(1.8)	(2.0)
Jamia Millia Islamia	19.5	91.9	10.7	53.9	30.2	145.8	-	-	0.3	0
	(51.2)	(36.0)	(28.2)	(21.1)	(79.4)	(57.1)			(0.9)	
Average	12.9	40.4	9.3	35.8	22.2	76.2	-	1.4	1.6	5
	(39.7)	(31.4)	(26.2)	(24.8)	(65.9)	(56.1)		(2.0)	(2.4)	(3.0)
Standard Deviation	7.8	23.0	6.8	22.7	-	-	-	2.7	2.3	11
	(13.0)	(10.2)	(5.3)	(7.6)				(3.3)	(2.8)	(6.0)
Coefficient of	60.5	56.9	73.1	63.4	14.5	40.1		192.9	143.8	219.0
Variation%	(32.7)	(32.5)	(20.2)	(30.6)	(17.5)	(8.9)		(165.0)	(116.7)	(184.0)

(*Contd.*)

TABLE 4.10 (*Contd.*)

Items of Expenditure	Furniture		Library		Other Misc. Items		Total on Non-Salary Items		Total Recurring Expenditure	
Institutions	1975-76	1985-86	1975-76	1985-86	1975-76	1985-86	1975-76	1985-86	1975-76	1985-86
	6		7		8		9		10	
C.I.E.F.L.	-	0.6	Neg.	0.5	14.7	20.0	14.8	30.8	32.1	87.0
		(0.7)	(0.1)	(0.5)	(45.7)	(23.0)	(45.7)	(35.4)	(100.0)	(100.0)
School of Mines	-	-	1.6	4.6	40.3	118.9	46.4	123.5	67.6	241.7
			(2.3)	(1.9)	(59.6)	(49.2)	(68.6)	(51.1)	(100.0)	(100.0)
Gujarat Vidyapeeth	-	-	0.3	10.6	1.8	41.1	2.1	51.7	15.9	89.5
			(1.8)	(11.8)	(11.3)	(45.9)	(13.1)	(57.8)	(100.0)	(100.0)
Tata Instt. of	0.6	4.8	0.1	3.4	4.3	25.0	5.0	33.2	15.6	82.3
Social Sciences	(3.8)	(5.8)	(0.6)	(4.1)	(27.8)	(30.4)	(32.2)	(40.3)	(100.0)	(100.0)
B.I.T.S.	-	-	4.8	8.4	21.3	48.8	31.9	90.3	85.7	182.4
			(5.6)	(4.6)	(24.8)	(26.8)	(37.2)	(49.5)	(100.0)	(100.0)
Gurukul Kangri	0.1	0.1	0.1	3.3	2.0	7.9	2.4	14.8	11.2	49.0
	(0.2)	(0.2)	(1.0)	(6.7)	(18.0)	(16.1)	(21.0)	(30.2)	(100.0)	(100.0)
Jamia Millia Islamia	-	29.8	2.4	4.2	5.1	75.7	7.8	109.8	38.0	355.6
		(11.7)	(6.4)	(1.6)	(13.3)	(29.6)	(20.6)	(42.9)	(100.0)	(100.0)
Average	0.1	5.0	1.3	5.0	12.8	48.2	15.8	64.9	38.0	141.1
	(0.6)	(2.6)	(2.5)	(4.5)	(28.6)	(31.6)	(34.1)	(43.9)	(-)	(-)
Coefficient of	200.0	204.0	130.8	62.0	102.3	73.4	100.0	60.9	69.5	55.2
Variation (%)	(216.7)	(161.5)	(92.0)	(80.0)	(57.7)	(35.1)	(51.3)	(20.3)	(-)	(-)

Notes: Figures within parenthesis indicate percentage to total
Neg. = Less than 0.1 lakh
— Nil

Source: Calculated on the basis of unpublished data obtained from the University Grants Commission, New Delhi.

(Rs. in Lakhs)

Items of Expenditure	Salaries of Research Guiding & Teaching		Salaries of Administrative & Other Staff		Total on Salaries		Grants to Colleges		Apparatus, Chemicals etc.	
Universities	1975-76	1985-86	1975-76	1985-86	1975-76	1985-86	1975-76	1985-86	1975-76	1985-86
	1		2		3 = (1+2)		4		5	
Andhra	64.6	275.0	81.8	449.9	146.4	724.9	2.6	0.6	11.4	13.4
	(24.1)	(27.0)	(30.5)	(4.2)	(54.6)	(71.2)	(1.0)	(0.1)	(4.2)	(1.3)
Gauhati	29.3	97.8	31.3	109.5	60.6	207.3	Neg.	0.7	1.1	0.4
	(25.8)	(27.6)	(27.6)	(30.9)	(54.6)	(71.2)		(0.2)	(1.0)	(0.1)
Sardar Patel	16.5	63.0	10.7	45.5	27.2	108.5	-	Neg.	6.3	14.2
	(28.4)	(35.5)	(18.4)	(25.6)	(46.8)	(61.1)			(10.9)	(8.0)
Kurukshetra	61.4	118.2	20.9	205.0	82.3	323.2	0.2	-	47.2	6.6
	(32.4)	(20.9)	(11.0)	(36.2)	(43.4)	(57.1)	(0.1)		(24.9)	(1.2)
Karnataka	45.8	221.4	31.8	155.6	77.6	377.0	38.3	-	1.9	4.0
	(22.2)	(40.2)	(15.4)	(28.2)	(37.6)	(68.4)	(18.6)		(0.9)	(0.7)
Kerala	22.8	78.3	40.9	346.6	63.7	424.9	0.6	5.8	7.1	0.6
	(15.7)	(10.1)	(28.1)	(45.0)	(43.8)	(55.1)	(0.4)	(0.8)	(4.9)	(1.1)
Dr. H.S. Gaur	33.1	82.5	24.3	95.3	57.4	177.8	0.1	-	5.9	14.4
	(36.8)	(23.7)	(27.0)	(27.4)	(63.8)	(51.1)	(0.1)		(6.6)	(4.1)
Vikram	9.2	25.6	22.8	83.3	32.0	108.9	-	-	Neg.	0.5
	(14.3)	(13.1)	(35.5)	(42.8)	(49.8)	(55.9)				(0.3)
Bombay	53.0	121.6	66.9	355.0	119.9	476.6	-	-	5.8	25.6
	(18.4)	(15.1)	(23.2)	(44.1)	(41.6)	(59.2)			(2.0)	(3.2)
Poona	34.3	145.4	30.1	157.1	64.4	302.5	0.2	-	4.6	9.8
	(21.5)	(27.1)	(18.9)	(29.3)	(40.4)	(56.4)	(0.1)		(2.9)	(1.8)
Average	37.0	122.9	36.2	200.3	73.2	323.2	4.2	0.7	9.1	9.8
	(23.9)	(24.0)	(23.6)	(35.4)	(47.5)	(59.4)	(2.0)	(0.1)	(5.8)	(2.2)
Coefficient of variation (%)	48.1	57.9	57.5	64.8	47.4	55.8	271.4	242.8	143.9	73.5
	(28.5)	(37.9)	(30.5)	(21.2)	(16.0)	(9.8)	(275.0)	(200.0)	(122.4)	(104.5)

(Contd.)

TABLE 4.11 (*Contd.*)

Items of Expenditure	Furniture		Library		Other Misc. Items		Total on Non-Salary Items		Total Recurring Expenditure	
Universities	1975-76	1985-86	1975-76	1985-86	1975-76	1985-86	1975-76	1985-86	1975-76	1985-86
	6		7		8		9 = (4+5+6+7+8)		10 = (3+9)	
Andhra	0.1	1.8	14.5	24.0	93.5	253.2	122.1	293.0	268.5	1017.9
	(Neg.)	(0.2)	(5.4)	(2.4)	(34.8)	(24.8)	(45.4)	(28.8)	(100.0)	(100.0)
Gauhati	0.2	0.7	4.7	10.3	46.9	135.1	74.9	147.2	113.5	354.5
	(0.2)	(0.2)	(4.1)	(2.9)	(41.3)	(38.1)	(46.6)	(41.5)	(100.0)	(100.0)
Sardar Patel	0.4	1.2	3.6	12.8	20.6	40.9	30.9	69.1	58.1	177.6
	(0.7)	(0.7)	(6.2)	(7.2)	(35.4)	(23.0)	(53.2)	(38.9)	(100.0)	(100.0)
Kurukshetra	1.5	0.5	7.8	19.9	50.6	216.9	107.3	243.1	189.6	566.3
	(0.8)	(0.1)	(4.1)	(3.5)	(26.7)	(38.3)	(56.6)	(42.9)	(100.0)	(100.0)
Karnataka	0.6	0.5	8.2	17.0	79.6	152.3	128.6	173.8	206.2	550.8
	(0.3)	(0.1)	(4.0)	(3.1)	(38.6)	(27.7)	(62.4)	(31.6)	(100.0)	(100.0)
Kerala	1.6	2.0	1.2	6.6	71.3	321.1	81.8	344.1	145.5	769.0
	(1.1)	(1.1)	(0.8)	(0.9)	(49.0)	(41.8)	(56.2)	(44.9)	(100.0)	(100.0)
Dr. H.S. Gaur	-	-	1.8	0.4	24.7	155.5	32.5	170.3	89.9	348.1
			(2.0)	(0.1)	(27.5)	(44.7)	(36.2)	(48.9)	(100.0)	(100.0)
Vikram	0.1	-	2.2	2.7	29.9	82.7	32.2	85.9	64.2	194.8
	(0.1)		(3.5)	(1.4)	(46.6)	(42.4)	(50.2)	(44.1)	(100.0)	(100.0)
Bombay	3.7	0.8	15.0	27.4	143.9	274.2	168.4	328.0	288.3	804.6
	(1.3)	(0.1)	(5.2)	(2.4)	(49.9)	(34.1)	(58.4)	(40.8)	(100.0)	(100.0)
Poona	0.6	0.9	9.9	25.1	79.8	197.5	95.1	233.3	159.5	535.8
	(0.4)	(0.2)	(6.2)	(4.7)	(50.0)	(36.9)	(59.6)	(43.6)	(100.0)	(100.0)
Average	0.9	0.8	6.9	14.6	64.1	182.9	87.4	208.8	158.3	531.9
	(0.5)	(0.2)	(4.2)	(2.9)	(40.0)	(35.2)	(52.5)	(40.6)	-	-
Coefficient of Variation %	122.2	75.0	69.6	62.3	56.0	45.1	50.3	43.5	48.1	48.8
	(10.0)	(100.0)	(40.5)	(65.5)	(21.0)	(20.5)	(14.5)	(14.3)	-	-

Note: Figures within parenthesis indicate percentages to the total Expenditure.

4.4.2 *Expenditure on Apparatus, Chemicals, etc.*

On an average, the expenditure on equipment, apparatus, chemicals, etc. is estimated to be in the range of 2.5 to 3 per cent. The coefficient of variations (CVs) indicated that the universities, however, differ a great deal in the extent of allocation of funds for the above purposes. A comparison of the share of expenditure by different types of universities over the period 1975-85 show that whereas the allocation for CUs and DUs has marginally increased, the same sharply declined for SUs.

4.4.3 *Expenditure on Furniture*

Of the total expenditure, about one per cent is spent on furniture by most of the CUs and DUs. The expenditure by the SUs under this item was as low as 0.2 per cent in 1985-86 as against 0.5 per cent in 1975-76.

4.4.4 *Expenditure on Library*

The average expenditure on libraries is estimated to be 4, 4.5 and 3 per cent, respectively, for CUs, DUs and SUs for the year 1985-86. The CVs in respect of allocation of funds for libraries have emerged to be somewhat higher for SUs than for CUs and DUs.

4.4.5 *Miscellaneous Expenditure*

The expenditure on miscellaneous items like electricity and water charges, telephone, postage, expenditure on hostels, etc. are the major heads of expenditure which, in 1985-86, accounted for 42, 31.6 and 35 per cent, respectively, of the total expenditure in respect of the CUs, DUs and SUs. Except for SUs, the share of expenditure on the above items has shown a rising trend. The analysis of expenditure on miscellaneous items does not lend any guidance in regard to spending patterns by different universities, on various items of expenditure. Table 4.12 presents the relevant details of the miscellaneous expenditure with respect to a few universities for which budgets could be easily acquired for the purposes of relevant analyses. Table 4.13 presents per student expenditure on different items under miscellaneous heads. Obviously, there is no discernible trend in expenditure on such items across various universities.

TABLE 4.12: Expenditure of Major Items Under Non-Salary Category 1986-87

(*Rs. in Lakhs*)

Items of Expenditure	UNIVERSITIES							
	B H U	Delhi	J N U	Kurukshetra	Annamalai	A M U	Ravishankar	Madras
General Administration	17.08 (1.63)	1.54 (0.39)	N.A.	48.40 (29.07)	21.56 (8.43)	12.90 (3.06)	18.72 (15.07)	3.11 (0.59)
Examinations	30.58 (2.93)	123.37 (31.22)	3.07 (1.30)	53.68 (32.24)	71.06 (27.78)	34.86 (8.27)	55.35 (44.57)	146.76 (28.05)
Library	49.18 (4.71)	82.66 (20.92)	31.70 (13.42)	19.61 (11.78)	4.87 (1.90)	31.19 (7.40)	2.93 (2.36)	19.12 (3.65)
Hostel	1.32 (0.13)	N.A.	0.57 (0.24)	0.04 (0.02)	44.96 (17.58)	5.39 (1.28)	0.15 (0.12)	0.37 (0.07)
Scholarship/Fellowship	60.55 (5.80)	13.59 (3.44)	67.42 (28.53)	8.51 (5.11)	31.76 (12.42)	17.52 (4.15)	1.59 (1.28)	1.77 (0.34)
Electricity	184.77 (17.69)	N.A.	52.07 (22.04)	24.50 (14.71)	9.86 (3.85)	75.43 (17.89)	2.74 (2.21)	4.33 (0.83)
Water	49.53 (4.74)	N.A.	7.73 (3.27)	N.A.	N.A.	8.07 (1.91)	N.A.	N.A.
Works Department	85.80 (8.22)	N.A.	37.95 (16.06)	N.A.	N.A.	47.33 (11.23)	N.A.	25.25 (4.83)
Health Centre	32.53 (3.12)	N.A.	N.A.	N.A.	N.A.	N.A.	N.A.	N.A.
Liveries & Uniform	32.29 (3.09)	8.62 (2.18)	N.A.	N.A.	N.A.	14.93 (3.54)	N.A.	N.A.
Contribution to P.Fund	126.01 (12.07)	N.A.	N.A.	N.A.	N.A.	N.A.	N.A.	N.A.
Others	374.63 (35.87)	165.43 (41.85)	35.78 (15.14)	11.77 (7.07)	71.72 (28.04)	173.98 (41.27)	42.72 (34.39)	322.54 (61.64)
Total	1044.27 (100.0)	395.21 (100.0)	236.29 (100.0)	166.51 (100.00)	255.79 (100.0)	421.60 (100.0)	124.20 (100.0)	523.25 (100.0)

Note: N.A. indicates non-availability of data in the concerned break-up. However, these could be accounted for under the 'others' or sometimes

TABLE 4.13: Per Student Expenditure on Selected Items of Expenditure 1986-87

(In rupees)

University Non-Salary By Items	B H U	Delhi	J N U	Kurukshetra	Annamalai	A M U	Ravishankar	Madras
General Administration	175	9	N.A.	1173	368	173	2162	200
Scholarships, Fellowships	619	80	1719	25	542	236	184	114
Electricity Charges	762	294	1327	594	168	877	316	278
Water Charges	282	20	197	26	33	108	25	15
Stationery & Printing	168	74	139	37	129	152	132	243
Telephone	117	50	151	43	9	39	154	201
Liveries & Uniforms	330	47	111	65	1	201	4	
Others	571	123	1465	323	117	374	858	492

Note: N.A. Not available. These seem to have been included under the category 'Other Items'.

Source: Compiled on the basis of data available in the annual accounts/budgets of the respective universities.

4.5 Analysis of Expenditure: Econometric Results

In the foregoing analysis an attempt was made to discern the pattern of distribution of financial resources across the major heads of expenditure. The observations have, however, been made on the basis of simple ratios and or *inter-se* percentages of different items of expenditure in the total expenditure for each category and level of analysis. Because of year to year fluctuations in the relevant ratios for various reasons, the conclusions based on such methods of analysis, as above cannot be fully relied upon. Also, from the view point of policy formulation, the above method of analysis does not provide a single ratio or a set of ratios which could be adopted with or without modifications as norms of expenditure for different educational purposes.

In order to overcome the above shortcoming, the approach of regression analysis was employed. This methodology establishes a relationship between two or more variables which could be said on the *a priori* grounds to be inter-related. The use of this method of analysis provides an idea of the strength of relationship between two or more variables and indicate the extent to which each measurable variable exert its influence on the dependent variable whose behaviour is sought to be studied. In the econometric exercises undertaken by us, an effort was made to quantify the extent to which the expenditure on different items like salaries of teaching and non-teaching staff, equipment and appliances and other miscellaneous expenditure, account for in the total expenditure on higher education. The results of econometric exercises demonstrated as under:

(i)(a) The analysis of time series data pertaining to all the universities in India for the period 1969-70 to 1979-80 indicated that of the total expenditure, payments of salaries to teaching and non-teaching staff accounted for 30.2 and 23.3 per cent respectively. The share of equipment was merely 5 per cent. The remaining share (40.7 per cent) of expenditure was incurred on miscellaneous items. This is evident from the regression coefficients as in Equation-1 of Table 4.14.

(b) The results for cross-sectional analysis of data, for the year 1979-80, for 15 major states emerged out to be consistent with the evidences discussed above. In the total expenditure, the shares of salaries of teaching and non-teaching staff were 32.1 and 22.7 per cent respectively. Likewise, the expenditure on equipment and appliances, scholarships and library, respectively, accounted for 5.5, 4.2 and 1.8 per cent of the total expenditure on universities. The remaining expenditure of 31.3 per cent was incurred on miscellaneous items.

It is, thus, evident from both the time-series as well as cross-sectional analysis that the salaries of non-teaching staff and miscellaneous expenses account for more than 50 per cent of the total expenditure on universities. The proportion of such non-academic expenses is moreover rising over time.

(ii) An attempt was also made to ascertain whether the pattern of expenditure among a cross-section of universities conform to the observations made above. To this end in view, the method of regression analysis was employed to obtain the relevant results for the universities of Andhra, Gauhati, Sardar Patel, Karnataka, Kerala, Dr. H.S. Gaur, Vikram, Bombay and Poona. These universities were chosen on the considerations of both the quality of available data as well as the regional representation. The data was obtained from the UGC. The regression coefficient with respect to data for 1985-86 (as in equation-3) indicated for the above universities that of the total expenditure while the share of salaries of teaching staff was 23.2 per cent, the share of payment to non-teaching staff was as high as 40.4 per cent. The expenditure on equipment and appliances and library was 3.3 and 1.1 per cent, respectively. The expenditure on miscellaneous items was about 28 per cent. Obviously, for the above 10 universities, the non-academic expenditure comprising the payment of salaries to non-teaching staff and other expenses on miscellaneous items account for about 68 per cent of the total expenditure on these universities. These evidences, therefore, establish a *prima facie* case for observing fiscal prudence but also indicate the area which ought to be looked into from the point of view to effecting economy and ensuring efficiency in expenditure.

TABLE 4.14: Econometric Results of Expenditure Analysis

Time-Series Analysis (1969-70 to 1979-80) - All India (Equation - 1)

$$\text{Log E (India)} = 0.5427 + \underset{(21.09)}{0.3017 \text{ Log St}} + \underset{(14.12)}{0.2330 \text{ Log Snt}} + \underset{(6.08)}{0.0509 \text{ Eq}} + \underset{(19.40)}{0.4075 \text{ Log Misc}}$$

$R^2 = 0.99$

Cross-Sectional Analysis (1979-80) - By States (Equation - 2)

$$\text{Log (States)} = 0.7576 + \underset{(12.57)}{0.3205 \text{ Log St}} + \underset{(6.27)}{0.2270 \text{ Log Snt}} + \underset{(4.12)}{0.0549 \text{ Log Eq}} + \underset{(2.60)}{0.0422 \text{ Log Gr}}$$

$$+ \underset{(1.13)}{0.0183 \text{ Log Lib}} + \underset{(13.75)}{0.3126 \text{ Log Misc.}}$$

$R^2 = 0.99$

Cross-Sectional: Analysis (1985-86): By Universities (Equation -3)

$$\text{Log E (universities)} = 0.6560 + \underset{(8.02)}{0.2318 \text{ Log St}} + \underset{(7.57)}{0.4037 \text{ Log Snt}} + \underset{(2.61)}{0.0326 \text{ Log Eq}} + \underset{(0.64)}{0.0111}$$

$$\text{Log Lib} + \underset{(4.70)}{0.2789 \text{ Log Misc.}}$$

$R^2 = 99$

Abbreviations

E = Expenditure on Universities and the subscripts indicate the sample size i.e. all India, Statewise and University wise data.

St = Expenditure on salaries of teaching staff

Snt = Expenditure on Salaries of non-teaching staff

Eq = Expenditure on equipment and appliances

Lib = Expenditure on Libraries

Gr = Payments of student grants like scholarships and fellowships

Misc = Miscellaneous expenditure like stationery, stamps and postage, telephone etc.

4.6 Concluding Observations

The aspects of management and utilization of resources are much less satisfactory than desired, especially, in a developing country like India which suffers from scarcity of funds. First, a little probing into the question of how the physical and financial resources are utilized would reveal that the major expenditure on higher education, about 60 per cent or even more, is accounted for by the staff salaries, of which nearly 50 per cent involves payment to non-teaching staff. Further, the expenditure on non-salary items which include *inter alia* student support services, has been declining overtime. The expenditure on miscellaneous items like electricity, water charges, telephone, etc., has been rising. Second, the academic staff of universities are not utilized to the extent stipulated by the UGC. The evidences, moreover, show that teacher-student ratio in a large number of universities is very low, about 1:10, which indicate the possibility of improving students' learning since a teacher has to concentrate on a small number of students. Alternatively, economies of scale could be generated by increasing student numbers. There are also those colleges which have high teacher-student ratio due to enrolment pressure which adversely affects quality of education. This reflects lack of planning at the regional and institutional level as well, which adversely influences, cost-effectiveness of the educational programmes. Third, the capacity utilization of infrastructure facilities like classrooms, labs and libraries is merely about 60 per cent which obviously indicate a colossal waste of resources that have been deployed for creation of such facilities.

It emerges from the foregoing that due to allocative inefficiency there is much to be desired as far as the financial accountability of the university system is concerned. There are those institutions which are characterised by abundance of physical and financial resources as is evident from budgetary surpluses and under utilization of facilities whereas some others are suffering from inadequacy of funds and necessary infrastructure as already discussed in Chapter 3. In the following Chapter, 5, we shall examine the extent to which unit costs of education vary across the institutions due to inefficient allocation and utilization of funds.

5

COSTS OF HIGHER EDUCATION
An Analysis of Internal Efficiency

This chapter seeks to (a) workout and analyse the costs of education by major categories; (b) examine the extent of variations in costs across the teaching facilities/departments; and (c) identify the reasons for differences in per student costs of higher education. An attempt shall also be made to assess the internal efficiency of universities in management of resources as judged from the m onetary costs of producing a graduate in a given year.

At the outset, it may be reiterated that none of the funding agencies are using acceptable norms or formula for distribution of resources across various heads of expenditure including administrative and secretarial staff and other contingency expenses. For instance, the UGC heavily relies on Visiting Committee's Reports which indicate *inter-alia* the requirements of universities for development purposes while the non-plan expenditure especially of the Central universities is fully provided for an actual expenditure basis. The study of the various Reports which are available with the Commission provide no clue to the effect as to what procedure and methodolgy various committees have adopted for recommending the resource transfer to the universities. The development grants of colleges especially those which are affiliated to Delhi University are worked out on the basis of the guidelines which the UGC has evolved in respect of non-teaching staff. Almost all the States have also developed grants-in-aid codes for determining their shares in the total expenditure, especially in respect of the Plan grants while the non-Plan grants are fully provided in the form of block grants for the approved items of expenditure. The magnitude of funds worked out on the basis of the codes are, however, found inadequate since the codes have hardly been revised for decades and are also not linked with the phenomenon of rise in prices. It has, therefore, been observed that for ameliorating financial hardship of universities 'no formula based on economic and educational indicators like prices, enrolment size, location of institution, teaching hours, student-teacher ratio, etc., which could be broadly applied to all the institutions in India has been evolved so far'.[1] As a result of which, a great deal of distortions in the requirement and availability of funds for executing the programmes of teaching and research are caused. Since the funding agencies like the UGC and the Central and the State Departments of Education have not evolved any uniform criteria of resource allocation, the costs of education, even in respect of comparable programmes of teaching and research, widely vary across the universities. This, therefore, constitutes a major deficiency in the mechanism of distribution of funds as the principles of equity and efficiency in resource allocation are not duly satisfied. And due to differential treatment in allocation of resources, quality of teaching and research vary greatly across the universities. Another difficulty that arise due to *adhoc* allocation of funds is that persistent diseconomies in management of universities become a rule rather exception because those institutions which are over funded continue to enjoy a better financial health whereas others being under funded suffer from either perpetual deficit or sacrifice the quality of education. Therefore, an attempt is made below to examine the extent to which the unit costs of education differ owing mainly to the lack of uniform method of resource allocation for comparable programmes of studies. An idea of unit cost would lend perspective on development of cost norms, based, of course, on the average level of expenditure on different programmes of studies and other supporting facilities. This would also enable us to assess the validity of our new mechanisms of funding, as suggested in Chapter 7. To be more precise, the advantages of unit cost analysis may be underscored below.

5.1 The Concept of Unit Cost and its Uses

The unit costs analysis is particularly useful to educational planners as it shed light on inter-university and intra-university differences in the patterns of spending on various programmes of studies within the educational system.

The concept of unit costs denotes the amount of recurrent expenditure spent per student in a given year. The unit costs are calculated either for the educational system as a whole or preferably for certain levels of education, or even for particular institution or for a particular programme of study and other related expenditures. The unit costs indicate the cost of educating one student for one year at the level of the chosen disaggregation. With the help of unit costs, it is possible to make all sorts of comparisons: from one year to the next; from one institution to the other and so on. As a summary statistics, unit costs reveal vital aspects of educational finances. It is, therefore, important to exercise a great deal of care in computing unit costs. Since the unit costs are used primarily for comparisons, it is imperative that it should be calculated in the same way for each type and level of educational programme. Indeed, the unit costs, itself indicate very little of interest, it is only when the relevant comparisons are made that they become useful for planning and policy making purposes.

In view of such an important role of unit costs in guiding policy, an attempt has been made to work out per student costs of education for different universities. Before the results are discussed, the methodology including the nature and quality of data, sample size, etc., may be briefly described below.

5.2 The Methodology and Data Base

An attempt has been made to work out the unit costs (per student) of education at the levels of university, faculty and department of studies. For each of such classifications, the break-up of per student expenditure on salaries of teaching and non-teaching staff, academic support services (other than salaries) and general administration has also been provided. To do this, the methodology which we have employed to ensure comparability of results is as under:

The unit costs analysis of an educational system require two sets of data. While one pertains to enrolment, the other relates to expenditure. As regards enrolment, a university offers various types of courses of studies at different levels. It is, therefore, important to obtain segregated data on enrolment in respect of each course and level of study. Almost every university compiles such data which may be had either from the Annual Report of a university or from the university departments, or the Annual Report of the U.G.C.

The difficulty, however, arises in obtaining data on expenditure that corresponds to each course and levels of study as well as different functions like salaries of staff, labs, equipment and library facilities etc., which are essential constituents of an educational programme. The lack of detailed disaggregated expenditure and the absence of any ingenious technique to overcome the problem arising from data constraints, are the major factors which contribute to weaknesses of exercises pertaining to the unit costs analyses. This study is no exception. An attempt has, however, been made to estimate the institutional expenditure incurred in educating one student for one year in various universities by different programmes of studies. In this context, the following aspects relating to the nature and quality of data, the procedure of classification, etc., may be noted.

(i) Since the desirable break-up of expenditure is not available, the enrolment data have been standardised by using weights with respect to one student at the given level. As we know that at each successive level of education, the amount of time and that of senior faculty rises due mainly to 'value added' in educational level of students who require a somewhat higher corresponding inputs in terms of teaching and research. In order to provide the needed inputs institutions incur higher costs in terms of payment of salaries as well as other supporting facilities. In view of this, the following weights which are based on our judgement about the normative distribution of expenditure for different types and levels of degree/diploma courses have been used for standardisation of enrolment data.

Table 5.1: Weights for Standardization of Enrolment Data

Levels of Education	Weight
1. Ph.D.	2
2. M.Phil	1.5
3. Postgraduate	1.0
4. Graduate	0.5
5. Certificate/Diploma	0.25

(ii) As the focus of the study is on working out the costs of education by discipline, the differential weights for science and non-science subjects are not assigned.

(iii) The unit costs reflect the expenditure on per student per year at postgraduate level i.e. M.A./M.Sc., etc., since the proportion of students at this level is higher which is due to the choice of universities selected by us for the study.

(iv) For the universities which form our sample, the affiliated colleges are out of our purview, while the constituent colleges, faculties/departments etc. have been duly included in the study.

(v) The physical information relating to enrolment, staff strength, etc., and the financial data pertaining to payment of salaries and other expenditures have been compiled from the Annual Reports and Budgets of the respective universities.

(vi) The analysis pertains to the year 1986-87.

(vii) Given the usual time constraint, the availability of relevant data was the main basis of selection of different universities. Care has, however, been taken to select both the Central as well as the State universities. In the category of former are the universities of Aligarh, Banaras, Delhi, Jawaharlal Nehru. The University of Annamalai, Kurukshetra, Madras and Ravi Shankar belong to the latter category.

A word about different items of expenditure used in this study may be mentioned.

(i) Academic expenditure refers to (a) payment of salaries and allowances to teaching and supporting staff attached with the department; and (b) expenses on academic support services, other than salaries, which include such items of expenditure as are necessary for expediting the process of learning and teaching. The items of expenditure included in this category are furniture, equipment, chemicals, stationery, postages, books and journals etc., as shown by various departments and faculties of universities.

(ii) (a) Expenditure on general administration refers to salaries and allowances of non-teaching staff and other non-salary expenditures which are incurred to run the general administration of a university. It includes the expenditure incurred on the office of Vice-Chancellor, pro-Vice Chancellor, Registrar, Finance and Accounts, Library, Examination, etc.

(b) The sum of expenditure incurred on salary items is generally very large. The non-salary items in general administration are maintenance and repair of land, building, furniture, equipment, expenditure on fuel, water, electricity, health and medicine, stationery, postage and other contingencies.

Needless to emphasise, in order to make the unit costs comparable across the universities as well as to reflect the costs of each major component of education, suitable adjustments in data have been made as indicated below.

First, the proportion of expenditure on account of examinations are generally very high in most of the universities and it is more so, for the affiliating universities especially in the States sector . Using the enrolment data attributable to affiliated colleges, the expenditure data have been cleansed on *pro rata* basis. Per student cost of general administration has thus been adjusted to reflect the cost on a comparable basis for all the universities in the sample.

Second, the appropriation of administrative costs attributable to each department/faculty has been made on the basis of their respective size of expenditure on salary and non-salary items. For instance, on the basis of *inter-se* percentages of expenditure of each department/faculty in the total university expenditure, the expenditure on general administration has been distributed across the departments/faculties. The size of administrative costs in some of the universities is estimated to be very high. For the reasons of limited information, it was difficult to identify the causes of high administrative costs.

5.3 The Results of Unit Costs Analysis : Inter-University Comparisons

The major conclusions based on the unit costs analyses may be summarised below:

First, the Central and the State universities differ a great deal in respect of allocation of resources for various comparable programmes of studies. The computation of the unit costs (per student) by faculties of Arts, Sciences, Commerce and Management, etc., demonstrate considerable differences in the degree as well as the magnitude of expenditure on salaries of teaching and non-teaching staff, academic support services and general administration. Table 5.2 presents the summary statistics on the unit costs of higher education for different faculties. The detailed break up of the unit costs are presented in Appendix Table 5C1 through 5C6. The disciplinewise unit costs under the above heads similarly differ; thereby indicating, the lack of uniformity in the pattern of allocation of funds even for the comparable teaching and research departments. The extent of variations in the expenditure on a student at post-graduate level in a particular discipline may be seen in Appendix Table 5D1 through 5D14, which provide detailed break-up for various disciplines belonging to the groups of Arts, Humanities, Social

Sciences and Sciences, etc. A summary statement of the unit costs by departments is presented in Tables 5.3 and 5.4. Using a different set of data and without standardizing the enrolment at various levels, an attempt was also made to workout the per student recurring ex penditure for the years 1975-76 and 1984-85 for the Central, the State and Deemed to be universities. The results may be seen in Appendix Tables 5E 1 through 5E 3, which reveal, as discussed above, large variations. There is, however, no discernible pattern to reflect the type of universities or nature of studies or source of revenue which cause a high or low cost of education.

Second, the unit costs of general administration, including the salary and non-salary expenses, have generally emerged out to be very high even higher than the expenses on teaching in most universities. This is true for both the affiliating and non-affiliating universities as may be seen in the above mentioned tables. Since the expenditure on examination especially in the affiliating universities, is generally very high, the higher magnitude of unit costs reflect the expenditure attributable to examinations.

Third, the evidences conclusively indicate that even though there is parity in the scale of pay of the teaching staff throughout the country, the differences in per student teaching costs are very wide, let alone the payments to supporting staff or the provision for physical facilities which are hardly determined on a uniform basis among the universities. Unlike the Central Universities, service conditions of non-teaching staff in the State universities differ a great deal which affect the per student costs of non-academic services.

Fourth, when an attempt was also made to identify the reasons for differences in the costs on account of academic and other support services as well as the general administration, the data revealed that the operating costs on account of payments of salaries to teaching and non-teaching staff were higher due to a very low ratios of students to teachers and students/teachers to supporting staff. The relevant ratios could be seen at the bottom of the different Appendix tables. In other words, these indicators indicated the scope for generating economies of scale by either increasing the number of students or reducing the teaching and non-teaching staff so as to generate savings on account of payment of salaries.

TABLE 5.2: Per Student Recurring Cost by Faculty of Study, 1986-87

(*In Rupees*)

University Faculty	Delhi	Aligarh	Banaras	Madras	Annamalai	Kurukshetra	Ravishan-kar	J N U	Coefficient of variation (%)
Arts	3335 (3112)	8040 (9108)	4737 (7592)	13247 (43316)	8751 (15551)	2599 (6245)	2500 (10819)	4282 (8429)	64 (98)
Science	5878 (5499)	6804 (7709)	9274 (14863)	17447 (50404)	3677 (6747)	6525 (15675)	4703 (20347)	12004 (23620)	55 (81)
Law	1957 (1827)	3463 (3935)	1622 (2590)	2659 (10923)	-	4021 (9663)	2000 (8706)	-	36 (63)
Commerce and Management	3070 (2882)	2993 (3395)	1413 (2273)	4660 (19132)	3011 (5539)	2196 (5264)	-	-	37 (99)
Education	7247 (6731)	-	3531 (5683)	-	2833 (5198)	3101 (7452)	-	-	49 (16)
Engineering & Technology	-	9932 (11253)	16149 (25871)	-	4048 (7427)	-	-	-	60 (66)
Average	3883 (3629)	10859 (12306)	11005 (17635)	10364 (42577)	3592 (6589)	3415 (8204)	3149 (13627)	5283 (10396)	56 (85)

Note: Figures in parantheses indicate the unit costs of general administration attributed to the respective faculties.

(-) Faculty does not exist.

TABLE: 5.3 Per Student Recurring Cost by Department of Study, 1986-87 (Faculty of Arts and Social Sciences)

(In Rupees)

University Department	Delhi	Madras	Ravishankar	Kurukshetra	Annamalai	Cofficient of variation (%)
1. Economics	3274	5539	2227	2383	2799	41
	(3078)	(22764)	(9773)	(5723)	(5134)	(85)
2. English	2646	1448	-	1542	6596	79
	(2475)	(5198)		(3706)	(12096)	(73)
3. Political Science	1093	4052	-	2129	4170	52
	(1029)	(16655)		(5115)	(7675)	(87)
4. Geography	4074	5786	1540	4647	N.A.	45
	(3826)	(23803)	(6674)	(11167)		(78)
5. Hindi	1563	6007	-	1760	N.A.	81
	(1117)	(25451)		(4232)		(129)
6. History	1601	10383	893	1587	2953	113
	(1488)	(43719)	(3862)	(3813)	(5421)	(154)
7. Philosophy	2226	2077	8461	1820	N.A.	88
	(2097)	(8523)	(36615)	(4375)		(124)
8. Psychology	2961	6053	2547	2597	N.A.	48
	(2737)	(25026)	(11013)	(6234)		(87)

Note: 1. Figures in paranthesis indicate the unit costs of general administration attributed to the respective faculties.
2. (-) Department does not exist.
3. N.A. Not computed due to non-availability of data.

TABLE 5.4: Per Student Recurring Cost by Department of Study, 1986-87 (Faculty of Sciences)

(*In Rupees*)

University Department	Delhi	Madras	Annamalai	Ravishankar	Kurukshetra	Cofficient of variation (%)
1. Physics	4396 (4115)	8860 (36420)	3346 (6137)	5169 (22373)	9353 (22447)	44 (73)
2. Chemistry	2465 (2299)	4414 (18145)	4021 (7379)	3864 (16716)	9109 (21880)	53 (61)
3. Botany	8152 (7611)	10231 (42054)	3092 (5672)	-	3746 (8976)	55 (108)
4. Zoology	8042 (751)	5068 (20833)	2200 (4033)	-	8452 (20271)	49 (66)
5. Geology	7020 (6533)	10214 (41982)	5473 (10044)	4215 (18238)	-	38 (83)
6. Mathematics	3737 (3503)	10047 (41308)	N.A.	5623 (24550)	6769 (7440)	40 (90)

Note: 1. Figures in parantheses indicate the unit costs of general administration attributed to the respective faculties.

2. - Department does not exist.

3. N.A. Not computed due to non-availability of data.

The major attributable reasons for variations in the unit costs of general administration are discussed below.

5.4 Causes of Variations in Unit Costs

(i) The universities vary in respect of teaching and research loads and there are those universities which are mainly unitary while others are largely affiliating. The extent of diversification of university activities as well as proportions of students pursuing scientific and technical education also differ which cause differences in the requirements for teaching and research, including student support services.

(ii) Unlike the uniform norms like educational qualifications for recruitment of teaching staff throughout the country and the scales of pay as laid down by the UGC, there is neither uniform norm for appointment of non-teaching staff nor there is any standard scale of pay for such staff. The non-teaching staff of the State universities are governed by the States' by-laws which differ very widely for various reasons. Thus, because of differences in service conditions of non-teaching staff in different States, the level and magnitude of payment of salaries to such staff differ. This naturally influences the unit costs of higher education and contributes to inter-state and inter-university differences in costs of education.

(iii) Under the existing approach of financing non-plan expenditure, there is hardly any attempt to make a fresh assessment of either the need for continuing the old schemes and the staff employed thereon or the scope to reorient the schemes initiated in the previous Plans so as to remove obsolscence and improve the relevance of the progress. Even though some programmes may not be relevant to the needs of the society or the market economy, the pursuance of the concept of non-plan finance hardly allows for redeployment of physical and financial resources. This, therefore, keeps on adding to the total financial burden on the funding agencies without corresponding improvement in efficiency in use of resources.

(iv) The use of modern office management methods are at a low key in most of the universities; as a result of which, labour intensity and the corresponding payments to non-teaching staff have increased considerably. Moreover, unlike other sectors of the economy, the education sector has hardly been benefiting from the modern technologies for promoting the teaching and learning process. As a result, this sector has not taken the advantage of productivity gains due to low cost and efficient technologies.

(v) The impact of all these factors on university finances has been that the non-academic expenditure has got unduly magnified.

The implications of the foregoing discussions for policy formulations are: First, the aspects of planning and management of resources both physical and financial for the university system as a whole, especially at the university level, ought to be closely looked into from the view point of devising an efficient and equitous resource allocation policy for the entire university system in India. Second, the expenditure on non-academic activities including the payment of salaries to non-teaching supporting staff and expenditures on non-salary items like stationery, postage and telegrams, purchase and maintenance of furniture and equipment and chemicals, honorarium, books and journals, advertisement, etc., are generally very high in most of the universities. As there is no discernible trend in spending on such items as discussed above, by different universities, there is ample scope to check the growth of expenditure on such activities as above so as to release funds for further investments on the programmes having direct bearing on the quality of teaching and research; and or to ensure effective utilization of funds. In essence, this requires improvements in internal efficiency of universities, a concept to which we shall return to in the following discussions.

5.5 Assessing Internal Efficiency of Universities

The concept of internal efficiency refers to economic use of physical and financial resources within the educational system or an institution to realise the objective of producing educational output (i.e. student) whereas the concept of external efficiency refers to the use of educational outputs by the economy and society in accelerating the pace of development. Much of the discussions and the conclusions drawn therefrom, in the preceding section, pertain to internal efficiency in utilization of resources as the relevant comparisons of unit costs in respect of the comparable programmes lend desirable perspective about the extent of efficient use of funds for given level (or unit) of output under the alternative system of production. The need for modifying the existing approach of planning and management of resources as revealed from wide variations in unit costs is duly corroborated by the empirical studies[2] which indicate that the facilities already created in the universities are not fully utilized for various reasons. For instance, an assessment of the extent of utilization of facilities has demonstrated that:

(i) The academic staff are not fully utilized to the extent desirable in a number of universities. The student-teacher ratio being very low in most of the universities, there is considerable scope for increasing the quantity of university output i.e. students as well as for improving the quality of education since a teacher has to concentrate on a relatively small number of learners.

(ii) The teaching cost not only vary from one university to another but is unduly high in most of the universities as compared, of course, to the institutions which can be called representative ones. A major reason attributable to this phenomenon is that the teachers, especially at senior levels, are recruited and promoted without having due regard to the needs of universities on account of teaching and research loads. In view of low student-teacher ratio, it is possible to minimise the teaching costs by way of rationalising teachers' recruitment and promotional policy for university teachers; which, in effect, would help contain the expenditure on salaries. Needless to point out, the UGC's merit promotion scheme and the similar schemes adopted by the universities for instance, the *en masse* promotion of 3000 lecturers as Readers in Delhi University in 1991-92, have played havoc with the university system, especially by way of misallocating limited resources towards, consumption rather than investment areas.

(iii) The non-academic costs, as measured by the expenditure on supporting non-teaching staff, are also unduly high in terms of both percentage share as well as the absolute per student costs as discussed before. This is due mainly to a high teaching to non-teaching staff ratio. The expenditure on non-academic activities could be checked by reducing labour intensity in servicing the academic staff, who are engaged in carrying out the programmes relating to teaching and research. In other words, the use of educational technologies, which is at the low key in most universities, could duly ensure cost-effectiveness of teaching programmes.

(iv) The capacity utilization of infrastructure facilities such as classrooms, laboratories and libraries is merely about 60 per cent as assessed for a sample of institutions which is obviously much lower than what would be desired in a developing country like India which suffers from deficiency in both physical and financial resources.

(v) Even though the causes of under-utilization of infrastructure facilities are not easily identifiable, the evidences conclusively indicated deficiency in the existing mechanism of planning and management of resources.

5.6 Some Policy Inferences

In conclusion, it may be said that a concerted effort ought to be made so as to ensure efficient and effective utilization of scarce resources that have been invested for the development of higher education and research. The issue being raised here is precisely related to financial accountability of the system of providing higher education. This issue is, therefore, concerned with both the institutions which receive the funds for creation of facilities with a view to providing educational service to the society as well as the funding agencies like the Department of Education of the Central and the State Governments, the UGC, etc., which are responsible for ensuring optimal utilization of public funds for the approved educational activities.

As the financial resources for higher education have generally increased at a higher rate than the rise in national income and prices, as discussed in Chapter 4, the planners should necessarily be concerned with the management and utilization of existing facilities. Because, if the resources are under-utilized or mis-utilized, it would have serious repercussions for the development of the system of higher education, as its credibility in respect of external efficiency would be adversely affected for the following reasons. First, under-utilization of facilities would lead not only to a general loss of income and wealth but also a relatively low quality and quantity of inputs in the process of human resource development which would, in turn, affect the standard of output i.e. students. Second, the health and vitality – physical and mental – of human resources have significant bearing on employability of university graduates for various categories of crucial jobs that are to be effectively handled for ensuring national development. A poor quality of education and training would adversely affect the ability of graduates to efficiently perform their duties as workers, managers, administrators, etc., which would, in effect, influence productivity and production. And if there is no growth in income, how can services like education be financed for human development?

As the resources are scarce and every socio-economic sector of economy has to compete for limited funds, any sector which is not utilizing its resources optimally and is not raising its credibility by way of complying with the functional requirements expected of it, such a sector would be unable to attract funds from the national pool of resources. Eventually, the development oriented programmes of such a sector would get jeopardised. This is precisely a kind of disease from which, to some extent; the system of higher education has been suffering. A remedy to this problem lies in making the system somewhat more accountable to the society, specially by way of: (a) ensuring better utilization of facilities; (b) enhancing the quality of teaching and research; and (c) improving the relevance of education to the contemporary needs of the society and the economy. In short, Cost-effectiveness of university programmes ought to be improved.[3]

These objectives could, however, be realised by adopting a sound method of funding, which should take into account all the relevant factors that have significant bearing on the costs of education. The assessment of financial requirements merely on the basis of various analyses of past trends, as has been the practice in India, does not seem to lend desirable guidance for working out additional investment requirements of universities. Therefore, in addition to the well-known determinants of educational expenditure like the number of students, teaching and research facilities, etc., the resource allocation criteria ought to attach due weightage to the degree of utilization of available facilities as well, so as to ensure efficient management of resources as well as financial accountability of universities to the funding agencies. Such an approach would naturally create conditions whereby the university would have to formulate their own meaningful plans for development.

While the universities are largely responsible for preserving, disseminating and generating knowledge and technical know-how as well as for providing alternative policy options for national development, the contemporary university situation is such that they are to be told now about the imperative need for carrying out exercises in physical and financial planning, with a view ensuring allocative efficiency of scarce resources, so that the people who pay for education can duly seek the value for money. To this end in view, the mechanism of ensuring better management of financial resources while raising the level of performance in teaching and research would be discussed in Chapter 7.

REFERENCES

1. Singh, A. and Sharma, G.D. (1981) *University and College Finance*, AIU.
2. See Author's (1989) 'Assessing the Extent Use of Educational Facilities,' *Journal of Higher Education*.
3. See Author's (1993) *Unit Costs of Higher Education: An Efficiency Study of Universities*, AIU.

6

THE POLICY AND COSTS OF IMPLEMENTATION
An Assessment of Budgetary Needs Upto 2000 A.D.

In this chapter an attempt is made to briefly state the policy on higher education and work out the budgetary requirements for implementation of the programmes, which have already been approved by the National Parliament in 1986. At the outset, against the backdrop of the prevailing scenario of university development, the salient features of the policy are described. Subsequently, the relevant exercises pertaining to projection of enrolment and financial requirements are carried out. To the extent possible, the budgetary outlays for different programmes are indicated separately for the period 1990-95, which largely cover the current Eighth Five Year Plan. The level of enrolment for different types of education has been projected upto A.D. 2000.

6.1 Preliminary Observation

Ever since the inception of the planning era, in 1951, a commendable progress has been made in respect of expansion and diversification of higher education system in India. As already discussed in Chapter 2, the development of higher education has been regarded as 'crucial factor for survival' (National Policy on Education (NPE) 1986). The health and vitality of universities are thus considered as important indicators of national development. In the planning for educational advancements considerable emphasis has, therefore, been laid on the promotion of tertiary education but the paucity of financial resources due to the low stage of economic development and high competing claims on limited funds by priority sectors of growth has generally posed insurmountable difficulties in providing for financial sustenance to the system. With the growing realisation about the value of education in socio-economic well-being of people and its consequent impact on widening of the base of elementary and secondary education, the pressure of demand for higher education is increasing and in the foreseeable future it would be much more than what has been observed in the past since the demand for trained and skilled manpower is expected to rise. This also means that the financial burden of protecting the system from degradation would increase and/or the present under investment on education would perpetuate. As long as the budgetary requirements of other socio-economic sectors particularly for alleviating nutritional and health poverty and eradicating illiteracy remain duly higher, the possibilities of raising the level of funding for higher education, commensurate with its requirement, especially from the traditional Government sources would be distinctively dim. The recent economic reforms in which focus has been laid on deregulation and privatisation of the economy duly support the view that HEIs would not receive substantial Government support to ameliorate their financial conditions.

In fact, this is precisely what has been happening in the recent times. It may also be argued that for the unsatisfactory state of affairs the HEIs are themselves responsible at least to the extent to which their performance with regard to cost-effectiveness of programmes have been below the expected level. It is mainly for this reason that despite the key role assigned to higher education in expediting the process of modernization by way of providing various types and levels of manpower to all the socio-economic sectors of development, the developments in this field have been extremely uneven. In this context, the Education Commission (1966) has observed that:

> "There is a general feeling in India that the situation in higher education is unsatisfactory and even alarming in some ways, that the average standards have been falling and that rapid expansion has resulted in lowering quality. Many realize how serious are the actual conditions academic and physical, that obtain in colleges and universities. Even those who are broadly aware of the situation fail to notice its poignancy because they have become used to such conditions."

Even after a lapse of two decades, the conditions have not changed. NPE-1986: Programme of Action (p.71) has observed that the system:

"Presents an uneven, often conflicting picture of great institutions with a large number of universities and colleges where all norms of academic conduct are undermined, several thousands of schools in which teachers and students are engaged not only in observance of their expected roles but which radiate excellence, and also those which do not open on time, are unkempt and where the teaching and learning processes have little chance to germinate; large numbers of teachers who inspire their pupils and are known for their learning, but also teachers who thoughtlessly ignore their obligations, sometimes altogether absenting themselves from the institutions; most sophisticated systems of pupil evaluation, with an examination system which is fast losing its credibility. . . ."

NPE (1986) has described higher education as a 'crucial factor for survival' because of its contribution to national development through dissemination of specialised knowledge and skills and also because of its potentiality to provide people with 'an opportunity to reflect on the critical social, economic, cultural, moral and spiritual issues facing humanity.' Being at the apex, the system of higher education also exercises an abiding influence upon the lower stages of education and, to a very great extent, determines the standards of education at these stages. It is, therefore, essential that higher education should be helped to develop on sound lines.

With a view to ameliorating the educational system, the policy, therefore, stipulates that 'urgent steps will be taken to protect the system from degradation so as to make it dynamic as never before'. This, however, has its own implication for cost and finance of higher education, to which we shall return to later. Let us in the following section indicate the major thrusts of the policy on higher education as contained in the NPE 1986.

6.2 **Thrust Areas**

The development of higher education in the next 10 to 15 years has to be primarily based on the consolidation and expansion of existing facilities as also to enable it to become 'dynamic as never before, constantly entering uncharted areas'. It should also be given the requisite freedom and responsibility to innovate in teaching and research. It has also to restructure its courses of study in order to be in tune with the emerging socio-economic and cultural realities of the country. The main areas of concern in the development of higher education which have relevance for the next 10 to 15 years are:

6.2.1 *General Higher Education*

(a) emphasis on autonomy of colleges and departments, provisions of means to interact across boundaries of institutions and funding agencies, better infrastructure, more rationalised funding for research, integration of teaching, research and evaluation (POA; P.38);
(b) encouraging the Open University System in order to augment opportunities for higher education, ensure access and promote a flexible and innovative system of education; and
(c) consolidating the new pattern of the Rural Universities and encouraging its development on the lines of Mahatma Gandhi's revolutionary ideas on education so as to take up the challenges of micro-planning at the grass-root levels for the transformation of rural areas.

6.2.2 *Technical and Management Education*

(a) to restructure technical and management education in the light of the anticipated scenario by the turn of the century, with specific reference to the likely changes in the economy, social environment, production and management processes, the rapid expansion of knowledge and the great advances in science and technology;
(b) greater induction of improved technologies and supply of technical and managerial manpower to the infrastructure and services sectors as well as the unorganised rural sector;
(c) promotion of continuing education, covering emerging as well as established technologies;
(d) emphasis on distance learning programme;
(e) training in entrepreneurship to promote self-employment;
(f) encouraging research for development; and
(g) promotion of individual and institutional excellence.

In pursuance of the above salient features of the policy, the UGC and other agencies responsible for the development of higher education, have made vigorous efforts to implement the policy, especially with regard to improvement in quality and relevance of education. The financial costs of various schemes initiated by the UGC, for instance, particulary after the adoption of new policy are substantial. The break up of expenditure already incurred by the UGC on different new schemes are, however, not available. Given this limitation, an attempt is made to translate the stipulated policies on higher education into financial costs. The entire period begining from the year of implementation of policy to the year A.D. 2000 is proposed to be covered. In order to gain an idea of the degree of reliability of our projection, suitable tests would be carried out and, accordingly, the results would be interpreted to draw relevant conclusions. It is important to mention that while the projections of financial requirements would largely be made on the basis of automatic increase in enrolment and the prevailing costs of education, the needs for resources on account of discretionary changes like upgradation of quality or a mix of various categories and levels of education would be determined partly on trend and sound judgement bases. The methodology of estimation of financial requirements for different programmes is outlined below.

6.3 **Methodology of Estimation**

As already discussed in Chapter 3, financial requirements of HEIs are provided largely on the basis of the past trend mainly for meeting the non-plan (i.e. maintenance) expenditure while the plan grants are provided on the basis of sound judgement of the need as mutually assessed by the Committees constituted for the purpose by the funding agencies as well as HEIs. There, is, however, no scientific norm or formula evolved by the funding agencies to channelise resources to HEIs for financing approved programmes. In absence of any valid criteria of determination of financial requirements, we have had to rely on the approach of extending the observed trend in growth of enrolment and financial costs, on the assumption that the past trend would replicate in future too. Wherever necessary and desirable, appropriate adjustments in data were made as pointed out below. Specifically, the following approach of estimating financial resources for the future was followed.

In educational system, the students number is the major determinant of the costs of education since the required number of teaching and non-teaching staff are usually derived from enrolment. The requirement for supporting facilities like classrooms, labs, libraries, etc., are determined on the basis of a set of variables, namely, enrolment, various categories and levels of university staff which are generally derived from enrolment and academic staff and different programmes of teaching and research. In view of this, the number of students who might seek admissions, as in the past, to various courses of studies at tertiary level was estimated by using a semi-log enrolment function, with respect to time, of the following type –

$$\text{Log } E = a + bt$$

Where:

E = enrolment

t = time

a and b are constant and regression coefficient, respectively.

In essence, this approach known as 'regression method' establishes relationship between two or more variables; and such relationships are subsequently used for projection purposes by substituting appropriate values for the explanatory variable i.e. time in the context of the above formulation. Obviously, it is assumed that the time factor captures the influence of all the variables like demographic structure, growth in income, sectoral changes in the economy influencing the demand pattern for educated and trained manpower, etc., which could be said to exert their impact on the dependent variable i.e. enrolment. For the purpose of projection of enrolment, we may confess, it would have been desirable to make use of such data as graduation rates from one level of education to another, ratios of distribution of students across the major disciplines and the extent of wastage and stagnation at various levels of education. Since these data were not easily available and that the constraints of time at our disposal did not allow for making our own calculations, the above mentioned formulation was tried on the assumption that behaviour of the factors having significant bearing on the educational scenario would continue to be consistent and, therefore, the past trend would replicate in the foreseeable future too. As expected, the above semi-log function with respect to time provided, when it was fitted to the data, the robust results as judged from the criteria of goodness of the fit. The estimated equations with respect to different categories of enrolment, as discussed below, were used for projection of student enrolment for respective cetagories.

In order to workout the costs of education under each category of enrolment, unit costs (i.e. per student) of education were estimated separately using the actual enrolment and expenditure data for the respective category of enrolment. The unit costs, thus estimated for the year 1986-87, were applied to work out the costs of education at the price level obtaining during the above period. It follows that given the quality and quantity of education in the above year, the financial costs at the constant prices have been estimated. A great deal of concern has, however, been expressed in the NPE-1986 for improving the quality and relevance of education. This aspect was, therefore, treated separately and adequate financial provision was made for each programme. Thus, the estimated requirements reflect both the growth in expenditure due to automatic increase in enrolment and the increase in outlays on account of discretionary interventions for raising the quality and relevance of programmes.

This broad approach has been uniformly applied to both general higher education as well as technical education and management education, although a number of appropriate adjustments have been made in order to improve the reliability and objectivity of the results. A mention of such adjustments would be made while discussing projections of enrolment for different categories of education. No attempt has, however, been made to show the data by levels of education i.e. undergraduate or post-graduate, an idea of which could be easily obtained by studying the pattern of transition ratios with respect to each level and discipline of education.

6.3.1 *Enrolment Projection*

General Higher Education

On the basis of actual enrolment data for ten years i.e. 1977-78 to 1986-87, the relevant enrolment functions were estimated for such courses as Arts, Science, Commerce, Education, Law and others (Social Work, Rural Studies, etc.). The estimated functions are as under:

(1) Log E_1 (Arts) $3.0047 + .0163\ t$; and $r = 0.96$
(2) Log E_2 (Science) $2.6491 + .0221\ t$; and $r = 0.98$
(3) Log E_3 (Commerce) $2.6418 + .0273\ t$; and $r = 0.99$
(4) Log E_4 (Education) $1.8342 + .0075\ t$; and $r = 0.84$
(5) Log E_5 (Law) $2.1909 + .0134\ t$; and $r = 0.97$
(6) Log E_6 (Others) $1.2089 + .0135\ t$; and $r = 0.88$

The actual data, for estimation of the above functions, as contained in various issues of University Development in India brought out by the University Grants Commission, were used. Based on these functions enrolment levels were projected as presented in Table 6.1.

TABLE 6.1: Enrolment in General Higher Education

(in thousands)

Year	Arts	Science	Commerce	Education	Law	Others	Total
	1	2	3	4	5	6	7 = (1+2+3+4+5+6)
Actual							
1977-78	1121	473	463	73	159	16	2304
1978-79	1107	492	492	71	167	18	2383
1979-80	1076	509	515	73	177	19	2468
1980-81	1114	534	552	71	174	18	2463
1981-82	1191	579	626	71	174	18	2659
1982-83	1260	624	667	74	183	18	2982
1983-84	1338	693	700	75	195	21	3072
1984-85	1372	670	735	77	196	22	3072
1985-86	1439	784	763	82	207	21	3216
1986-87	1484	725	786	85	214	22	3316
Projected							
1987-88	1528	780	875	83	218	23	3507
1988-89	1586	821	932	84	224	23	3691
1989-90	1647	864	992	85	232	24	3844
1990-91	1710	909	1057	87	239	25	4037
1991-92	1775	956	1125	88	247	26	4217
1992-93	1843	1006	1198	90	254	27	4418
1993-94	1913	1059	1276	92	262	27	4629
1994-95	1987	1114	1359	93	270	28	4851
1990-95	*9228*	*5044*	*6001*	*450*	*1272*	*133*	*22128*
1995-96	2063	1172	1447	95	279	29	5085
1996-97	2141	1233	1541	96	288	30	5329
1997-98	2233	1298	1641	98	297	31	5588
1998-99	2308	1366	1747	100	306	32	5859
1999-2000	2397	1437	1861	102	316	33	6146
1995-2000	*11132*	*6506*	*8237*	*491*	*1486*	*155*	*28007*

The course-wise *inter se* percentages of the projected enrolment for the period 1989-90 to 1999-2000 reveal that the ratio of enrolments in Science and Commerce to the total enrolment in general higher education is rising, whereas the corresponding shares of Arts, Education are declining as might be observed from Table 6.2. Keeping in view the policy perspectives for promoting science and technology based education the following adjustments were made:

First, as the NPE 1986 emphasises on the need to widen the science-based courses of studies, it was assumed that the proportionate share of enrolment in sciences would increase even at faster rate than what was observed, while the respective shares of enrolment in Commerce, Education, Law and others would follow more or less the observed trend. In other words, of the additional enrolment, a significant proportion would get absorbed in Science disciplines which would mean that the proportion of enrolment in Arts-based courses would be somewhat lesser than the observed trend.

Second, in view of the policy emphasis on consolidation of existing facilities rather than expansion and/or creation of more facilities, it was assumed that at least 10 per cent of the additional enrolment would be absorbed within the existing facilities. Accordingly, on the basis of this assumption, the estimated additional enrolment was scaled down by 10 per cent and the resulting enrolment, as indicated below, would have to be covered under expansion programme of the next plans upto AD 2000.

TABLE 6.2: Desirable Shift in the Level of Enrolment

(In' 000)

	Arts	Science	Commerce	Education	Law	Others	Total
Projected							
1989-90	1647	864	992	85	232	24	3844
	(42.9)	(22.5)	(25.8)	(2.2)	(6.0)	(0.6)	(100.0)
1999-2000	2397	1437	1861	102	313	31	6146
	(39.1)	(23.4)	(30.2)	(1.7)	(5.1)	(0.5)	(100.0)
Desirable							
1999-2000	2148	1688	1854	104	313	31	6146
	(35.0)	(27.5)	(30.2)	(1.7)	(5.1)	(0.5)	(100.0)

Note: Figures within parantheses indicate percentages to the total.

TABLE 6.3: Enrolment Level after Adjusting for Consolidation Factor

(In'000)

	Arts, Sci. & Commerce	Edn.	Law	Others	Total
i) Additional enrolment (between 1989-90 & 1999-2000)	2187	19	81	7	2294
ii) Additional enrolment to be absorbed within the existing facilities (10% of i)	219	2	8	1	230
iii) Additional enrolment to be provided with new facilities by 2000 A.D. (i-ii)	1968	17	73	6	2064

Third, the base of distance learning system has gradually been widening. The proportion of enrolment in distance education to total enrolment in higher education was 8.5 per cent in 1986-87. The share of distance learners has risen to 10 per cent by 1989-90. On present reckoning and also the recent policy emphasis, it was assumed that the proportion of distance learners would rise to 20 per cent by A.D. 2000, though there might be considerable variations in the rates of increase in distance learners for different courses. This would also mean that of the additional enrolment as high as 60 per cent would be diverted to DLS programmes. Thus, on the assumption of increasing proportion of learners under distance education from 10 per cent in the beginning of 1990 to 20 per cent by the end of A.D. 2000 adjustments in the total additional enrolment were accordingly made. The course-wise figures of additional students who are expected to be catered to through the conventional and distance education system are shown below.

Fourth, of the total estimates, thus made, it was assumed that 40 per cent would be covered by the year 1995 and the remaining 60 per cent would be covered during the subsequent five years i.e. 1995-2000 since the enrolment pressure would rise overtime. Thus, the following is the net additional burden during 1990-95 which largely cover the period of current Eighth plan and during which period the facilities should be provided.

TABLE 6.4: Distribution of Student Load in Conventional and Distance Education System, During 1990 - 2000 A.D.

(In '000)

	Arts, Sci. & Commerce	Edn.	Law	Others	Total
i) Additional Enrolment to be covered by 2000 A.D.	1968	17	73	6	2064
ii) Conventional Education	788	7	29	2	826
iii) Distance Education	1180	10	44	4	1238

TABLE 6.5: Additional Student Load During 1990-95

(In '000)

	Arts, Sci. & Commerce	Edn.	Law	Others	Total
Conventional Education	315	2	12	1	330
Distance Education	472	4	17	2	495
Total	787	6	29	3	825

6.3.2 *Financial Estimates*

In order to arrive at financial estimates for the above projected enrolment as in Table 6.5, the relevant unit costs for different courses were applied to the above enrolment estimates. The latest issue of *Education in India*, Volume II, 1979-80 provides unit costs (all-India) separately for (i) Arts, Science and Commerce, (ii) Education (including training), (iii) Law and (iv) Others (including rural studies and social work, etc.) for the year 1979-80. It may be mentioned that the coursewise unit costs, as provided in the above document, are mainly for collegiate level institutions which cater to about 88 per cent of the total enrolment in higher education. On the basis of the enrolment and expenditure in university level institutions and the existing unit cost differentials between colleges and universities, unit costs for higher education as a whole were worked out which were subsequently used for estimating future requirements. Since the educational plan expenditure has increased over the last decade at the rate of about 10 per cent per annum which is also close to rise in prices, we have escalated the unit costs at the rate of 10 per cent per annum to indicate the costs at 1989-90 prices for the period 1990-95.

The unit cost of distance education was worked out on the basis of the data available for the School of Correspondence and Continuing Education, University of Delhi; which is the oldest institution of the type in the country. Assuming that the unit cost for this School would be a fairly representative one, we have used it to indicate the overall costs of distance education programmes. The outlays for continuing schemes as well as new schemes are discussed below.

6.4 **Expenditure on Continuing Schemes**

6.4.1 *Expansion and Development*

(i) Teaching and non-teaching Costs

The total teaching and non-teaching cost is obtained by multiplying the estimated enrolment by the course-wise per student expenditure as discussed above. Table 6.6 shows the estimated expenditure.

(ii) Quality Improvement Programmes

The measures for improving the quality of teaching and research have to be taken on a continuing basis. For the fresh enrolment, specific provision has to be made for improving the teaching and the learning process. It is, therefore, deemed essential to provide additional funds to the extent of 20 per cent of the total teaching and non-teaching costs. Thus, the 20 per cent of (i) above comes to Rs.26.15 crores.

(iii) Restructuring of Courses

The relevance of the various courses of studies and research programmes to the contemporary needs of society has always been the prime concern of the educational system. Due attention has to be paid, therefore, to the need of restructuring of undergraduate and postgraduate courses, especially among the colleges which cater for about 88 per cent of the total enrolment in higher education. In view of the major role of the colleges in higher education, at least Rs. two lakhs per college is proposed to be made available to 5000 colleges of 7121 existing colleges in the country for meeting additional expenditure arising out of the restructuring of undergraduate and postgraduate courses so that educational requirements of the country for economic and social development are duly provided for. On this assumption, the total requirement under this head comes to Rs.100 crores (at the rate of two lakhs per college for each of at least 5000 colleges).

TABLE 6.6: Estimate of Expenditure for the Period 1990-95

Programme	Estimated enrolment during 1990-95	Per Student expenditure at 1989-90 Prices	Total expenditure
	(In'000)	(In rupees)	(Rs. in lakhs)
	(i)	(ii)	(iii)
1. Conventional Education			
(a) Arts, Science and Commerce	315	2787 (1280)	8779
(b) Education	2	6307 (2896)	126
(c) Law	12	1407 (646)	169
(d) Others	1	14680 (6740)	147
		Sub-Total	9221
2. Distance Education	472	817	3856
		Total (1+2)	13077

Note: Figure within parenthesis indicate per student expenditure at 1979-80 prices.

6.4.2 *Development of Universities and Colleges*

Adequacy of infrastructural facilities is a *sine qua non* for the development of universities. The NPE has duly emphasised the need for expansion of facilities in the existing universities. Without making adequate provisions for teaching and research facilities, it is not possible to improve the standard of higher education and research and its relevance to the society and economy. It is, therefore, desirable to provide at least Rs. 2 crores for each university, including its constituent colleges, to equip itself with the necessary facilities so as to contribute effectively to growth and propagation of knowledge. The total requirement for at least 150 universities, out of 190 in 1991, comes to Rs. 300 crores.

Likewise, in order to improve the academic and physical facilities in colleges it is deemed desirable to provide special assistance at the rate of Rs.10 lakhs for each college to at least 3000 colleges. The total cost would be Rs.300 crores.

6.4.3 *Programmes for Research*

The significance of original and applied research into various aspects of development hardly needs any elaboration. It must, however, be mentioned that the present position of socio-economic, political and cultural development, which is characterised as underdeveloped, warrants for massive effort for bringing research inputs into the policy-making as well as the process of implementation of the approved programmes. An amount of Rs. 400 crores is, therefore, be earmarked for the purpose of research in university sector during the period under discussion.

6.4.4 *Fellowships and Scholarships*

As an accepted policy, the needy as well as meritorious students should be encouraged by way of providing adequate amount of fellowships and scholarships. At least 10 per cent of the estimated cumulative enrolment of about 22 lakhs for 1990-95 should be provided on an average of Rs.300 per month per student so as to enable them to meet their academic and other expenses. The total requirement under this category of expenditure comes to about Rs.6.6 crores.

6.4.5 *Orientation and Training of Teachers*

The NPE has laid special emphasis on establishment of Academic Staff Colleges and as many as 48 such colleges have already been established with a view to conducting orientation programmes for college teachers. The number of teachers at present is about 2.4 lakhs in universities and colleges. If at least 15 per cent of them are covered under the training programme, and the cost of short-term and long-term training is Rs. 10,000 per teacher, the total requirements during the period would be Rs. 36 crores.

6.4.6 *Research Councils and Co-ordinating Agencies*

The research councils and co-ordinating agencies like ICSSR and ICHR, etc., require adequate funds for promoting the activities which they have been carrying out. The various departments of education with the Central and the State Governments and agencies like UGC, also require to be strengthened in terms of management and administration of educational programmes. A provision of about Rs.200 crores is, therefore, to be made for research councils and co-ordinating activities.

Thus, in all the total requirements for the continuing schemes would be Rs.1499.52 crores or say Rs.1500 crores.

6.5 New Schemes in General Higher Education

6.5.1 *Promotion of Research in Higher Education*

The NPE lays great emphasis on research as an essential component of higher education because of its role in generating new knowledge and insights as well as stimulating dynamism to the educational process. The accent in research in higher education will, therefore, be on, among other things, for enabling the universities to grapple with significant scientific problems of industry and other national agencies. For this purpose, it is necessary to strengthen the existing infrastructure and enhance the funding of research in universities. It would also be necessary to set up co-operative research facilities in the universities and to foster formal links with various research agencies to link education with research and to identify tasks that could be undertaken within the university system. An amount of Rs. 75 crores is suggested for these programmes.

6.5.2 *Modernisation of Equipment and other Technologies*

The equipment and appliances in most of the university institutions are obsolete and outdated. It is, therefore, necessary that the universities should be provided financial assistance to modernise their equipment in order to help them keep pace with the rapid scientific and technological advancements. Further, the universities also need to be helped to take advantage of recent developments in the field of educational technology for improving students' learning. For this purpose, a sum of Rs.200 crores is suggested (at the rate of Rs. 2 crores for 100 universities).

6.5.3 *Student Support Services*

The availability of hostels, play-fields, equipment for games and sports, etc., is abysmally low in universities and colleges. It is, therefore, necessary to augment these facilities. It is suggested that an amount of Rs.100 crores may be provided for these programmes in the Eighth plan.

6.5.4 *Quarters for Teaching Staff*

In view of the acute shortage of staff quarters for teachers in the institutions of higher education, at least 10,000 staff quarters should be built-up during the period 1990-95. For this purpose funds should be judiciously distributed between universities and colleges, at the rate of Rs. 2 lakhs per quarter. A sum of Rs. 200 crores, therefore, should be allocated for providing staff quarters.

6.5.5 *Development of Autonomous Colleges and University Departments*

The NPE 1986 (pp.14-15) clearly stipulates that 'autonomous colleges will be helped to develop in large numbers until the affiliating system is replaced by a free and more creative association of universities with colleges. Similarly, the creation of autonomous departments within universities on a selective basis will be encouraged'. Keeping in view the policy objective, it is proposed to develop 500 affiliated colleges and about 100 selected university departments as autonomous institutions with freedom to frame courses of studies and to adopt their own systems of evaluation. A sum of Rs.60 crores is suggested for this purpose (i.e. at the rate of Rs.10 lakhs per college/department).

6.5.6 *Rural Institutes/Universities*

The NPE has envisaged the development of a pattern of education related to the needs of rural communities. For this purpose, it is proposed to set up Rural Universities/Institutes which would seek to integrate all aspects of education and training with productive and creative activities, horizontally across disciplines of sciences, technology, humanities and social sciences and vertically across all stages of education: primary, secondary and higher education.

It is proposed to develop 30 institutions at the rate of Rs.3 crore per institution as rural institutions. An amount of Rs.90 crores is proposed for this scheme.

6.5.7 *University Adult Education Programmes*

In spite of concerted efforts made to promote literacy among the adults, the situation is far from satisfactory in that it is characterised by 'low level of literacy among persons treated as literate, widespread disuse of literacy skills often resulting in relapse of illiteracy, scanty opportunities for continuing education and access of information' (POA-p.130).

The university institutions have, therefore, to be enabled to expand their extension activities through the vast body of students and teachers as also to undertake research studies in various problems of adult education like curricular development, methods of teaching and evaluation, planning and development of adult education, etc. A sum of Rs. 25 crores is suggested for this purpose, (at the rate of 5 lakhs per annum for 100 universities).

6.5.8 *Central University in Assam*

As per the decision of the Government of India, a Central University is to be set-up at the Barak Valley, in Assam. A sum of Rs.25 crores has been provided for this purpose.

6.5.9 *National Testing Service*

The POA (p.150) has emphasised the necessity for establishing a National Testing Service/National Evaluation Organisation which would work as a 'quality control mechanism to organise nation-wide tests on a voluntary basis so that norms can be evolved for comparability of performance and also for conducting independent tests'. A sum of Rs.10 crores has been provided for this scheme.

Thus, the total outlay for General Higher Education, under both continuing as well as new schemes, comes to Rs.2285 crores (i.e. Rs.1500 crores + 785 crores, respectively). For schemewise details, please see Appendix 6.1.

6.6 **Technical and Management Education**

The data on enrolment in Technical and Management education were compiled in four categories viz., IITs, Colleges for Engineering/ Technical Education, Polytechnics and Business Management. While enrolments in IITs for the period 1990-95 and 1995-2000 were projected on the basis on actual data available for the period 1975-76 to 1984-85, enrolments in colleges for engineering/techology Education and Polytechnics for the same period were projected on the basis of actual data available for the period 1977-78 to 1986-87. As regards enrolment in Business Management, these were projected only up to the year 1994-95. The reasons for doing so were mainly two. Firstly, for Business Management, actual enrolment data at the all-India level were available for seven years only i.e. 1976-77 to 1982-83. Secondly, since the base year enrolment in Business Management was relatively smaller and it started increasing leaps and bounds over the next few years, the trend could not be relied upon for long-term projections. Table 6.7 provides projected enrolments for IITs, colleges for Engineering/Technical Education and Polytechnics up to A.D. 2000, while Table 6.8 provides projected level of enrolments for Business Management upto 1994-95.

6.6.1 *Continuing Schemes*

6.6.2 *Expansion and Development*

(i) Teaching and Non-Teaching Costs

The institution-wise *inter se* percentages of the projected enrolments for the period 1989-90 to 1999-2000 reveal that while the ratio of enrolment in colleges for Engineering/Technical to total enrolment in higher education (General plus Technical and Management Education) has increased, the corresponding ratios relating to IITs and Polytechnics have declined (Table 6.7).

TABLE 6.7: Enrolment in Technical Education

(in thousands)

Actuals	IITs		Colleges for Eng./Tech.Edn.	Polytechnics
	(E1)		(E2)	(E3)
1975-76	10.5	-	-	-
1976-77	10.7	-	-	-
1977-78	11.1	1977-78	103.7	123.2
1978-79	11.5	1978-79	111.7	114.2
1979-80	11.4	1979-80	118.6	127.8
1980-81	11.6	1980-81	128.9	99.1
1981-82	11.9	1981-82	130.2	119.1
1982-83	12.2	1982-83	142.4	98.3
1983-84	11.8	1983-84	153.1	113.0
1984-85	11.9	1984-85	159.0	147.6
1983-84	11.8	1985-86	164.3	124.5
1984-85	11.9	1986-87	169.4	198.5
Projected				
1985-86	12.4	-	-	-
1986-87	12.6	-	-	-
1987-88	12.8	1987-88	185.3	150.5
1988-89	13.0	1988-89	195.9	155.9
1989-90	13.1	1989-90	207.2	161.5
1990-91	13.3	1990-91	219.0	167.3
1991-92	13.5	1991-92	231.6	173.3
1992-93	13.7	1992-93	244.8	179.5
1993-94	13.9	1993-94	258.9	185.9
1994-95	14.1	1994-95	273.7	192.6
1990-95	*68.5*	*1990-95*	*1228.0*	*898.6*
1995-96	14.3	1995-96	289.4	199.5
1996-97	14.5	1996-97	306.0	206.6
1997-98	14.8	1997-98	323.5	214.0
1998-99	15.0	1998-99	342.1	221.7
1999-2000	15.2	1999-2000	361.7	229.7
1995-2000	*73.8*	*1995-2000*	*1622.7*	*1071.5*

Note: Projections have been made on the basis of Semi-log Enrolment (E) function with respect to Time (T). The function is of the type log (E) = a+ bt, and the respective equations for (1) IITs, (2) Colleges for Eng./Tech. Edn. and (3) Polytechnics have been as follows:

(1) $\text{Log } E_1 = 1.0239 + .0063\, t$; and $r = +0.91$

(2) $\text{Log } E_2 = 2.0017 + .0242\, t$; and $r = +0.99$

(3) $\text{Log } E_3 = 2.0092 + .0153\, t$; and $r = +0.52$

Source: (i) Enrolment data of IITs were collected from the Technical Education Division of the Ministry of HRD, Govt. of India.

(ii) Enrolment data of the Colleges for Engg./Tech. Education were collected from the various issues of *University Development in India*, University Grants Commission, New Delhi.

(iii) Enrolment data of Polytechnics were collected from various issues of *Selected Educational Statistics*, Ministry of HRD, Govt. of India.

TABLE 6.8: Enrolment in Business Management

Year (T)	Enrolment (E_b)
1976-77	906
1977-78	974
1978-79	1000
1979-80	1509
1980-81	2386
1981-82	2672
1982-83	4193
Projected	
1983-84	4855
1984-85	6343
1985-86	8287
1986-87	10827
1987-88	14145
1988-89	18480
1989-90	24143
1990-91	31543
1991-92	41210
1992-93	53839
1993-94	70340
1994-95	91897
1990-95	*288829*

Note: Projection has been made on the basis of Semi-log Enrolment (Eb) function with respect to Time (t). The function is of the type log (Eb) = a+bt, and the equation was found to be as follows:

$$\text{Log}\,(E_b) = 2.7574 + 0.1161\,t;\ \text{and}\ r = +0.97$$

Note: We did not project the enrolment data beyond 1994-95, because actual figures were available only for seven years i.e. 1976-77 to 1982-83.

Source: Enrolment data were collected from various issues of *Education in India*, Ministry of HRD, Govt. of India.

Keeping in view the policy perspectives, certain modifications were made to the above figures so as to allow for adjustments due to discretionary measures, Table 6.9. Firstly, the ratio of IIT enrolment to total enrolment in higher education was fixed at 0.23 per cent. Secondly, the ratio of enrolment in the colleges of Engineering/ Technical Education to total enrolment in higher education was raised from projection-based 5.36 to 6.00 per cent. Thirdly, the ratio of enrolment in Polytechnics to total enrolment in higher education was raised from projection-based 3.40 to 5.00 per cent. In view of the above, the additional enrolments in different categories of Technical Education between 1989-90 and 1999-2000 were estimated as Table.6.10.

TABLE 6.9: Discretionary Adjustments in Trend Enrolment

(*In '000*)

Year	IITs	Colleges for Engg./Tech. Education	Poly-technics	General Higher Education	Total Enrolment in Higher Education (General plus Tech. & Management
1	2	3	4	5	6
Projected					
1989-90	13.1	207.2	161.5	3894	4275.8
	(0.31)	(4.85)	(3.78)	(91.06)	(100.00)
1999-2000	15.2	361.7	229.7	6146	6752.6
	(0.23)	(5.36)	(3.40)	(91.01)	(100.00)
Desirable					
1999-2000	16.9	405.2	337.6	5992.9	6752.6
	(0.25)	(6.00)	(5.00)	(88.75)	(100.00)

Note: Figures within parenthesis indicate percentages to the total.

TABLE 6.10: Additional Enrolment Pressure

(*In '000*)

IITs	Colleges for Engg./Tech. Education	Polytechnics
3.8	198.0	107.9

It is assumed that at least 45 per cent of these additional enrolments should be covered by the end of 1995. The additional enrolment figures in different categories of Technical Education upto the above period were estimated as presented in Table 6.11.

TABLE 6.11: Additional Enrolment in Technical Education to be Covered by 1995

(*In '000*)

IITs	Colleges for Engg./Tech. Education	Polytechnics
1.7	89.1	48.6

As regards Business Management, only seven years' (i.e. 1976-77 to 1982-83) actual enrolment data, as pointed out before, were available for projection. Therefore, the projection was restricted upto the year 1994-95 only, and the additional enrolment in Business Management was estimated to be as in Table 6.12.

TABLE 6.12: Enrolment in Business Management

(*In '000*)

Year	Enrolment
1989-90	24.1
1994-95	91.9
Additional Enrolment During 1989-90 to 1994-95	67.8

(ii) Unit Costs of Technical Education

The per student expenditure for various institutions were estimated on the basis of information collected from various sources/publications. For instance, the per student expenditure for IITs, polytechnics and Business Management were calculated on the basis of data collected from the Technical Education Division of the Ministry of Human Resource Development. The per student expenditure for Colleges of Engineering/Technical Education was worked out on the basis of expenditure and enrolment data as available in *Education in India*, 1979-80, Ministry of Human Resources Development. The per student expenditure so calculated was thereafter increased as before, at a simple annual rate of 10 per cent to determine its value at 1989-90 prices. The total estimated expenditure on Technical and Management education for the period 1990-95 was therefore estimated to be as follows (Table 6.13).

(iii) Quality Improvement Programmes

A provision of 20 per cent of the total teaching and non-teaching Costs (i.e. of 366.1 crores as above) is provided for quality improvement programmes for the fresh entrants. The outlay on this account comes to Rs.73.22 crores. Thus, the total requirement for expansion and development programmes is worked out at Rs.439.32 crores.

TABLE 6.13: Financial Requirements for Technical Education, 1990-95

	Estimated enrolment (In '000)	Estimated per student expenditure at 1989-90 prices (In Rs.)	Estimated total expenditure (Rs. in crores)
IITs	1.7	84652	14.39
Colleges for	89.1	15298	136.31
Engineering/Technical Polytechnics	48.6	9737	47.32
Business Management	67.8	24790	168.08
	Total		366.10

6.6.3 *Direction and Administration*

The All India Council for Technical Education has been invested with the statutory authority for planning, formulation and the maintenance of norms and standards, accreditation, funding of priority areas, monitoring and evaluation, etc., and ensuring the co-ordinated and integrated development of technical and management education. Besides, it is proposed to develop the Technical Manpower Information System. Further, selected institutions will be given autonomous status. A sum of Rs.100 crores is proposed for these schemes during the period 1990-95. For relevant break-up of expenditure for different schemes see Appendix 6.2.

6.6.4 *Training*

It is proposed to further develop the Regional Engineering Colleges and Central Institutions like Technical Teacher's Training Institutes, National Institute of Training for Industrial Engineers, National Institute of Foundry and Forge Technology and School of Planning and Architecture, etc. Programmes of curriculum renewal to systematically phase out obsolescence and to introduce new technologies or disciplines will be taken up. Polytechnics for women, weaker sections especially in rural areas are proposed to be established. A sum of Rs.270 crores is provided for these schemes.

6.6.5 *Research and Development*

It is proposed to strengthen the research and development in the Indian Institutes of Technology, Institute of Management, etc., in order to focus on improving present technologies, developing new indigenous areas and enhancing production and productivity. It is also proposed to set up a system for watching and forecasting technology. Emphasis will be laid on further developing post-graduate courses in the Departments of Engineering and Technology in the existing universities. Networking System will be established between technical education and industry, R&D Organisations, programmes of rural and community development, and with other sectors of education with complementary characteristics. A sum of Rs.210 crores is proposed for the schemes under this head.

6.6.6 *Development of Engineering/Technical Colleges and Institutions*

The major thrust will be on modernisation and removal of obsolescence in curriculum in engineering institutions, creation of infrastructure in areas of emerging technologies, strengthening of facilities in technical institutions, improvement in the existing community polytechnics, industry-institutions linkages, etc. It is also proposed to provide larger facilities for hostels, staff quarters, libraries and laboratories. A sum of Rs.380 crores has been proposed for the purpose. Thus the total requirement for the Continuing Schemes would work out to Rs.1399.32 crores.

6.7 New Schemes in Technical and Management Education

6.7.1 *Community Polytechnic*

(i) It is proposed to establish at least 300 additional community polytechnics in the country at the estimated cost of Rs.15 lakhs per institution. A sum of Rs.45 crores has been provided for this purpose.

(ii) With a view to achieving the objectives of setting up of one special institute for relevant/useful technology and rural development in each state for promoting R&D, development of technology, conducting a variety of programmes for rural development and act as resource institution to community polytechnics and other institutions involved in transfer of technology and Rural/Community development, an amount of Rs.30 crores is suggested for the period 1990-95.

6.7.2 *Computerisation*

Although computers are fast penetrating into all professions and walks of life, many institutions of technical and management education do not have adequate computer facilities for both instructional and training purposes. A sum of Rs.50 crores has been provided for computerisation of institutions/departments imparting technical and management education.

6.7.3 *Entrepreneurship Development Programmes*

Special incentive programmes will be drawn up in order to bring about attitudinal changes among students towards self-employment and equipping them with relevant skills. An amount of Rs.75 crores has been provided for this scheme.

6.7.4 *Promotion of Individual and Institutional Excellence*

Under this head, a package of programmes is envisaged which includes scholarships, fellowships, staff development schemes, improving teaching quality by making the emoluments and service conditions of teachers better, provision of computer facilities, establishment of learning resource centres, modernisation and removal of obsolescence, etc. These are to be provided to selected institutions/individuals in the field of technical and management education over and above the general provision for modernization and removal of obsolescence in such institutions. An amount of Rs. 25 crores is proposed for this scheme.

6.7.5 *Implementation of Central Schemes Under AICTE*

The following major programmes are envisaged under the statutorily recoganized All India Council for Technical Education:

(i) Establishment of New Boards of Studies in the newly emerging areas of technology, continuing education, distance learning and educational technology.

(ii) Restructuring of the co-ordinating Committee of the AICTE.

(iii) Setting up of Board of Accredition to prescribe guidelines and norms for accreditation of programmes and institutions.

(iv) Evolving of feasible staff appraisal system incorporating necessary norms for accountability.

(v) Integration of educational content of vocational education and craftsmen training.

An amount of Rs.25 crores has been provided for this purpose.

6.8 Other Schemes

There were a few schemes like setting up of an Indian institute of Technology in Assam and the Longowal Institute of Engineering and Technology in Punjab, installation of Super Computer at the Indian Institute of Science, Bangalore, establishment of Educational Consultant India Ltd. (EDCIL) in New Delhi, and initiation of New Quality Improvement Programme (QIP) upon which some expenditures were incurred during the Seventh Plan. A sum of Rs. 87 crores has been proposed for supporting these schemes during the period 1990-95.

Thus, the total plan outlay on Technical and Management education, under continuing, new and other schemes, works out to be Rs. 1736.32 crores. For scheme-wise details of allocation, please see Appendix 6.2.

6.9 Centre-State Share in Plan Outlays

Table 6.14 presents a summary statistics of financial requirement under different programmes and also indicate the break-up for the Centre and the States. Of the total estimated expenditure of Rs. 4021 crores for the period 1990-95 towards the implementation of NPE (1986), 62 per cent of the total financial burden would be borne by the States while the remaining share would be met by the Centre (Table 6.14). This has been calculated on the basis of existing *inter se* percentages of expenditure incurred by the Centre and the States for the promotion of the general and technical higher education. As may be observed in the above mentioned table, the burden of general higher education largely, about 80 per cent, devolves on the States whereas the Centre has extended its contribution, about 60 per cent, for the promotion of technical and management education. As compared to the growth in expenditure under the above categories our estimates demonstrate that for effective implementation of the NPE, the allocation for general higher education is required to be doubled while the expenditure on technical education is needed to be enhanced by about two and a half times of the existing level of expenditure at 1989-90 prices. Even though the above estimates are very conservative and have been made largely on trend approach and partly on the basis of our judgement, as discussed before, they would prove to be a valuable guide for determining the magnitude of allocation for various programmes that have national approval for implementation so as to improve cost-effectiveness of higher education and its contribution to national development. It must, however, be emphasised that while the success in strengthening higher education would largely depend on the ability to finance the relevant new schemes, it is the efficient utilization of non-plan i.e. maintenance expenditure, which holds the key to the contemplated educational reforms.

TABLE 6.14: Distribution of Financial Burden on the Centre and the States, 1990-95 (at 1989-90 Prices)

(In Rs. Crores)

Type of Education	Total	Centre	States
1. General Higher Education	2285 (100)	457 (20)	1828 (80)
a) Annual Average Increase over Five years	457	91	366
2. Technical & Management Education	1736 (100)	1042 (60)	694 (40)
a) Annual Average Increase over Five years	347	208	139
3. Total (1+2)	4021 (100)	1528 (38)	2498 (62)
a) Annual Average Increase over Five years (1a+2a)	804	299	505

Note: Figures in parenthesis indicate percentages to the total as obtaining in 1989-90.

7

PERFORMANCE AND ACCOUNTABILITY OF HIGHER EDUCATION INSTITUTIONS

New Approaches of Funding

The financial problems of HEIs may be classified into three broad categories. First, despite the substantial contributions which the Central and the State governments are making towards the financing of higher education and research, the finances of HEIs are inadequate as they have not increased commensurately with the rise in enrolment, increase in prices and the growing requirements for modernization and diversification of tertiary education. Second, the stresses and strains in the Centre-State budgetary relations have left their scars on the financing of universities and colleges also, which is attributable due mainly to disproportionate distribution of fiscal powers and responsibilities in respect of development oriented educational projects. Third, the priorities within higher education have got distorted. In an attempt to equalize educational opportunities, too little attention has been paid to nurturing of excellence in higher education and promotion of research, which are crucial for raising productivity and production in every sphere of human activity. In view of this, the National Policy on Education (1986) has observed that higher education 'Contributes to national development through dissemination of specialised knowledge and skills. It is, therefore, a crucial factor for survival'. Therefore, the 'development oriented objectives of Indian society can be realized only by making investments in education of an order commensurate with the nature and dimension of the task'. This observation, it may be noted, has been made against the backdrop of prevailing fiscal deficiencies; as discussed in chapters 3 and 4, which impinge upon the effectiveness of the programmes on higher education and research. In this Chapter, an attempt is made to briefly outline the alternative methodologies of distribution of limited resources such that cost-effectiveness of higher education programmes could be ensured. At the outset, against the backdrop of challenges faced by HEIs, the prevailing methods of allocation of resources may be critically examined so as to justify the need as well as the validity of new mechanism of funding.

7.1 **The Challenge of University Development**

The experiences of most countries demonstrate that without technological innovation and its application by the educated and trained manpower of all types and levels, it is not possible to improve productivity to expedite the process of economic development. Creation of new knowledge including technical know-how falls largely under the domain of HEI which are also responsible for dissemination, preservation and application of knowledge such that well-being of people can be improved. The challenge of human development before HEIs has, however, been a formidable task for the following reasons.

India has the second largest system of higher education and one of the lowest per capita income in the world. It enrols more than four million students which constitute about 6 per cent of the population in the age group of 18-23 years. This enrolment ratio may be regarded as one of the lowest as the European countries enrol in the range of 25 to 40 per cent. More than 85 per cent of HEIs expenses are financed by the Government and the costs of education and training have been rising. A major problem is how to provide financial sustenance for the system. This problem is especially acute because:

(i) A large section of the population is yet to be covered by the educational network of programmes to provide elementary education, to which the Constitution of India is committed. The costs of educating a university graduate is as high as 70 to 100 times the cost of educating a primary school student;

(ii) In terms of the quality and relevance of educational programmes, the credibility of HEIs has been eroded as reflected from the growing number of "unemployable graduates";

(iii) More than three-fourths of the beneficiary groups of higher education are drawn from the top one-fourth higher income group, which indicates inegalitarian character of the system; and

(iv) Heavy subsidization of higher education by the State has come into sharp criticism, especially on grounds both of social justice and economic efficiency. The system has helped perpetuate the concentration of income and wealth in the hands of a few who are generally and traditionally the beneficiaries of the system.

These shortcomings of the university system will get further accentuated if the programmes of teaching and research are not updated to remove obsolescence and to make them relevant to social and economic needs. In addition, an appropriate financial policy is required to be formulated so as to equalise educational opportunities without unduly subsidizing the education of rich and/or burdening the economy by ignoring priority areas of programmes such as elementary and adult education. The policy should, moreover, aim at rectifying the deficiency in infrastructural facilities, from which most of the universities suffer. Their ability to keep pace with the advances in technological knowledge as well as to enhance the quality of teaching and research programmes is limited and will remain so unless (i) adequate funds are channelised for their development; and (ii) conditions are created for efficient utilisation of funds and for improving cost-effectiveness of higher education. The pressure on universities for providing relevant courses and appropriate training to a growing number of graduates, who generally seek employment in the industrial and allied sectors, is increasing while the costs of such services are also rising. The growing awareness among the masses, particularly about the role of universities in addressing to the regional and local problems through their extension programmes, has added to the gravity as well as urgency of the problem of financing new university programmes.

In carrying out the multiplicity of functions in academic and applied areas, a huge amount of investment is required and the Government sources which meet university expenses to the tune of 85 per cent or even more are unlikely to assure any increase in the current level of funding due to both a high competing claims by other sectors including the removal of illiteracy and poverty alleviation programmes and the lack of adequate level of accountability of the system to the society, as pointed out above. Therefore, alternative methods and sources of funding are required to be explored. We venture to do it here below.

7.2 A Critical Assessment of Mechanisms of Financing Education

The responsibility of planning, management and financing of education is jointly shared by the Centre and the States. The burden of financing education of all types and levels, however, largely falls on the States. Of the total expenditure on education, in 1986-87, 88 per cent was borne by the States. The corresponding figures for higher education-technical and non-technical were 60 and 80 per cent, respectively. Within the overall framework of arrangement of sharing resources between the Centre and the States, financial resources to various types of institutions are channelised through different agencies of the above levels of Governments. For instance, the Institutions of National Importance like IITs are fully funded by the Department of Education of the Ministry of Human Resource Development. The Central and some of the 'deemed to be' universities are directly funded by UGC. The State universities, which are in majority and enrol about 95 per cent of the students in higher education are funded by the States as far as non-plan expenditure is concerned, while the plan outlays are shared on 'matching basis' by the States and UGC. The Agricultural universities are largely financed by the Indian Council of Agricultural Research. The Central Ministries of Agriculture, Industry, Urban Development and Health also extend financial assistance to the above HEIs for carrying out specific teaching and research programmes. Evidently, there are multiple of Governments' agencies which have been entrusted with the responsibility of financing general as well as professional education. Due to the lack of proper cooperation and coordination of activities as well as the deficiencies in the mechanisms of allocation of funds, a number of problems arise as discussed below.

7.2.1 *Inequity in Distribution of Funds*

On *a priori* reasoning, it could be argued that the objective of empowering different levels of governments and their agencies to plan, monitor and finance various types and levels of educational institutions, is not only to promote teaching and research in different fields of study but also to cater for educational and training needs of various clientele groups which would, otherwise, have not been covered under the control of a particular level of Government or its agencies. In practice, however, we observe that because of lack of coordination or demarcation of areas of activities, the educational programmes of the Central and the State universities are, in their larger parts, common and overlapping in terms of both the nature and types of courses as well as the clientele group. The block grants provided to universities are determined on incremental or deficit basis which hardly take into account all the requirements arising from the need to modernize facilities and to cope with inflationary pressures. As a result of *ad-hoc* nature of allocation of funds, simultaneous existence of budgetary deficits in some, and surpluses as well in some others, are observable among the universities. An analysis of data for the last five years in respect of 80 universities has demonstrated that while as many as 45 universities suffered from budgetary deficits in varying degrees, at least 35 of them emerged out with surpluses.[1] This is inspite of the fact that a number of universities are found to be making inefficient use of available facilities and that a significant share, about 25 to 40 per cent of the total expenditure is accounted for by non-academic activities as discussed in Chapter 4 of this study. Briefly, in other words, inspite of theoretical parity of degrees awarded by HEIs, the magnitude of financial inputs differ a great deal as the unit costs analyses demonstrate in Chapter 5. Such differences consequently affect the students' learning and efficiency of institutions. The unit costs of technical education for a comparable degree course, for instance, at universities of Roorkee, Banaras, Aligarh and IIT Kanpur, all in the same State of Uttar Pradesh, considerably differ simply because they fall under the jurisdiction of different funding agencies of the government, and these agencies do not have scientific and uniform method of distribution of resources for even comparable educational programmes. Obviously, it reflects ineffective planning and lack of coordination of academic activities, which distorts the fiscal policy for investment in education for human development.

7.2.2 *Fiscal Mis-match and the Centre-State Responsibility*

There are considerable variations in development of education system across the States as the economically backward States are lagging much behind than others due mainly to lower level of expenditure and inadequate policy intervention by the UGC. The UGC's scheme of providing matching grants largely favours the economically advanced States which have been able to attract UGC funds due to their relatively higher financial capacity. Unfortunately, the UGC's scheme of funding HEIs is not linked with their academic performance or prudent fiscal management or efforts to establish effective linkages with the community and industry. Also, the location of Central universities has not been planned on any sound criteria either of manpower requirement of a region or promotion of excellence in frontier areas of knowledge. The haphazard promotion of such universities, mainly on political considerations is reflected from the fact that Union Territory of Delhi alone has, apart from an IIT, four Central universities[2] and some universities in this category located elsewhere in the country offer programme from nursery classes to wide range of post-graduate degrees from Agriculture to Medical Sciences. Unlike the financial treatment given to the Colleges in the country, all the 54 colleges of Delhi are, financed by the UGC on the pattern of the Central universities. Such an extra-ordinary treatment makes Delhi a higher education 'Heaven' because no other region of the country has this priviledge.

The UGC has, however, felt[3] that almost every Central University in the recent past has devised its own mechanism largely, under pressure from staff, to regulate service conditions, without caring for the growing financial burden, which UGC has to bear. Some of the notable instances of irregularities in extending benefits to staff, as cited by UGC, are: The conditions accompanying the revised pay scales of 1973 to stop the payment of remuneration for examinations and invigilations, and to give re-employment to teachers of 60 years of age (in Delhi University) have not been followed by the universities; Some universities still continue to operate the Merit Promotion Scheme even after the cut off date of May 1987; University of Delhi has amended its ordinance to facilitate *en masse* promotion of 3000 lecturers; Some universities have created such posts and the scales of pay which do not exist while some others have offered higher scale of pay to some staff without obtaining proper sanction of UGC. A number of universities have not amended their ordinances to make the age of retirement of non-teaching staff 58 years as required in the revised pay scale; Some universities offer special benefits or allowances to the staff without prior approval of UGC. Thus, the universities have accepted the revised scale of pay without complying with the accompanying conditions and that the wave of offering other incentives have led to similar demands by the staff of other universities. The cumulative effect of all these is that the financial liability of UGC has been increasing without corresponding improvement in the performance of universities. In effect, thus, the prevailing method of funding universities, mainly on the past trend basis, has not only invited financial troubles but has rendered the UGC approach ineffective.

7.2.3 *Declining Revenues from Fees*

The system of budgeting in universities is also deficient at least in one important respect. There is no incentive (or disincentive) for the universities to augment resources from different sources. The amount of money raised by them from tuition fee, for instance, was, till recently netted out from the block-grants determined by the funding agencies. As such, the responsibility of financing the entire university programme is generally assumed by the Government and a university, as a self government, hardly makes any worthwhile effort to raise funds for either improving quality of teaching and research or meeting the costs of new programmes. For the purpose of providing matching shares, the existing funding mechanism hardly takes into account, on reward basis, the extent to which an individual institution has made endeavours to raise funds from beneficiary groups. In this context, it is pertinent to point out that the question of revising fee structure and linking it to the costs of education has been debated at various fora. It has been conclusively said that 'there is no justification for subsidizing higher education to the extent it is being done today'.[4] Of the total costs of higher education, tuition fee constitute less than two per cent. Because of general rise in prices and the need for upgradation of infrastructure, the case for revising other user's charges on account of facilities like hostel, lab, library, etc. is equally strong. Even though the quality of education in most universities is deteriorating due to lack of infrastructure and paucity of funds, no worthwhile effort has been made on the parts of either universities to exercise their powers to suitably increase the rates of fees for different services or funding bodies like UGC to create conditions for rationalising the fee structure and for attracting funds from business and industry which view the university outputs from profit angle.[5]

7.2.4 *Indiscriminate Subsidy*

The financial dependence of universities on the Government has increased to the extent of 85 per cent of the total expenditure and the benefits of increased subsidy are inequitably distributed. As pointed out in Chapter 3, the Central and the 'deemed to be' universities are somewhat more dependent, to the tune of 90 per cent or even more as compared to the State universities which enrol about 95 per cent students in higher education. These universities together collect about 30 per cent of their financial requirements, as against 10 per cent for Central universities, from various admissible charges largely tuition fee. It follows that the extent of financial dependence of universities or subsidisation by the Government varies a great deal across various types of universities. While there are differences in the costs of education, even in respect of comparable nature among the institutions of similar types, per student costs by discipline are observed to be much higher among the institutions funded by the Centre/UGC, as is evident from the analyses in Chapter 5. This also means that the extent of Government's subsidy is more, about 90 to 95 per cent, in the Centrally funded universities as against 65 to 70 per cent in the State funded universities. Needless to say, there is no evidence to prove that educational services rendered by either the highly or lowly subsidised institution of higher learning cater to the needs of economically poor sections of the society. Conversely, the UGC has elsewhere admitted that "more than eighty per cent of the beneficiary of university system are drawn from the top thirty per cent of income group"[6] which obviously indicate that present system of funding universities is regressive. This is more so because, of the entire Government revenues, a major chunk, about 80 per cent of the total tax revenues, is collected through the excise duty, the incidence of which largely falls on poor people. In effect, thus, the prevailing mechanisms of funding universities, works as a negative transfer of resources from the poor to rich who largely benefit from the network of university system. Thus, the increase in financial dependence of universities on the Government has not necessarily assured them of equitous treatment and adequate funds for modernisation and expansions of educational programmes, which has, in effect, impinged upon the UGC's effort to maintain uniform standard of higher education. Also, due to the regressive nature of funding and inefficient distribution of resources across various types of universities, the prevailing policy of university development is contributing, it may be reiterated, to income inequality among those who benefit and those who don't. from the network of university system to improve their prospects of life time earnings.

7.2.5 *Utilization of Facilities*

The aspects of management and utilization of resources are also much less satisfactory than desired, especially, in the era of scarcity of funds.[7] First, a little probing into the question of how the physical and financial resources are utilized would reveal that the major expenditure on higher education, about 60 per cent for universities and 80 per cent for colleges, is accounted for by the staff salaries, of which about 50 per cent involves payment to non-teaching staff. Further, the expenditure on non-salary items which include student support services, has been declining overtime. The expenditure on miscellaneous items like electricity, water charges, telephone, etc. has been rising. Second, the academic staff of universities and colleges are not utilized to the extent stipulated by the UGC. The evidences, moreover, show that teacher-student ratio in a large number of universities is very low, about 1:10, which indicate the possibility of improving students' learning since a teacher has to concentrate on a small number of students. Alternatively, economies of scale could be generated by increasing student numbers in a class. There are also those colleges which have high teacher-student ratio due to enrolment pressure which adversely affects quality of education. This reflects lack of planning at the regional and institutional level as well which, ultimately, influences internal efficiency and cost-effectiveness of the educational programmes. Third, as pointed out before, the capacity utilization of infrastructure facilities like classrooms, labs and libraries is merely about 60 per cent which obviously indicate a colossal waste of resources that have been deployed for creation of such facilities. It emerges from the foregoing that due to allocative inefficiency there is much to be desired as far as the financial accountability of the university system is concerned. There are those institutions which are characterised by abundance of physical and financial resources as is evident from budgetary surpluses and under utilization of facilities whereas some others are suffering from inadequacy of funds and necessary infrastructure. There is obviously the case for making judicious allocation of funds.

7.3 New Approaches of Funding

In order to overcome the problems discussed above, we suggest below the two alternative approaches of funding higher education. While one relates to playing the game of distribution of resources within the existing rules, the other relates to changing the rule of the game. We first discuss the later one. The dominant consideration in both of these approaches is to seek value for money by orienting the scheme funding towards better performance.

7.3.1 *Direct Funding of Students*

In order to overcome the problem of growing diseconomies or to improve the cost-effectiveness of the educational programmes, it seems desirable to directly finance the students who have proven ability to benefit from higher education, rather than through the institutions as is being done today. The idea of direct funding of students is not new since this innovation has already been implemented by the UGC in respect of research students. From the point of ensuring accountability of universities to the society, the scope of this approach should be extended to cover all the students who seek to acquire university degrees. The reasons are as under.

The prevailing system of financing universities by the Centre and the State Governments allows for the simultaneous existence of the best or worst performing university departments since the funds are provided on the basis of the past trends rather than the realistic requirements for planned programmes or the performance of universities as judged from their quality of teaching and research. As such, there is no mechanism either at the Central or the State levels to ascertain the performance of a university *vis-a-vis* the average performance of other universities. Though there are differences in the levels of grants received by different universities in terms of per student costs, all of them continue to co-exist and make increasing claims on government funds and that without making the expected improvement in quality and relevance of education. This is because there is no effective measure either to regulate and monitor the quality of teaching by using financial mechanisms like fiscal incentives or to let the inefficient departments be routed out through the process of intense competition from the best performing institutions. Even though almost 50 per cent of the over 7000 odd colleges are characterised as non-viable, a number of colleges come into existence almost every year. There is, therefore, hardly any effort to rationalize and justify the ever increasing number of higher education institutions and expenditure incurred on them.

In order to improve their performance, it is desirable to increase competitiveness among universities, which is possible if the allocation of resources is linked through the students or beneficiary groups who would judge the performance of university departments from: (a) quality of teaching and research; (b) volume of output i.e. teaching and research load, and (c) relevance of educational and research programmes to the contemporary needs of the society and economy. An idea of much of these informations could be publicised by the universities themselves or the national agencies like UGC so as to enable the students to decide as to which institution is able to offer them a better package of education and training that he needs; and for which they have to pay partly or fully from their own or Government sources. The objectives of universities can also be realized by direct financing of planned number of students for various courses of studies, in which case students would receive loans or grants from the Government and they would be responsible for making payments towards the full costs of education. This approach is, of course, in contrast to the existing practice of financing education through universities/ institutions. The method by which various categories and levels of students should be fully or partly financed by parents, Government agencies, etc., require separate discussion and should be examined by a National Committee. Some of the advantages of financing higher education through students are pointed out below.

(i) Students would seek admission to the courses which they expect would ensure higher social and economic returns and would join such university departments that would provide the best education and training to them;
(ii) Students would compete for the limited government funds, in which case the students with proven capacity to learn would have the chance of receiving government support;
(iii) Since the students would be responsible to pay for their education fully or partly, they and their parents would become more vocal and would be genuinely concerned about the quality and relevance of education offered by the universities;
(iv) It would be possible to make obligatory, if required, for the beneficiary groups of students to serve for certain number of years, after completing the course work, on such priority areas as extension programmes pertaining to socio-economic development;
(v) This method would also effectively check brain-drain and minimise wastage of scarce resources invested on students pursuing professional degrees; and
(vi) In the context of rural development also, it could be possible to ensure that the rural areas do not suffer for want of adequate educated and trained manpower since the migration of educated

persons towards cities could be checked in the interests of balanced regional development of the country.

The UGC has already been following a somewhat similar approach of direct financing of students for research degrees in various disciplines. Many teaching departments have come to realise about their low quality of teaching as their students are not able to compete and qualify for research fellowships. Under the existing system of financing higher education through institutions, there is hardly any disincentive for the poor performance in teaching and research as the level of funding is hardly affected. As against this, financing of education through students would ensure: (a) a proper degree of competition across various teaching and research departments so as to attract adequate number of competent students in order to justify their existence; (b) enhance accountability of educational system to the society by way of improving the relevance of education and training programmes which is very much in demand in recent times; and (c) a reasonably high degree of responsibility on the part of students, parents, teachers, institutions and funding agencies for promoting the participatory role in strengthening the teaching-learning process for human resource development. The need of financing higher education through students arises also from the fact that of the total enrolment in higher education, only about 60 per cent pass out and of those who do so less than 25 per cent score above 50 per cent marks which itself is indicative of low quality of education. Obviously, the existing method of funding through institutions yields less than optimum results because a university, including its functionaries, has taken for granted that it would continue to receive the usual maintenance grants even in conditions of non-performance of accepted duties. This has been breeding mediocricity which ought to be checked by employing the above alternative funding approach, of which the ultimate objective is to vitalize the university system to enhance its contribution to national development. The exigencies of financial situation under which India is tightly gripped now than ever before, also suggest that funding of higher education should be need based, target oriented and judged on economic criteria of investment.

7.3.2 *Funding linked with Performance in Teaching and Research*

The Central Universities funded by the UGC and the Institutions of

National Importance like IITs financed by the Department of Education of the Central Ministry of Human Resource Development (HRD) are hardly provided funds on uniform criterion of efficiency and equity in resource allocation. This causes variation in the physical and financial inputs which consequently affect the outputs i.e. students scholastic achievements. Likewise, the existing method of resource allocation by the States in which non-plan expenditure is financed on increamental or past trend basis and plan grants are provided on matching basis, hardly takes into account such vital aspects as the relevance of educational programmes and the required level of facilities for ensuring high students' learning. At present, not only the limited resources get thinly spread over all the institutions but educational excellence and obsolete programmes get simultaneously funded by the UGC and other bodies. Because of such deficiency in the mechanisms of funding the Central and the State Universities, as above, it has not been possible to build them as entreprenurial organisations for promoting development schemes.

In view of the foregoing, an attempt is made below to outline an approach to distribute resources across the universities on the basis of the criteria of (a) quality of teaching and research; (b) students number and their compositions by discipline of study; and (c) the relevance of the schemes to the societal needs and manpower requirements. At the outset, it may be mentioned that for adopting the proposed approach, it would be necessary to (i) evolve appropriate positive and normative efficiency norms in respect of different indicators of academic performance; and (ii) suitably classify all the courses of study into proper cost heads such that full and/or part time students admitted to different departments of a university could be properly clubbed to reflect the load of student number at each cost head; thereby indicating the unit costs of their education for each discipline. Thus, based on the unit costs per equivant student, as attempted by us in Chapter 5, and the sound judgement of the funding agency about the desirability of promotion of education in a particular discipline and at different levels as well as the potentiality of a university department to provide quality education, the magnitude of funds that will be available for a university in specific discipline/cost head could be determined as per the method proposed below. However, the total amount thus determined for each discipline would represent the block grant to be earmarked to a university which would be free to devise its own method of internal allocation for different departments and programmes. Against this background, the new approach of funding which is largely consistent with the prevailing method of resource allocation may be outlined as under.

1. Of the total funds available for university development as may be indicated by the Planning Commission or the Ministry of HRD, 60 per cent should be earmarked for teaching and research and the remaining 40 per cent for meeting the overhead expenses including student support services, academic administration, etc.

1.1 Out of the funds for teaching and research, ratio of teaching and research should be 70:30.

1.2 The eligibility of a university under the teaching criteria should be determined by multiplying the national average unit costs of education in a particular discipline by the planned or fixed number of students for that university. The planned number of students under each discipline and its distribution across the university departments should be determined by the funding agency keeping especially in view the national requirements, the target number as proposed by a university and the potentiality of various departments to provide quality education as judged by the funding agency on the basis of past performance. The distribution of quota of students should essentially depend on the quality of teaching of a department which ought to be assessed by efficiency norms.[8] The sum total of funds, thus, determined for each discipline/cost head, would represent the amount that would be available to a University under teaching criterion.

1.3 Out of the total funds for research, 50 per cent should be distributed along the cost headlines on the basis of *inter-se* share of different disciplines/cost head under the teaching criterion. The remaining 50 per cent should be allocated on the basis of the indicators of quality research and its relevance to the societal needs, which ought to be assessed by the peer groups.

2. As regards the distribution of 40 per cent of resources earmarked for overhead expenses, 50 per cent should be allocated on the basis of the absolute student number and the remaining share should be distributed on the basis of *inter-se* percentage share of each university under the teaching and research criteria.

3. The block grant determined as per the above approach should not include the local taxes paid by the universities. The expenses on account of such payments as taxes and tarrifs should be provided by Government on 100 per cent basis. Likewise, on the basis of weighted students load for Arts, Science, Engineering and Medical education and assumed life of equipment, a lump-sum amount should be given to universities for repairing and replacing equipment. The financial requirements for such purposes should be worked out using both appropriate norms as well as sound judgement of needs for modernization. The grants for maintenance of buildings and major repairs should also be provided after inspection and assessment of the needs by organisations like CPWD.

The institutions which cater for special services like high quality of teaching and research, training for unemployed youth and education of backward classes/minorities should be duly provided with adequate funds so as to enable them to perform their special functions. The advantage of such an approach is self-evident. Under the proposed approach, it would be possible to provide for minimum funds atleast to the national average extent, for ensuring infrastructure facilities in all the institutions on a uniform basis, the institutions which demonstrate accountability by improving their performance in teaching and research would duly receive more funds than others. Moreover, the institutions will enjoy full autonomy to utilize the block grants as the funding agency need not interfere in the internal planning and management of resources. If an institution enrols more students than the planned number of students for which either facility with it exist or enough budgetary cushion has been provided, it would most likely do at the costs of sacrificing quality of education, in which case its prospect to attract funds in the future would diminish due to the loss of credibility. Since considerable significance is attached to research, the academic staff would be duly involved in research pursuits which positively affects the quality of teaching and students' learning. In brief, the approach of resource allocation, as discussed above, would ensure (a) uniform financial treatment of institutions while allowing for reasonable variations in costs of inputs of different courses of study; (b) accountability of institutions by way of promoting competitiveness in offering quality programmes, improving credibility and attracting funds. In effect, thus, the diseconomies in management of higher education institutions could be minimised and their contributions to socio-economic development could be enhanced.

7.4 Concluding Remarks

We may be briefly recepituate the foregoing discussions. The task of vitalizing higher education system is most urgent from the view points of both seeking value for money as well as removing obsolescence from the existing programmes. Due to ineffective planning and management of the system and lack of coordination between funding agencies, resources are not equitably distributed and efficiently utilized. The UGC being a statutory body has a vital role in promotion and maintenance of standards of higher education, but its success would depend on the extent to which it is able to distribute resources equitably and ensure its efficient utilization, diagnose the problems faced by the system and devise methods of resolving them. In the current regime of serious financial crunch and growing expenditure at the tertiary level especially on non-academic items, the UGC's concern for checking the such expenditure on account of salaries and wages to contain the further subsidization of higher education through regulating services conditions of university employees is quite understandable and is also in tune with the time trend.

But the staff matters are always ticklish and, therefore, it is not so easy to rationalize expenditure on salaries by regulating service conditions particularly when the employees are organised to promote their interests in the manner trade unions do. It becomes difficult to pursue development policies because any reform can be construed as interference in the university autonomy. This is precisely what has been happening in the context of the proposed amendments of UGC Act, which aims at bringing uniformity in appointment and promotion of Central university employees so as to contain growing expenditure on payment of salaries. We have suggested above that diseconomies in management of universities could be minimised by reforming the method of distribution of resources such that equity and efficiency in utilization of Government funds could be assured. In this context, we have outlined two alternative approaches of funding universities. In the first approach, the funding agency i.e. UGC would be required to directly finance in full or part the eligible students, rather than channelising funds through institutions as is the current practice. The students should be responsible to pay for the costs of education out of Government grants/loans or from their own sources. In this approach, UGC should finance education of those who have proven ability to benefit from higher education and/or belong to educationally and economically backward communities. A suitable mix of policy options, regarding educational subsidy should be accordingly formulated. With the direct funding of students, students and their parents would be free to choose the package of programmes offered by different institution, which, in turn, would be required to offer quality and relevant courses so as to improve their credibility, attract students and funds for running the institutions. As autonomous body, the institutions would have full freedom to govern and manage their affairs. The non-performing institutions would thus get discouraged as mediocrity would not be supported, as is being done today. In the second approach, the funding agencies would be required to promote entreprenuership among institutions by linking funds with their performance in teaching and research as well as relevance of various programmes. Since excellence breeds excellence, the efficiency norms and the manpower requirements of different sectors of economy should be the main criteria of providing block grants which ought to be determined and distributed by employing an equitous approach for comparable programmes. This approach would promote competitiveness among institutions and help remove obsolescence from the existing programmes. In both the alternative approaches, selective funding in terms of institutions, programmes and students is suggested with a view to ensuring cost-effectiveness of higher education system. In essence, HEIs would have to bid for limited government funds and their success would depend on the quality and relevance of their teaching and research programmes.

NOTES AND REFERENCES

1. See *Financial Deficit in Universities*, AIU, 1991.
2. These are: University of Delhi, Jawaharlal University, Indira Gandhi National Open University, and Jamia Millia Islamia.
3. This part of the discussion is based on the information collected from the UGC and various press reports which appeared during January to March 1992.
4. *Challenge of Education: A Policy Perspective*, para 3.40, Ministry of Human Resource Development.
5. It is however important to make atleast two important observations. First, the Central Government and some of the States have been contemplating to make necessary changes in the existing financial provision to allow the universities to raise funds from sources like fees and industry which would not be adjusted against the block grants provided by the UGC or the States. Second, a number of piece meal effort has been made by universities during the 1992-93 academic year for raising tuition fees and examination fees and other charges so as to augment funds. The Central budget for 1993-94 has made the provision for 100 per cent

exemption from Income Tax on donation to HEIs. But the ability of HEIs to attract fund would depend on its success in offering high quality of relevant programmes.

6. *Development of Higher Education: Policy Frame*, UGC, 1978.
7. For a detailed discussion on pattern of utilisation of funds, please see Chapter 4 of this study.
8. For a detailed discussion on development and use of efficiency norms, see 'Performance Indicators in Education', *Journal of Educational Planning and Administration*, Oct. 1991. by Zeenat S. Shafi.

8

AGENDA FOR REFORMS OF HIGHER EDUCATION

Policy Implications

There has been a good deal of debate recently as to how to resolve the problems currently confronting systems of higher education so as to enable it to respond to the educational and technological needs of the society and economy. The need for search of solutions has arisen from the fact that the old order, in terms of valued functions, institutional status system, traditional values has been shaken to its foundations and in parts destroyed. The world has changed and in such conditions to allow Indian universities to turn themselves into microcosms of a lost world would be as absured as to turn them into second rate businesses. If the occurrence of such a situation is to be avoided, the major issues for the future would be required to be identified and, to the extent possibly resolved so that the system can reasonably enhance its contributions to national development. Some of the major issues to which immediate attention would be paid are:

(a) The universities have very little capacity, or indeed will, to innovate and there are various factors responsible for weakening the system. Inadequacy of financial resources is, the single important factor which has impinged upon the efforts for creation of facilities and modernization of teaching and research programmes. Much of the time and efforts of universities are wasted in devising methods of managing with the resource crunch of financial deficits, especially in the regime of almost non-existence of alternative sources of funding or lack of sufficient options to exploit different sources of revenue since the universities are largely dependent on the Government for funds. This raises questions about (i) internal management of institutions of higher education and of specific measures for their revitalization; and, (ii) the total outlays of financial resources, their distribution among various sectors/departments of the system and how the costs will be shared between individuals, the State and the private sector.

(b) Curricula in certain fields of studies mainly in the technical and professional areas, particularly among the institutions of national importance like IITs are also closely tied to current labour market needs, while in others mainly universities and colleges they float indecisively, unclear as to purpose and objectives. This has created a situation in which we observe that there are shortages of technical manpower in certain professional categories while in others they are in abundance or in some respects unemployables. The question is how to redesign curricula to maintain the balance between general education and vocational specialization; and what measures should be taken to effectively implement the accepted design of course structure.

An equally important issue pertaining to the supply of educated and trained manpower is the challenge of meeting the demand for training and re-training of non-traditional students, especially adults, both for professional upgrading and recycling as well as for personal fulfillment in an increasingly technocratic society. If this challenge is not faced by the conventional university system, the non-university institution, largely in the private sector would venture, though belately, to fill up the vacuum with a profit motive, in which case the credibility of the system would get further eroded due to its failure to adequately respond to the societal needs.

(c) Uneven development of higher education across the regions and socio-economic groups poses a potential threat to destabilise the society and economy by both perpetuating disparities in distribution of income and wealth as well as creating social tensions and undermining democratic values. Equality of opportunity among all the sections of the society should be effectively ensured to enable the deprived groups to benefit from the network of higher educational programmes for the betterment of their social and economic lives.

(d) The concern for promoting research in universities has got diminished, even though they offer the best setting for interdisciplinary and multi-disciplinary research, because they cover wider range of subjects than do other establishments. The close association of teaching and research gives a special strength and vitality to universities. In order to ensure quality teaching and relevance of courses to the societal needs, considerable attention is required to be paid to various aspects of researches to avoid the risks of pushing the universities as a second rate business.

In the following paragraphs, each of the above issues and related themes will be discussed with a view to both developing policy perspectives as well as providing a background for modifying the approach of funding HEIs, which we propose to discuss in the subsequent chapters.

8.1 Perspective Planning of Higher Education

In view of vital role of HEIs in social and economic progress, a concerted effort should be made to plan and manage them, keeping especially in view the major constraints and the challenges before the nation and higher education system. India has unique characteristics of having the second largest system of higher education, after USA, and has one of the lowest per capita income in the world. There are about 4.5 million students enrolled in university system and about 90 per cent of them are full time students. Due to low per capita income of the country, the problem today is as to how to provide adequate finance for the sustenance of the system and provide education to an increasingly large number of students who demand it and are capable of benefiting from university education. In order to fulfil the constitutional commitment of universalization of elementary education, educational facilities at elementary and secondary levels are expanding and enrolments are also rising due to both public enlightment about economic value of education and increased accessibility to education as well as the general population pressure. With the widening of base of secondary education and improvements in rates of retention and pass out rates, the demand for higher education would accordingly rise; implying thereby, increased pressure on university system. If adequate resources for meeting the needs arising from either expansion and diversification or modernization of the system or both are not made available the degradation of standards of education would be the unavoidable consequence. In fact, this is precisely what has happened in the past. As the demand for education of all types and at all levels has tendency to increase over time, the investments on infrastructural facilities would have to be enhanced commensurate with the increase in the demand for higher education as well as the need for improving the relevance and quality of course contents. On the present reckoning, the enrolment level would rise to about 6 million by the end of this century and the relevant and adequate level of education and training would have to be provided in order to cope up with the needs of the job market to all those who seek it either through formal system or non-formal system. However, the inadequacies of infrastructural facilities like shortages of trained teachers, instructional materials, teaching equipment and library facilities, outmoded curricula and paucity of financial resources would pose formidable difficulties in imparting worthwhile education that would fulfil the perceived needs of the society and the economy. The question, therefore, boils down to exploring the possibilities of mobilising adequate resources for meeting the challenges of higher education as well as to devising method by which resources could be distributed for various programmes of studies such that efficiency in utilisation of funds and accountability of education system to the society could be optimised. A number of related issues would have to be dealt with simultaneously. Some of these are raised below.

8.1.1 *Institutional Planning*

There is no practice of pursuing perspective planning of physical and financial resources for the development of higher education in India. This aspect, needs to be given serious thought lest the existing problems should acquire unmanageable proportions. For instance, the number of colleges producing graduates are increasing beyond 7000 even though there are neither adequate basic facilities for teaching and research nor enough number of students to justify the existence of several hundred colleges. There are several university departments which lack infrastructure facilities and competent teachers, yet they are producing graduates who either remain unemployed or their productive capacity is much less than desired. The question, therefore, is whether or not the development of higher education should be planned on the basis of manpower planning approach which essentially means that the production of graduates and specialists should be regulated by the number required by the society and economy. This would in effect provide an effective solution to the existing problem of proliferation of non-viable colleges and swelling number of unemployable university graduates. The technical aspects of manpower planning approach are much easier to tackle in the mixed economies like India which have strong bases of the State and Central levels of planning. In accordance with the magnitude and location of financial investments by regions and socio-economic projects, manpower requirements of various kinds and levels could be determined and through the planning process adequate number of labour force with different levels of specialization would be produced by the HEIs. This would obviously entail preparation of perspective plan for the production of manpower which would duly take into account physical and financial resources as well as the nature of technologies to be employed for realizing optimum results.

8.1.2 *Diversion of Students Towards Vocational Stream*

In the context of the above, it must be pointed out that if the past trend of growth of student enrolment replicate in the future, the production and composition of arts and science including technology graduates would be highly imbalanced in terms of societal requirements.

The plans for educational development should lay emphasis on the following: A shift in the science: arts ratio to an approximate parity, as against the current ratio of 35:65, should be contemplated. This should be achieved not only by any absolute increase in the number of students in science ad technology but by a reduction in the number of students in arts and social sciences. The fact that the problem of unemployment is more pronounced among the arts and social science graduates and that an increasing number of graduates seek employment in the industrial and commercial sector, there is apparent need to have more graduates in technological subjects to meet the requirements of new industries and of a changing society.

In view of inadequacy of facilities for teaching and research at most university centres and the financial constraints with which most of them suffer, the relevant policy measures might envisage diverting of at least 50 per cent of students at +2 level towards vocational stream as against less then 10 per cent, at present. In so doing, not only the much desired quality of education would be improved by reducing the pressure on higher education but the base of educated and trained labour force could be enlarged, which would have a positive impact on productivity in all the economic sectors. Needless to say, vocational institutions should be vitalized by creating better facilities commensurate with the requirements of job market, particularly, in the vicinity of such institutions.

8.1.3 *Re-designing of Courses*

The rapid increase of knowledge suggests that content materials be more carefully selected and structured. It is also required that the reorganisation of curricula reflect not only the unique structure of the respective discipline but also student needs viewed in terms of developmental stages, social needs and learning conditions. Thus, in organising curricula, flexibility and varsality may be allowed for so that they translate educational ideas and goals into specific learning experiences relevant to individual learners. In spite of policy emphasis on the continuing improvement of curricula, the failure of the system to adapt itself to the global changes requires that a Curriculum Development Institute be established which should be responsible for research and development tasks from a long-term perspective. So far, we have relied on *ad hoc* approaches to develop model curricula with the support of the UGC. The experience show that because of the lack of will or certain impractibility in implementation of curricula, not many colleges and universities have adopted in them either in full or in part. A regular Institute should, therefore, be established. The major functions of the Institute should include basic studies, curricula development and evaluation. The outputs of the Institute would provide the much needed specialised feedback for redesigning and restructuring of courses in different disciplines and levels of education. The mechanisms of resource allocation should be specifically geared not only to facilitate the process of evaluation, revision and adoption of new course structure but also to discourage such universities which do not adopt new curriculum. In this context, appropriate changes in the teaching methods and training of teachers are of crucial importance, to which we return to below.

8.1.4 *Teachers and Innovations in Teaching Methods*

Amid the torrent of change in various aspects of life, teaching methods still remain very conventional in the empty wilderness of the blackboard and textbook. As the development trend continues, this labour intensive teaching will lose its relevance in the society of the future. It is imperative that new teaching methods be developed, drawing on various media and up-to-date learning theories so that effectiveness of teaching could be improved.

In the context of innovations of curricula and teaching methods, the role of teachers is of crucial importance as they are rightly regarded as kingpin of the education system. Even though the NPE 1986 has emphasised that 'norms of accountability will be laid down with incentives for good performance and disincentives for non-performance', there is no perceptible improvement in the collective behaviours of teachers towards teaching and research. As a result, the quality of teaching continues to be unsatisfactory. Teachers continue to teach old curricula and that for much less than the period stipulated by the UGC. Moreover, they excessively rely on traditional course contents and methods of teaching. In terms of policy stipulation that 'teachers will continue to play a crucial role in the formulation and implementation of educational programmes', they have belied the national expectations to bring about a revolutionary change in the system to enhance its accountability to the society. This is inspite of the fact that in pursuance of NPE 1986, considerable headway has been made in improving the plight of teachers. For instance, a better deal has been made in respect of recruitment, promotion, training and salary matters. All the new recruitments at lecturer level are being made out of those who have cleared UGC's prescribed test. This has eliminated much of the discrepancies in selection of teachers. The scales of pay of teachers *vis-a-vis* the salary benefits of other Government employees have been duly revised in favour of teachers and the same has been uniformly implemented in the country. The establishment of Academic Staff Colleges (ASCs) at different university centres provide better avenues for training of teachers on a continuing basis. All these measures have, however, not made desirable impact in respect of improving the accountability of teachers to the society in general which largely bears the salary burden and the institutions, in particular, which are entrusted with the responsibility of developing human resources. The aspects of evaluation of performance of teachers especially in respect of what they teach, how do they teach and its impact on learning achievements are to be closely examined for designing remedial measures. While the cooperation of teachers association is necessary in deciding upon any issue that affect teachers, the experiences show that there is a great deal of resistance on the part of teachers to modify the course contents and reform the modalities of teaching for effective learning. The university authorities can do nothing to cleanse the system either by improvement in quality of teaching or by discountinuing the programmes which are not cost-effective. In this context, the mechanisms of assessment of teachers performance should be evolved and universities be empowered to frame their own rules and regulations such that would allow to retain and attract competent teachers and shed off those who are assessed to be incompetent and inefficient in performing their duties. The modalities of assessment of teachers' performance and tenurial appointment on attractive terms, rather than on regular basis, as exists today, should be decided upon by peer groups. In brief, in the prevailing conditions in which teachers associations are functioning typically on the lines of trade unionists' approaches, the system requires to be endowed with academically sound teachers who should be appointed on tenurial basis with attractive salary package.

Moreover, almost every university has become a localised institution in terms of both students enrolment and appointment of teacher. This character of universities ought to be changed and their outlook should be more universal. A great deal of the purpose of promoting students and teachers mobility would be served if the universities enrol certain percentage of students and recruit teachers from other States so as to allow for cross fertilization of ideas, cultures and other educational pursuits. These measures, in effect form the backbone of national unity and integration, a goal which educational system should contineously pursue.

8.1.5 *Equalization of Educational Opportunity*

Indian society is characterised by glaring socio-economic disparities across the regions. In this context, education system can play a catalytic role for either reducing or increasing such disparities. If the benefits of education system are reaped by the economically better off sections, while the poor communities remain deprived, the disparities would get perpetuated or even widened. If, however, educational opportunities are equalized through positive discrimination and the socially and economically backward sections of society are enabled to acquire relevant knowledge and skill to improve their prospects of social mobility and employability in higher earning jobs, inequalities could then be easily reduced. Being apex educational institution, universities have a major responsibility and have significant potential to liquidate adult-illiteracy and provide better social and economic opportunity to women and other educationally backward communities so as to enable them to benefit from new knowledge and technology. This would, in turn, help them in making increasing contributions to the process of development as well as equitious distribution of its benefits. A number of policy measures have already been identified in our plan documents but our achievements, which are obviously much less than desired, reflect the extent of impact of such measures in ameliorating educational inequality across various groups and regions. This simply calls for a somewhat more vigorous effort to implement the programmes of equalizing educational opportunity. The involvement of teachers and students, for executing the relevant schemes, as well as the Government, for providing adequate funds should be explored. As pointed out above, because of the nature of influence of education and training in generation and distribution of income, disparities in provision of educational facilities and learning abilities should be minimised through policy interventions. And, this aspect should receive a higher priority in our planning process.

8.2 Resources for Higher Education

University system everywhere is experiencing a great deal of strain and stress in so far as resources are concerned. The reasons are not too far to seek. If the characteristics of the system remain somewhat inegalitarian or the quality and relevance of its programmes are not tailored to needs of the society and the schemes like liquidation of illiteracy and promotion of vocational and technical education dominate the plan priorities, the allocation of funds for higher education will be relegated to a lower policy emphasis. In other words, the system will have to compete for the limited funds and its competitive ability will obviously depend on the degree to which the system establishes its credible records by improving its performance and accountability to the society. The current financial scene of universities presents a mixed picture of light and shade. There are those institutions which suffer from perpetual financial deficits, while some others emerge with surpluses or are found to be not making optimum use of facilities with them. The evidences reveal that a majority of the universities suffer from budgetary deficits and for want of funds they are unable 'to undertake and execute innovative programmes in the areas of higher education and research. There are also those which emerge with surpluses in varying degrees, which indicate *inter alia* that because of ineffective planning and management of resources there is no proper correspondence between the requirement and available resources for university development. In fact, due to the absence of a valid criteria for distribution of funds, universities are not sure of the amount of block grants that they will receive on time; and, therefore, in such uncertain situation much of the valuable time of the Vice-Chancellor is wasted in the devising method to manage with the exigencies of financial situations. Also, the prevailing system of financing universities by the Centre and the State Governments allows for the simultaneous existence of the best or worst performing university departments, as judged from the quality of the graduates produced by them. Though there are differences in the levels of grants received by them, they continue to co-exist and make increasing claims on government funds because there is no effective mechanisms either to improve the quality of teaching by using the fiscal instruments or to let the inefficient departments be routed out through the process of intense competition from the best performing departments. The main reason for this is that the Centre and the State Governments provide funds mainly on the basis of past trend rather than their performance in teaching or efficient utilization of funds or the requirements for improving quality of educational programmes.

In order to increase the return from investments on HEIs, it is desirable, therefore, to increase competitiveness among them by way of linking the allocation of resources with peformance of university departments as judged from quality and quantity of graduates produced by them. The approach of allocation of resources for enhancing productivity and improving accountability has already been discussed in Chapter 7. An equally important concern pertaining to financial health of HEIs is that in the prevailing regime of financial stringency, it is imperative to search for alternative methods of funding, which should be justifiable on equity and efficiency grounds. In this context, the first and foremost tasks are to rationalise fee structure, withdraw subsidy from foreign studies, raise resources from industry and provide educational loans. We may briefly discuss the various measures for vitalizing financial health of HEIs.

8.2.1 *Measures for Economy in Expenditure*

(i) Reduction in non-Academic Expenditure

There is evidence of high and rising expenditure on non-academic activities, which include salaries of non-teaching staff and other miscellaneous expenses, among the institutions of higher education. The fact that there are three to four times more non-teaching staff than teaching ones, there is a case for reducing the dependence on secretarial and other non-academic staff by way of intensive utilization of the existing staff and employing modern office management techniques like the use of communication technologies, computers, etc., so as to reduce labour intensity of the System.

(ii) Optimum Utilization of Infrastructure

The scene in respect of educational infrastructural facilities present a sharp contrast between the institutions of higher education. While a number of institutions suffer for want of such facilities, the capacity utilization in many others is much less than desired. The evidence for a number of universities reveals that classrooms, libraries, labs, etc., on which huge capital expenditure have been made, are not fully utilized. There are also the institutes where the facilities are awfully poor. This is especially true for 'non-viable colleges' and most State universities especially from backward regions of the country. In many regions, including urban centres, the number of colleges and universities, which offer almost comparable educational programmes, are more than to justify their needs particularly on the grounds of the level of enrolment and duplicity of their programmes. With a view to efficient management of inputs and outputs, there is an urgent need to plan the development of higher education on the basis of (a) manpower requirements and (b) a reasonably high quality of teaching and research. Since the costs of education at tertiary level are generally very high, and at this level of education, it is the quality which should matter most, it is imperative to plan the development of higher education in such a way that the factors like existing and required facilities and their effective utilization are duly taken into account. Such an approach would surely help in not only making proper use of existing resources but also in avoiding uneconomic creation of facilities.

(iii) Sharing of Facilities

A considerable amount of money is devoted every year on the infrastructure facilities especially for the maintenance of national laboratories and libraries in various parts of the country. Currently, the services of such facilities are not optimally shared by different organisations located within the region. If a system is devised to utilize the services optimally by sharing the facilities and avoiding vertical expansion especially in respect of libraries and specialized laboratories which require huge investments, a large sum of money could be saved for further investments on improvements of quality of educational services.

(iv) Economising Expenditure on Examinations

The expenditure on the conduct of examinations accounts for, on an average, 15 per cent or even more, of the total university budget of the teaching and affiliating universities. Its influence on the university finances is, therefore, considerable. Now since the National Policy on Education 1986 has emphasised the need to delink degrees from the jobs and almost all the employers are conducting their own qualifying tests for various levels and categories of jobs, it seems undesirable to spend huge money on the conduct of uncredible examinations for determining the awards of degrees. And the fact is that a university degree, by and large, is no longer taken on its face value for either awards of scholarships or offer of employment opportunities by many employers in both public and private sectors. It is, therefore, worthwhile considering abolition of examinations in piece meal especially in general courses so as to save the money spent on the conduct of examinations. Instead of awarding formal degrees/diplomas, merely certificate of attendance or scores of internal assessment in different courses should be provided which could be used for determining the eligibility of a candidate for appearing in qualifying tests for scholarships, jobs, etc. What is being suggested here is to avoid duplicity of functions by university and the employers in their roles of assessing the worthiness of candidates for specific jobs. Such a step would not only generate considerable savings for reinvestment into the university system but also release more time for teachers to teach and carry out their own research programmes. Some universities are, however, able to mobilise funds through examination fees for financing the general university programmes. The question, however, is whether the use of such a mode of financing education is a proper one, especially when the sources like tuition fees and other user charges are yet to be fully tapped?

(v) Reducing the Costs of Admissions to Different Courses

In printing of prospectus and processing of application forms for admissions to various courses of studies, a considerable amount of money is spent by every university. This is more so because most of the students submit their applications to more than one university/college which unduly magnifies the work load and increases the expenditure on processing of applications. As the universities receive large funds from the Central pool of resources, irrespective of the routes through which money is channelised, there is a case for minimising wasteful expenditure by way of regulating the admissions to different courses in various universities and colleges by a Central agency. Like the practices of IITs, IIMs and other Medical Institutes in the country, all the seats in different courses of studies available with different universities/colleges could be pooled together. All the seats should then be rationed among the qualified students who would enrol themselves in order of their preferences for different colleges and universities. This would not only ensure uniform standards but also minimise the expenditure on processing of application forms and other related activities. Such an approach could be pursued, in the first instance, on regional basis which could later be extended to on the nationwide basis. In addition to minimising expenditure and ensuring uniform standards, this approach would promote mobility of students and teachers as stipulated by the National Policy on Education 1986.

(vi) Diverting Students to Distance Learning System (DLS)

The National Policy on Education 1986 has duly emphasised the need to promote distance learning system in the country. As the communication technologies like radio, TV, etc., have considerably improved and are generally available throughout the country, it is desirable to make a concerted effort to divert a significant proportion of learners to DLS, especially in the area of general higher education which constitutes about two-thirds of the total enrolment at tertiary level. In fact; the IGNOU and the UGC have already shown the way as to how teaching programmes could effectively be launched through TV. Moreover, the cost of distance higher education through postal correspondence is about one-forth of the conventional method of education and the same is largely self-financed. It is possible to improve the accessibility of higher education without unduly sacrificing the quality of teaching or increasing the amount of expenditure. Since the course structure and the students profile in DLS are somewhat comparable to that of conventional system, there should not be any problem relating to transition of students from the latter to the former. Thus, the diversion of students to DLS could minimise the growing expenditure on conventional universities. More importantly, as the DLS is largely self-financed, almost entire burden of financing education of additional students could be shifted on to the beneficiary groups. In effect, the promotion of DLS would greatly reduce the Government burden (or current subsidy) of supporting higher education.[1]

8.2.2 *Measures for Additional Resource Mobilization*

(i) Rationalisation of Fee Structure

The fee structure should be rationalised with a view to augmenting resources for higher education and also to recover, on equity grounds, a part of the total costs of education, the beneficiary of which belong to higher income groups. While the costs of education have been rising for different reasons, fees have remained more or less stationary even though the returns due to higher education in the form of individual earnings have also increased. Efforts should be made to devise and adopt such fee structure which should bear some relationship between what a student pays and what is spent on his education. In view of this, the rates of fees for various courses should be suitably increased particularly in professional courses which yield higher return over the life time earnings. There should not be genuine resentment from students since the expected benefits of education are much more than the expenditure they incur for receiving the subsidised education.[2]

(ii) Withdraw Subsidy to Foreign Students

Of late, most advanced countries, have begun to charge tuition fee on full costs basis from foreign students without unduly straining their relations with the home countries of students. The question is why should India not recover the costs of education of foreign students who generally come from better off countries as compared to India? There are about 13 thousand students, from different countries, who are receiving various types and levels of education in Indian universities. Our conservative estimate indicate that India is subsidising foreign students' education to the tune of Rs.10 crores per year. This sum of money, if recovered would be sufficient enough to run a university in India. The Aligarh Muslim University has already taken necessary steps to charge an amount of 300 U.S. dollars, and there is no reason why other universities should not follow it. While the collections of full costs fees from foreign students would greatly alleviate the financial crisis faced by the universities, the revenues interms of foreign exchange thus raised could be utilized for purchasing foreign books and journals, equipments which have become very costly due to devaluation of Indian rupee.[3] The damage caused to inter country relations, if any, could, however, be redressed through diplomatic ties and other cultural links, rather than educational subsidy at the cost of sacrificing the quality of higher education for want of funds.

(iii) Raising Resources from Industry

A concerted effort should be made to raise resources from non-traditional sources such as industries and other commercial concerns, which are making use of highly qualified and trained manpower produced by the institutions of higher education. Such an effort would greatly reduce the present financial burden on the Central and the State Governments. The funds from industries and other business houses could be tapped by (a) introducing such courses of studies and training programmes that are relevant to the manpower needs of industries for increasing productivity; and (b) undertaking consultancy research projects, the findings of which would be conducive in reorienting the industrial sector for reducing costs of production and increasing its profitability. Moreover, the public and private sector enterprises should be encouraged to sponsor a specified number of students especially in technical and professional fields, whom they can employ after their graduation. Such an approach would considerably reduce the financial burden of the Government while the relevance of education and training would naturally improve due to the programme linked sponsorship.[4]

(iv) Funding on 100 per cent Basis by UGC

In respect of the State universities, the UGC has been providing partial assistance on account of plan grants on matching basis. It seems desirable that for the programmes of crucial importance, from the point of view of national development, the UGC should provide financial support to the State universities on 100 per cent basis as is being done for the Central and some of the 'deemed to be' universities. As education is included in the Concurrent List of the Constitution, the States should have no objection in the implementation of a programme of national importance if it is funded on 100 per cent basis. This policy would go a long way in ensuring a somewhat uniform level of facilities as well as in improving the standard of education which is one of the main objectives of the UGC. The fiscal deficiency of the backward States needs to be particularly rectified by the UGC support.

(v) Educational Loans

With a view to ploughing back the investments that are being made in every plan, appropriate mechanism needs to be evolved for administering the scheme of interest-free loans which should be inflationary adjusted so as to expand the facilities for higher education. Under such a system, financial assistance should be made available from public funds in the form of loans to all the meritorious students as well as to those who would otherwise be deprived of higher education due to income constraints. Such assistance should be provided on the condition that they enter into a contract to repay the loans without interest after they enter into earning age. The payment schedule should be spread over the average earning span of life. For providing such loans, the criteria of minimum academic standards and minimum parental income should be developed. The management of such aspects should be entrusted to an autonomous financial body which may be named as 'Educational Opportunity Fund'. While such a scheme would ensure recovery of investments in education, the financial accountability on the part of both the students and the institutions would duly increase.

(vi) Review non-Plan Approach of Funding

The existing approach of financing non-plan expenditure hardly allows for reassessment of the need and relevance of the programmes which were initiated in previous Plans; and, therefore, resources are largely allocated on incremental/deficit basis to meet the payments on account of salaries of teaching and non-teaching staff. This approach needs to be examined afresh so as to ensure that the quality and relevance of education are duly improved and maintained at a higher level. By implication, it would also mean that in order to overcome the problem of resentment the teaching and non-teaching community who might resist the introduction and implementation of new schemes, the tenurial appointments should be preferred over the existing permanent/regular system of appointments. The availability of funds should, moreover, be linked with such factors as growth in enrolment, the need for modernization of teaching methods, the provision for student support services, rise in prices, etc.

8.3 **Conclusion**

To sum up, the recent economic reforms which have focussed on reduction in Government subsidy and deregulation of economic control have significant implications for university development. The university system is highly subsidised to provide the needed manpower for the economy. The system has, however, not been able to ensure (a) cost-efficiency and cost-effectiveness of its programmes; and (b) equalization of educational opportunities for different income groups of people. This has consequently impeded the national efforts to accelerate the rate of economic growth and ensure equitable distribution of benefits of development, since the influence of educated and trained persons on all the socio-economic activities is intense and pervasive. In order to rectify deficiencies in the system and to direct its activities in such a way as to improve efficiency and accountability of the system, the fiscal instruments are considered vital and effective. The mechanisms of resource allocation to different types of universities by various Central and States level agencies are neither based on scientific norms nor linked to the requirements for teaching and research. This has, in effect, led to uneconomic use of resources and has contributed to inefficiency in performance of universities. Consequently, economic growth and social progress are adversely affected. In distribution of funds for higher education, the accepted criteria of equity and efficiency are hardly adhered to, as a result of which the costs of even comparable programmes of education differ widely and there is hardly any incentive (disincentive) for better (poor) performance. The element of competition among the universities is lacking, therefore.

To remedy the situation, alternative method of funding has been suggested so as to enable the universities to enhance the quality of ongoing programmes and to launch market oriented courses while allowing students to pay for it. Currently, the education of students from higher income groups are heavily subsidised which contribute to perpetuation of socio-economic disparities. In the approach suggested above, the beneficiaries would pay according to their income ability or meet the educational expenses out of the interest-free loans while the education of poor sections of society would be suitably subsidised by the Government. The financial dependence of universities on Government would be gradually reduced somewhat and so would get minimised the government interference in the university autonomy. In this context, the measures for augmenting additional resources that have been suggested are: upward revision of fee structure especially in professional courses, full recovery of costs of education from foreign students, mobilization of resources from industry by way of initiating relevant programmes for managerial and technical staff of industries and other commercial organisations, undertaking consultancy projects from industry, revising user's charges like hostel, library and lab fees, etc. Among the measures suggested for economy in expenditure are to reduce the expenses on non-academic activities, to share facilities like national laboratories and libraries, etc., with other local institutions, to increase the capacity utilization of infrastructure like class rooms, labs, libraries, etc., to abolish the uncredible examination system so as to avoid duplication of academic testing service to save resources, to centralize the system of admission to various courses offered by colleges and universities on regional basis so as minimise the wasteful expenditure by reducing the duplication of activities relating to processing of applications, to divert students towards distance learning system which is largely self-financing and cost-effective as well. The important measures for raising additional resources include revision of fee structure especially for professional courses, withdrawal of subsidy to foreign students so as to generate foreign exchange reserve for import of educational equipment, books and journals, exploring the ways and means of funding by industry and commercial organisations which are beneficiaries of university programmes and introduction of the educational loans schemes on ment-cum-means basis so that funds could be ploughed back for re-investment in education for future generation. All these measures have significant potential to enhance the resource base and productivity of the system which is a must for accelerating the pace of economic and social development.

NOTES AND REFERENCES

1. See Authors *Economics of Distance Higher Education*, Concept Publishing Company, 1991.
2. The proportion of tuition fee to the total costs of higher education constitutes less than two per cent. Even though a number of colleges and universities have increased fees in the recent past by about ten times or so, the share of tuition fee in the total costs would be much less to off-set the escalation of costs due to rise in prices and budgetary cuts imposed by the Government.
3. It is learnt from reliable sources that , of late, most universities have begun to charge from each foreign student in varying amounts. These funds, thus raised, would be used for the purchase of books and journals from foreign publishers. Due to the foreign exchange crisis, the number of subscription of journals from abroad has substantially declined in most institutions.
4. For a detailed discussion on areas and forms of cooperation between universities and industry, with a view *inter alia* to raising funds for university development, please see Author's 'Universities and Industry in India: Is Collaborative Effort Succeeding' (with T.C. Sharma) *Industry & Higher Education*, 1991, September.

9

SUMMARY OF CONCLUSIONS

The primary function of higher education institutions (HEIs) are to generate and disseminate knowledge and to promote technological innovation and know-how. Planners, therefore, make concerted efforts especially with regard to allocation and management of physical and financial resources for ensuring the promotion of such programmes as teaching, research and training which are essential to the attainment of the manpower requirements of the society and economy. It is precisely in this context that the costs and finance aspects of higher education system become an interesting area of study, particularly from the view point of designing suitable fiscal instruments which should ensure equity and efficiency in provision of facilities financed out of public funds. The examinations of relevant policies and programmes become important more so because during the era of financial exigencies, the competing claims of various sectors of development are required to be objectively determined such that the inter-sectoral balance, particularly in the long-term perspective, is properly maintained. During the last four decades of planning, it has been observed that the factors like growth of population, widening basis of elementary and secondary education, endeavours to equalize educational opportunities, growing realization among the people about the socio-economic value of education and the growing need for qualified and trained manpower of different types and levels, have exerted considerable pressure of demand for higher education. Accordingly, commendable progress has been made with regard to expansion and diversification of university programmes. Yet, merely 6 per cent of the age specific population has been able to benefit from the network of educational programmes. This share is not likely to improve to any appreciable extent in the current decade, which would mean that the level of human capital formation as measured by the proportion of persons in the total labour force having a higher degree of knowledge, training and skill would continue to remain low for India as compared to the European countries where the corresponding proportion is in the range of 25 to 40 per cent. Since the developments in the field of higher education have been quite uneven as revealed from low performance and lack of accountability, under utilisation of facilities, inflexibility in the mode of functioning of most institutions, a great deal of effort is needed to be made to strengthen and vitalize the conventional system of higher education such that the contributions of the system to the national development could be desirably improved. In trying to rectify the deficiencies of an important sector of development like university system, it is imperative to examine the costs and finance aspects of higher education with a view to evolving perspectives on the sources and methods of financing university programmes and the extent of cost-effectiveness of such schemes so as to obtain an idea of the performance of fiscal efforts. In view of this, the present study is devoted to examine the entire gamut of resource allocation policy for development of university system in India. Specifically, the major objectives of the study are: to discuss the inter-relationship between higher education and national development; to discern the trend in allocation of resources for universities; to examine the pattern of utilisation of funds and to quantify the extent to which different factors account for university expenditure; to work-out unit costs of higher education by major disciplines; to estimate the financial requirements for higher education in the current Eighth Five Year Plan, taking particularly into account the implementation of policies and programmes approved under the National Policy on Education 1986; to recommend alternative methods of funding such that equity and efficiency of university system could be ensured; to indicate the areas and direction of reforms of higher education; and to suggest appropriate policy measures for economising expenditure and raising additional resources for improving the financial health of universities.

The analysis and study of the above aspects are based on comprehensive data base which pertain to both macro-level i.e. all India time-series data as well as micro-level i.e. university-wise cross-sectional data. To the extent possible, for the purposes of analysis of data, up-to-date information have been used. For instance, most generally, the time series physical data pertain to 1950-51 to 1988-89 while financial data relate to 1970-71 to 1985-86. The case of 24 universities belonging to the different categories namely, Central, State and 'deemed to be' universities is based on cross-sectional data for 1986-87. Also, certain aspects are compared at two points of time i.e.

1975-76 and 1985-86 so as to indicate the direction and extent of shift in allocation and utilisation of funds. Keeping in view the nature of data and the purpose of analysis as explained in each Chapter, appropriate statistical techniques have been employed so as to draw meaningful conclusions. For instance, in the case of time-series analysis, the approach of regression analysis has been employed to examine the trend of change and the extent to which different interrelated variables are exercising determining influence on the educational expenditure. The coefficient of variation has also been worked out in the context of cross-sectional data to demonstrate the degree of variation from the mean with respect to the specific indicator. In brief, each of the research questions has been objectively examined, to the extent possible, by fitting appropriate statistical tool to the available data on the subject matter of analysis. The major conclusions of various analytical exercises and statistical results are as under.

It is the development of human resources of a nation, not its capital nor its material resources, that ultimately determine the character and pace of economic and social development; which, in effect, influence the quality of life of people. In this context, higher education plays a crucial role of overseeing and providing guidance for development of education and training of various types and levels so as to constantly improve the knowledge and level of comptence of people, which essentially nurture and promote human capital formation. Such a role of higher education is considered crucial because the experiences of most countries have demonstrated that the promotion of education has preceded economic development. Thus, without the constant improvement in knowledge, technology and skills of the people, it is not possible, in the modern world, to accelerate the pace of development. Inspite of the fact that considerable effort has been made to expand and diversify the system of higher education, the achievements in this field have been much below the level required for increasing the tempo of development. The evidences show that influence of higher education on social and economic development has been quite mixed and not always consistant with the national policies. This, therefore, calls for initiating corrective measures to vitalize the various aspects of higher education, which have positive influence on raising productivity, reducing inter-regional and interpersonal socio-economic inequality and nurturing faith in the future of the country. By the same token, the aspects of higher education, which adversely affect the realisation of national objectives due to ineffective planning and deficiency in management of the system, should be eliminated.

The mechanism of funding higher education is largely responsible for uneven developments in this field. Even though the expenditure on higher education, in its larger part, is considered investment; and, therefore, much care is exercised in allocation of resources, there is no valid criteria for determining the physical and financial requirements for the development of HEIs in general and the specific programmes of teaching and research in particular. There are different types of HEIs which are funded by different Central and State level agencies. Eventhough much of the programmes carried out by them are comparable or there are considerable duplication of activities by them, the block grants provided to them are not determined on a uniform basis, employing normative or positive norms of expenditure for specific programmes. In brief, the evidences indicate the following:

(i) While the universities are largely dependent on the Government support for financing their programmes, the Central universities are relatively more dependent than other types of HEIs. The financial dependence in respect of all types of institutions has tended to rise over the past decade.

(ii) Inter-university differences in allocation of funds by the UGC are much higher in respect of the state and 'deemed to be' universities whereas the same are very low for the Central universities. The UGC has seemingly not tried to evolve an acceptable method of resource allocation whereby the institutions under its purview could be treated equitably in respect of the comparable programmes of teaching, research and training.

(iii) The extent of funds mobilised by different types of universities from non-government sources indicate large variations. And in this respect, the state universities are able to augment relatively more funds from non-government sources such as fees, endowments, etc., than other types of institutions. Obviously, higher education in Central universities is relatively more subsidised than others. It has also been observed that most of the state universities mainly of affiliating type, are able to generate resources from activities like conduct of examinations. Similarly, the conventional universities offering distance education programmes are also able to raise considerable amount of funds through various charges from distance learners. The amount, thus raised are utilized for meeting the maintenance expenditure of universities.

(iv) The share of income from tuition fees and utility charges on account of lab, hostel, examination, etc., has generally declined; thereby indicating, the lack of concerted efforts to augment resources from the beneficiary groups of higher education.

(v) In financing higher education, the contributions of the Centre have declined from 31 per cent in 1970-71 to 24 per cent in 1983-84 even though education has been included in the Concurrent list of the Constitution of India. In respect of technical higher education, its share has, however marginally increased to 38 per cent in 1984-85 as against 35 per cent in 1970-71. In all, at least three-fourths of financial burden of meeting the requirements of universities and other higher education falls on the State Governments, which also means that the health and vitality of higher education in India is heavily dependent on fiscal capacity of the States as well as their perception about the relative role of higher education in promoting economic and social development.

It has also emerged that inspite of the substantial contributions which the Central and the State governments are making towards the financing of higher education and research, the finances of universities and colleges are inadequate as they have not increased commensurate with the rise in enrolment, rate of inflation and increased requirements for modernisation and diversification of tertiary education. The absence of valid criteria or scientific norms are the main reason for underestimation of resource requirements. The existing arrangements under which the Centre and the States are financing universities have quite often given rise to diverse and dilatory practices and procedures between the two levels of governments, so much so that the attention of the government's gets diverted from ensuring a sound financial base for HEIs. The fact that development schemes of a majority of the State universities are financed on matching basis by the UGC and the States, the implementation of most of the schemes suffer because of the lack of adequate support from the States. The States do not provide matching shares because of either paucity of resources or low priority for general higher education or the fear of impending financial burden which devolves on the States after the plan period is over. Also, a number of state universities are observed to have been resorting to financial and accounting gimmick whereby the plan outlays are being utilized for non-plan purposes, mainly the payment of salaries to the teaching and non-teaching staff. Thus, the developmental activities pertaining to the relevance and quality of educational and training schemes get hampered.

As pointed out above, the main source of distortion in the allocation of funds is lack of objectivity in determination of requirements of HEIs. An analysis of budgetary positions of 80 universities for the last 5 years has, for instance, revealed that as many as 45 universities suffered from deficit while 35 of them experienced a surplus. As many as 78 of these universities had deficit budgets for varying years during the period of analysis; and at least 10 universities suffered from perpetual deficit for all the five years. The magnitude of deficits also varied a great deal across the universities. These evidences demonstrated the lack of planning and management of financial resources either by the funding agencies or by the universities themselves. It, therefore, recommends for modification in the existing mechanisms of distribution of funds while taking duly into account the aspects of utilization of funds by HEIs.

An endeavour has also been made in the present study to examine the pattern of growth and utilisation of expenditure. The major exogeneous factors which account for growth in expenditure are: the pressure of social demand and the market forces influenced by the general economic conditions under which various educational inputs are purchased by the institutions. Of the various factors that are internal to the system and are responsible for determining the size of expenditure are: the nature and extent of use of educational technologies, the structure and level of salaries of staff, the degree of wastage and stagnation, and the extent of utilisation of facilities. All these factors are influenced by the forces that are within the control of the education system and have significant bearing on the growth of expenditure.

The evidences demonstrated that on an average 4.7 per cent of GNP was spent on education and income elasticity of expenditure emerged out to be above unity (1.25), which indicated more than proportionate increase in educational expenditure in relation to national income. The corresponding income elasticity coefficient for higher education emerged out to be 1.32, the break-up of Centre and the States being 1.03 and 1.40, respectively. This indicated a relatively high fiscal effort by the States than the Centre in promotion of high education for the period of analysis, on an average 0.57 per cent of GNP was spent on higher education as against 4.7 per cent for the overall education system. As the econometric exercises have revealed, the phenomenon of rise in prices has adversely affected the real value of expenditure on education. An analysis of inter-State variations in educational efforts, as measured by the share of expenditure in the State Domestic Product (SDP), revealed that there is general increase in efforts by the Indian States. The economically better off States are, however, much ahead of others which are relatively backward. There seems to be no desirable level of fiscal intervention by the Centre to nullify the fiscal deficiency of the backward States so to enable them to expedite the sources of educational development. A low level of educational effort could also be attributed to the perception of various States about the role of education in development.

A major chunk of expenditure on higher education i.e. about 70 per cent is accounted for by the salaries of staff, of which the share of teaching and non-teaching staff is 48 and 22 respectively in the total expenditure. The remaining expenditure is on non-salary items which include equipment, appliances, books and journals and other miscellaneous expenses. The share of payment of salaries has been rising which is largely attributable to the indexation of salaries to rise in prices and partly to perpetuation of labour intensity of the education system. The respective shares of expenditure of different types of HEIs, however, differ considerably. While the payment of salaries is the major determinant of expenditure, the share of payments to non-teaching staff is very significant, and in some institutions more than the academic staff salary. Further, the expenditure on non-salary items especially student support services has been declining. It follows that the aspects of management and utilization of resources are much less satisfactory than desired, especially, in a developing country like India which suffers from scarcity of funds. First, a little probing into the question of how the physical and financial resources are utilized would reveal that the major expenditure on higher education, is accounted for by the staff salaries, of which nearly 50 per cent involves payment to non-teaching staff. Further, the expenditure on non-salary items which include *inter alia* student support services, has been declining overtime. The expenditure on miscellaneous items like electricity, water charges, telephone, etc., has been rising. Second, the academic staff of universities are not utilized to the extent stipulated by the UGC. The evidences, moreover, show that the teacher-student ratio in a large number of universities is very low, about 1:10, which indicates the possibility of improving students' learning since a teacher has to concentrate on a small number of students. Alternatively, economies of scale could be generated by increasing student numbers. There are also those colleges which have high teacher-student ratio due to enrolment pressure which adversely affects quality of education. This reflects lack of planning at the regional and institutional level as well, which adversely influences cost-effectiveness of the educational programmes. Third, the capacity utilization of infrastructure facilities like class-rooms, labs and libraries is merely about 60 per cent which obviously indicate a colossal waste of resources that have been deployed for creation of such facilities.

It emerges from the foregoing that due to allocative inefficiency there is much to be desired as far as the financial accountability of the university system is concerned. There are those institutions which are characterised by abundance of physical and financial resources as is evident from budgetary surpluses and under utilization of facilities whereas some others are suffering from inadequacy of funds and necessary infrastructure.

Since the analysis of unit costs of higher education is of immense importance from the view point of examining effectiveness of planning and management of resources, an endeavour was made to evolve a methodology of estimating comparable per student costs of higher education across the universities. The relevant comparisons of costs by disciplines would enable a university to gauge its fiscal behaviour *vis-a-vis* the performance of other institutions. The results for a cross-section of universities are also helpful for planners or funding agencies in identifying the areas of under or over investment for effective management of resources. Our exercises have demonstrated that even though there is theoretical parity in the degrees/diplomas awarded by the different types of universities, there is no uniform basis for allocation of resources as revealed from the differences in costs of inputs without any justification for quality reasons. Some of the important conclusions that have emerged are: First, there is no discernible pattern to reflect the type of universities or nature of studies or source of revenue which cause a high or low cost of education. Second, the unit costs of general administration, including the salary and non-salary expenses, have generally emerged out to be very high in relation to the costs of teaching in most universities. Third, even though there is parity in the scale of pay of teaching staff as the UGC's pay scales have been implemented throughout the country, the differences in per student teaching costs are very wide. This is attributable to variations in student-teacher ratios, within a given discipline, across the universities. Similarly, per student expenses on supporting staff also differ a great deal which can be ascribed *inter alia* to the differences in service conditions and payments of salary to different levels of administration and secreterial staff. Fourth, the operating costs on account of payment of salaries to teaching and non-teaching staff were higher due to a very low ratio of students to teachers and student/teachers to supporting staff. Also, the extent of utilisation of infrastructure like classrooms, labs, libraries, etc., emerged out to be much less than desirable. These evidences indicated the scope for generating economies of scale by either increasing the number of students or reducing the teaching and non-teaching staff so as to generate savings on account of payment of salaries. The analyses of unit costs thus corroborated the observations made in the foregoing paragraphs.

The implication of the above findings for policy formulation is that a concerted effort ought to make for ensuring efficient and effective utilisation of resources that have been invested for the development of higher education and research. Since this question is related to financial accountability of the system of providing higher education, the funding agencies as well as the receipient institutions ought to pay due attention to the aspects of uses of funds so as to seek the value for money.

The National Policy on Education, 1986 stipulated for vitalizing the higher education system so as to make it somewhat more responsive to socio-economic needs of the country. A number of policy measures have been undertaken to improve the continuing programmes while some new schemes have also been launched to improve performance and accountability of the system. Against the backdrop of major thrust areas as identified in the policy, an attempt has been made to work-out the financial costs of implementation of the programmes of higher education. To this effect a methodology of projection of enrolment by major categories has been developed; and accordingly, enrolment has been projected up to A.D. 2000. Also, as per the discretionary changes, as indicated in the policy suitable adjustment has been for such factors as shift in enrolment towards science and technical courses as well as distance education programmes. On the basis of the unit costs as obtaining for different courses of study and the desirable level of escalation of costs for raising the quality of education, estimate of financial requirements for general as well as management and technical higher education, at 1989-90 prices, has been worked out for the period up to

1995 which largely cover the current Eighth Five Year Plan. The relevant methodology and projected level of enrolment up to A.D. 2000 provide the desirable guidance for estimating financial requirements for the future. Briefly, using a semi-log function with respect to time, enrolment in major fields of study, namely, Arts, Science, Commerce, Education, Law, etc., have separately been projected till A.D. 2000. Since the National Policy on Education (NPE) 1986 has placed emphasis on the need to widen the science based courses of study, the enrolment data has marginally been adjusted in favour of science and professional courses. Likewise, suitable adjustment has been made for the factors like intensive use of existing facilities, diversion of students from conventional to distance learning system. The enrolment level, thus obtained indicate the number of students in different courses for the year of projection. To estimate the financial requirements, the relevant per student costs as obtaining for different courses have been applied to the estimated enrolment figures, which yield the projected financial requirement for the given period. In view of the perceived need for improving the quality and relevance of higher education, an appropriate level of increase in the total costs has been provided for with respect to the continuing programmes. The requirements for the new schemes have been worked out separately, applying appropriate norms and sound judgement based on the available facts and proper justification. Thus, the additional requirements for the continuing and new schemes as well as the break-up for each for the various programmes has been indicated separately. It shows that during the period 1990 to 1995 the total outlays for general higher education, under both continuing as well as new schemes, comes to Rs.2285 crores at 1989-90 prices (i.e. Rs.1500 crores of 785 crores, respectively). This is, of course, in addition to the recurrent maintenance expenditure which has been rising at the rate of 6-7 per cent per annum.

A similar approach has been adopted to estimate the requirements on account of technical and management education. Of the total estimated expenditure of Rs.1736 crores during 1990-95 about Rs.1400 crores would be required for continuing schemes while the remaining expenditure would be incurred on new schemes and other programmes as indicated in the policy documents.

It may also be pointed out that of the total estimated expenditure of Rs. 4021 crores for the period 1990-95 towards the implementation of NPE 1986, 62 per cent of the total financial burden would be borne by the States while the remaining share would be met by the Centre. On the present reckoning, the burden of financing general higher education to the extent of 80 per cent would devolve on the States while the corresponding share of technical and management education would be merely 40 per cent as the Centre has largely been investing (about 60 per cent) in technical and management education. Moreover, for effective implementation of the policy, the plan allocation for general higher education is required to be doubled while the expenditure on technical education is needed to be enhanced by about two and half times of the existing level of expenditure at 1989-90 prices. The above estimates are, however, very conservative that had to be made keeping in view the economic limitation of the country and its relative prioritisation of various sectors of development.

The method by which resources are provided, however, plays a crucial role in streamlining the functioning of HEIs. The concern for improving the performance and accountability of HEIs has never been as high as today. This calls for identifying the factors which have been contributing to degradation of the higher education system or impinging on its efforts to effectively cope with the challenges of development. Against the backdrop of major shortcomings from which the system is suffering, an endeavour has been made to describe alternative methods of funding higher education with a view to improving performance. In view of the major deficiences in the mechanisms of financing the programmes of higher education, namely, inequity in distribution of funds across the various HEIs, mis-match between availability of funds and educational responsibilities, lack of effective method of sharing costs of education among the beneficiary groups, indiscriminate subsidy or lack of target orientation in provision of educational services, under-utilisation of infrastructure facilities, etc., alternative methods of allocation of limited resources has been suggested so as to overcome the problems indicated above. Of the two suggested methods, while one relates to playing the game of distribution of resources within the existing methods and procedures, the other relates to changing the rule of the game. The latter may be termed as direct funding of students, in which the limited resource should be provided on merit-cum-means basis to students in the form of grants/loans. The students who have proven ability to benefit from higher education programmes should choose the package of education and training programmes offered by different institutions. The institution for providing educational loans should, in turn, charge full fee from the students who would pay largely out of government grants and partly from inflationary adjusted interest free loans raised through financial institutions. The institution for providing educational loans may be named as Educational Opportunity Fund. The students' loans should be linked to earnings of students and it should be repayable during the entire span of working life. Such a method of funding would make the students/parents economically concious of the education that they buy for themselves or for their wards and would, therefore, be duly vocal about the quality and relevance of programmes offered by the HEIs. The HEIs, in turn, would not take for granted that irrespective of their performance they would continue to be funded by the Government, as happens today. Rather, they would have to compete for attracting students and their success in this regard would depend on the quality and relevance of programmes offered by them. The method of direct funding would also allow various public and private sector organisations to sponsor able students in different professional catagories in more or less the same proportion as they annually employ the staff. In effect, thus, keeping in view the manpower requirements of various sectors of development, the Government should empower the students of proven ability to choose an institution and the relevant programme; and the scheme of financing should be suitably devised on merit-cum-means basis such that the burden of the costs of education is shared in inverse proportion of income of the beneficary groups.

The best and worst performing institutions simultaniously exist today due to indiscriminate method of funding. The second method, therefore, relates to the distribution of funds among the institutions on the basis of their performance in teaching and research which should be assessed by the peer groups on the basis of efficiency norms. Instead of thinly spreading the limited funds among a large number of institutions, the resources should be distributed in accordance with the national average performance of institutions in a given field of study and their eligibility for funds should, accordingly be determined on requirements basis. Keeping in view the quality and relevance of various programmes, in each of the disciplines, the eligibility of an institution for funds would depend on its performance in teaching and research, as per the detailed scheme outlined in the study. The allocation of funds linked to the performance of HEIs would duly improve their accountability to the society, which is the need of the hour. In short, fiscal instruments ought to be properly used for ensuring better performance of HEIs by way of improving cost-effectiveness of educational programmes since the expenditure on higher education in its larger part constitute investment.

In a diverse and complex system of higher education as in India, it is not so easy to bring about reforms for the development of the system. Yet, the responsiveness of the system to the socio-economic requirements of the country should be invariably improved. An endeavour has been made to identify the areas and direction of reforms that may be contemplated in the ensuing future with a view to both improving planning and management of HEIs as well as rationalising the funding of various programmes. From the view point of perspective planning of HEIs, due attention should be paid to such aspects as (a) institutional planning in relation, of course, to manpower requirements; (b) diversion of students towards vocational courses which are generally very cost-effective; (c) re-designing of courses so as to improve relevance of programmes; (d) improvement in teaching methods so that students' learning achievement could be improved; and (e) equalisation of educational opportunity such that the benefits of development could be equitably distributed across the socio-economic groups and regions. An equally important aspect of perspective planning and management of HEIs is to reform the structure and method of funding. At least two sets of measures have been suggested. While one relates to economy in expenditure, other pertains to additional mobilization of resources. Based on the relevant findings of the present study, it has been suggested that some resources could be saved by (i) reduction in non-academic expenditure; (ii) optimum utilisation of facilities; (iii) sharing of facilities between national institutions; (iv) economising expenditure on conduct of examinations; (v) reducing costs of processing applications for admissions to different courses; and (vi) diverting students to distance learning system which is economical and cost-effective. Of the various measures suggested for additional resource mobilization are (i) upward revision of fee structure and various user's charges; (ii) withdrawal of subsidy to foreign students; (iii) mobilization of funds from industry and other commercial organisations; and (iv) promotion of educational loans scheme so as to plough back resources for reinvestment in education. In recommending the above measures, as discussed in detail in the present study, due care has been taken of the various policy measures taken by the Government recently to deregulate the Indian economy so that cross-fertilisation of various sectors of economy, including higher education, could be optimised so as to accelerate the pace of economic growth and social development.

APPENDICES

APPENDIX 4.1

Recurring Expenditure by Level of Education in India

Year	Elementary Education (including Pre-primary Education	Secondary Education	Higher Education (including Research Institute)	Vocational/ Professional Special and Other Education	Total Expenditure on Education
1	2	3	4	5	6 (2=3+4+5)
1950-51	46.3 (50.8)	20.5 (22.5)	18.5 (20.3)	5.8 (6.4)	91.1 (100.0)
1960-61	116.9 (45.4)	68.9 (26.8)	57.0 (22.1)	14.6 (5.7)	257.4 (100.0)
1970-71	407.4 (42.4)	270.0 (28.1)	270.9 (28.2)	12.8 (1.3)	961.1 (100.0)
1980-81	1392.1 (40.4)	1012.2 (29.4)	999.5 (29.0)	38.8 (1.2)	3442.6 (100.0)
1981-82	1660.3 (41.4)	1178.0 (29.4)	1124.4 (28.0)	48.8 (1.2)	4011.5 (100.0)
1982-83	1942.1 (41.6)	1358.6 (29.2)	1298.2 (27.9)	61.5 (1.3)	4660.4 (100.0)
1983-84	2209.0 (41.9)	1441.4 (27.3)	1558.5 (29.6)	61.0 (1.2)	5269.9 (100.0)

Source: Annual Report (1991-92), Ministry of Human Resources Development.

APPENDIX 4.2

Expenditure on Education by all Departments 1970-71 TO 1984-85

(*Rs. in crores*)

	CENTRE			STATES*			TOTAL		
	Plan	Non-Plan	Total	Plan	Non-Plan	Total	Plan	Non-Plan	Total
1970-71	35.4	30.5	65.9	83.3	821.7	904.9	118.6	852.2	970.8
1971-72	48.8	45.6	94.4	125.8	882.1	1007.8	174.6	927.6	1102.2
1972-73	64.8	52.3	117.1	173.9	1000.3	1174.2	238.6	1052.6	1291.2
1973-74	88.4	57.9	116.3	243.8	1089.9	1333.7	302.2	1147.8	1450.0
1974-75	57.3	88.1	145.4	117.2	1522.8	1640.0	174.5	1610.9	1785.4
1975-76	65.5	107.6	173.1	181.4	1730.7	1912.1	246.9	1838.3	2085.2
1976-77	85.8	125.4	211.2	228.4	1909.1	2137.5	314.2	2034.5	2348.7
1977-78	98.5	129.1	227.6	294.2	2184.1	2478.3	392.7	2313.2	2705.9
1978-79	133.8	157.1	290.9	423.5	2373.3	2796.8	557.3	2530.4	3087.7
1979-80	115.0	167.7	292.7	276.5	2862.2	3138.7	391.5	3029.9	3421.4
1980-81	119.6	209.8	329.4	348.6	3343.8	3692.4	468.2	3553.6	4021.8
1981-82	167.0	220.8	387.8	397.4	3650.7	4048.1	564.4	3871.5	4435.9
1982-83	272.5	285.5	558.0	592.8	4585.6	5178.4	865.3	4871.1	5736.4
1983-84	305.4	317.4	622.8	766.7	5125.2	6891.9	1072.1	5442.6	6514.7
1984-85	416.6	351.2	767.8	968.4	5851.7	6820.1	1388.0	6202.9	7587.9
1985-86 (RE)	477.7	464.0	942.7	964.2	7158.2	8122.4	1441.9	7622.2	9064.1
1986-87 (RE)	638.1	481.0	1119.1	1441.8	7622.2	9064.0	2079.9	8103.2	10183.1

Note: * Including Union Territories.

Source: Various issues of *Analysis of Budget Expenditure on Education*, Ministry of Human Resource Development, Govt. of India, New Delhi.

APPENDIX 4.3

Trends in Plan and Non-plan Expenditure (Revenue Account) on University & Other Higher Education (Non-Technical) — Centre, States & Union Territories

(Rs. in crores)

Years	Centre			States & Union			Total		
	Plan	Non-plan	Total	Plan	Non-plan	Total	Plan	Non-plan	Total
	(1)	(2)	(3)=(1+2)	(4)	(5)	(6)=(4+5)	(7)	(8)	(9)=(7+8)
1970-71	22.04 (67.94)	10.40 (32.06)	32.44 (100.00)	10.85 (14.07)	66.27 (85.93)	77.12 (100.00)	32.89 (30.02)	76.67 (69.98)	109.56 (100.00)
1971-72	23.26 (68.27)	10.81 (31.73)	34.07 (100.00)	14.90 (16.99)	72.79 (83.01)	87.69 (100.00)	38.16 (31.34)	83.60 (68.66)	121.76 (100.00)
1972-73	27.65 (70.72)	11.45 (29.28)	39.10 (100.00)	17.68 (16.23)	91.23 (83.77)	108.91 (100.00)	45.33 (30.63)	102.68 (69.37)	148.01 (100.00)
1973-74	23.38 (64.16)	13.06 (34.84)	36.44 (100.00)	23.97 (18.83)	103.35 (81.17)	127.32 (100.00)	47.35 (28.91)	116.41 (71.09)	163.76 (100.00)
1974-75	21.95 (43.25)	28.80 (56.75)	50.75 (100.00)	11.10 (7.13)	144.64 (92.87)	155.74 (100.00)	33.05 (16.01)	173.44 (83.99)	206.49 (100.00)

(Contd.)

Appendix 4.3 (*Contd.*)

Years	Centre			States & Union			Total		
	Plan	Non-plan	Total	Plan	Non-plan	Total	Plan	Non-plan	Total
	(1)	(2)	(3)=(1+2)	(4)	(5)	(6)=(4+5)	(7)	(8)	(9)=(7+8)
1975-76	32.10 (50.17)	31.88 (49.83)	63.98 (100.00)	15.95 (8.92)	162.94 (91.08)	178.89 (100.00)	48.05 (19.78)	194.82 (80.22)	242.87 (100.00)
1976-77	40.81 (54.25)	34.44 (45.75)	75.28 (100.00)	22.97 (10.70)	191.79 (89.30)	214.76 (100.00)	63.81 (22.00)	226.23 (78.00)	290.04 (100.00)
1977-78	44.90 (54.54)	37.42 (45.46)	82.32 (100.00)	35.31 (13.35)	229.26 (86.65)	264.57 (100.00)	80.21 (23.12)	266.68 (76.88)	346.89 (100.00)
1978-79	51.25 (48.57)	54.27 (51.43)	105.52 (100.00)	41.82 (13.86)	259.99 (86.14)	301.81 (100.00)	93.07 (22.85)	314.26 (77.15)	407.33 (100.00)
1979-80	31.06 (36.40)	54.28 (63.60)	85.34 (100.00)	30.76 (8.68)	323.45 (91.32)	354.21 (100.00)	61.82 (14.06)	377.73 (85.94)	439.55 (100.00)
1980-81	32.45 (32.85)	66.32 (67.15)	98.77 (100.00)	42.13 (10.97)	341.77 (89.03)	383.90 (100.00)	74.58 (15 45)	408.09 (84.55)	482.67 (100.00)
1981-82	40.69 (37.09)	69.00 (62.91)	109.69 (100.00)	41.60 (8.89)	426.53 (91.11)	468.13 (100.00)	82.29 (14.24)	495.53 (85.76)	577.82 (100.00)

(*Contd.*)

Appendix 4.3 (*Contd.*)

Years	Centre			States & Union			Total		
	Plan	Non-plan	Total	Plan	Non-plan	Total	Plan	Non-plan	Total
	(1)	(2)	(3)=(1+2)	(4)	(5)	(6)=(4+5)	(7)	(8)	(9)=(7+8)
1982-83	46.44	79.70	126.14	61.14	493.23	554.37	107.58	572.93	680.51
	(36.82)	(63.18)	(100.00)	(11.03)	(88.97)	(100.00)	(15.81)	(84.19)	(100.00)
1983-84	48.82	92.38	141.20	70.37	565.42	635.79	119.19	657.80	776.99
	(34.58)	(65.42)	(100.00)	(11.07)	(88.93)	(100.00)	(15.34)	(84.66)	(100.00)
1984-85	74.42	104.87	179.29	99.59	643.01	742.01	174.01	747.88	921.89
	(41.51)	(58.49)	(100.00)	(13.41)	86.59)	(100.00)	(18.88)	(81.12)	(100.00)
1985-86 (R.E.)	81.72	123.00	204.72	70.42	831.45	901.87	152.14	954.45	1106.59
	(39.92)	(60.08)	(100.00)	(7.81)	(92.19)	(100.00)	(13.75)	(86.25)	(100.00)
1986-87 (B.E.)	87.65	125.30	212.95	79.20	878.20	957.40	166.85	1003.50	1170.35
	(41.16)	(58.84)	(100.00)	(8.27)	(91.73)	(100.00)	(14.26)	(85.74)	(100.00)

Note: Figures within parantheses indicate percentages to respective totals.
Source: Same as in Appendix 4.2

APPENDIX 5C-1

UNIT COSTS ANALYSIS - PER STUDENT (EQUIVALENT), 1986-87 (FACULTY OF ARTS)

(*In Rs.*)

Items of expenditure / University	Delhi	Aligarh	Banaras	Madras	Annamalai	Kurukshetra	Ravishankar	JNU	Cofficient of varia -tion (%)
i. Expenditure on Salaries the Faculty Staff:	3017 (46.8)	7723 (45.0)	4628 (37.5)	9657 (17.0)	7592 (31.2)	2545 (28.8)	2281 (17.1)	3911 (30.8)	54
of which:									
(a) Teaching Staff	2408 (37.3)	6050 (35.3)	3548 (28.8)	8841 (15.6)	4523 (18.6)	1978 (22.4)	1544 (11.6)	3302 (26.0)	60
(b) Non-teaching Staff	609 (9.5)	1673 (9.7)	1080 (8.7)	816 (1.4)	3069 (12.6)	567 (6.4)	737 (5.5)	609 (4.8)	75
ii. Academic Support Services (Other than Salaries)	318 (4.9)	317 (1.9)	109 (0.9)	3590 (6.4)	1159 (4.8)	54 (0.6)	219 (1.6)	371 (2.9)	155
iii. General Administrative Expenditure	3112 (48.3)	9108 (53.1)	7592 (61.6)	43316 (76.6)	15551 (64.0)	6245 (70.6)	10819 (81.3)	8429 (66.3)	81
Total (i+ii+iii)	6447 (100.0)	17148 (100.0)	12329 (100.0)	56563 (100.0)	24302 (100.0)	8844 (100.0)	13319 (100.0)	12711 (100.0)	72
- Teacher-Student Ratio	1:20	1:6	1:24	1:8	1:8.4	1:15	1:10	1:11.5	
- Teaching to Non-teaching Staff Ratio	1:0.84	-	-	1:1	-	1:0.8	-	1:0.4	
- Non-teaching Staff to Student Ratio	1:23.5	-	-	1:7.2	-	1:17.1	-	1:29	

Note: 1. Figures in parenthesis indicate the percentage to total cost.
2.* Including payments of salaries to non-teaching staff and other non-salary items.
3.(-) Not computed due to non availability of data.

APPENDIX 5C-2

UNIT COSTS ANALYSIS - PER STUDENT (EQUIVALENT), 1986-87 (FACULTY OF SCIENCE)

(*In Rs.*)

Items of Expenditure / University	Delhi	Aligarh	Banaras	Madras	Annamalai	Kurukshetra	Ravishankar	JNU	Coefficient of Variation (%)
1	2	3	4	5	6	7	8	9	10
i. Expenditure on Salaries of the Faculty Staff; of which:	4078 (35.8)	5701 (39.3)	7900 (32.7)	15042 (22.1)	3421 (32.8)	5558 (25.0)	4286 (17.1)	6949 (19.5)	56
a) Teaching Staff	2139 (18.8)	3307 (22.8)	5473 (22.6)	9480 (13.9)	2736 (26.2)	3725 (16.8)	2807 (11.2)	4374 (12.2)	55
b) Non-teaching Staff	1939 (17.0)	2394 (16.5)	2427 (10.1)	5562 (8.2)	685 (6.6)	1833 (8.2)	1479 (5.9)	2575 (7.3)	61
ii. Academic Support Services (Other than Salaries)	1800 (15.8)	1103 (7.6)	1374 (5.6)	2405 (3.5)	256 (2.4)	967 (4.4)	417 (1.7)	5055 (14.1)	92

(*Contd.*)

APPENDIX 5C2 (*Contd.*)

Items of Expenditure \ University	Delhi	Aligarh	Banaras	Madras	Annamalai	Kurukshetra	Ravishankar	JNU	Coefficient of Variation (%)
iii. General Administrative Expenditure	5499 (48.4)	7709 (53.1)	14863 (61.7)	50404 (74.4)	6747 (64.3)	15675 (70.6)	20347 (81.2)	23620 (66.4)	77
Total (i+ii+iii)	11377 (100.0)	14513 (100.0)	24137 (100.0)	67851 (100.0)	10424 (100.0)	22200 (100.0)	25050 (100.0)	35624 (100.0)	66
1. Teacher-Student Ratio	1:18	1:12	1:8	1:5	1:12	1:15	1:5	1:9	
2. Teaching to Non-teaching Staff Ratio		1:1.5	-	-	1:2	-	1:0.8	-	1:1.2
3. Non-teaching Staff to Student Ratio	1:11.7	-	-	1:2.2	-	1:6.1	-	1:7.7	

Note:
1. Figures in parenthesis indicate the percentage to total cost.
2. * Including payments of salaries to non-teaching staff and other non-salary items.
3. (-) Not computed due to non availability of data.

APPENDIX 5C-3

UNIT COSTS ANALYSIS - PER STUDENT (EQUIVALENT), 1986-87
(FACULTY OF COMMERCE & MANAGEMENT)

(*In Rs.*)

Items of Expenditure \ University	Delhi	Aligarh	Banaras	Madras	Annamalai	Kurukshetra	Coefficient of Variation (%)
i. Expenditure on Salaries of the Faculty Staff;	2720	2838	1406	4577	2863	1984	39
	(45.7)	(44.4)	(38.1)	(19.2)	(33.4)	(26.6)	
of which:							
a) Teaching Staff	1906	2042	1406	3313	2776	1608	34
	(32.0)	(31.9)	(38.1)	(13.9)	(32.4)	(21.6)	
b) Non-teaching Staff	814	796	-	1264	87	376	68
	(13.7)	(12.5)	(5.3)	(1.0)	(5.0)		
ii. Academic Support Services (Other than Salaries)	350	155	07	83	154	212	73
	(5.9)	(2.4)	(0.2)	(0.4)	(1.8)	(2.8)	
iii. General Administrative Exp.	2882	3395	2273	19132	5539	5264	89
	(48.4)	(53.2)	(61.7)	(80.4)	(64.8)	(70.6)	
Total (i+ii+iii)	5952	6388	3686	23792	8550	7460	72
	(100.0)	(100.0)	(100.0)	(100.0)	(100.0)	(100.0)	
1. Teacher-Student Ratio	1:16	-	1:28	1:7	1:12.1	1:11	
2. Teaching to Non-Teaching Staff Ratio	1:0.8	-	1.1	-	-	1:0.8	
3. Non-Teaching Staff to Student Ratio	1:25.6	-	1:13.1	-	-	1:13.9	

Note: 1. Figures in parenthesis indicate the percentage to total cost.
2. * Including payments of salaries to non-teaching staff and other non-salary items.
3. (-) Not computed due to non availability of data.

APPENDIX: 5C-4

UNIT COSTS ANALYSIS - PER STUDENT (EQUIVALENT), 1986-87 (FACULTY OF EDUCATION)

(*In Rs.*)

University Items of Expenditure	Delhi	Banaras	Annamalai	Kurukshetra	Coefficient of Variation (%)
1	2	3	4	5	6
i. Expenditure on Salaries of the Faculty Staff; of which:	6513 (46.6)	3436 (37.3)	2443 (30.4)	2979 (28.2)	48
a) Teaching Staff	4538 (32.5)	3436 (37.3)	2112 (26.3)	2495 (23.6)	34
b) Non-teaching Staff	1975 (14.1)	- (4.1)	331 (4.6)	484	98
ii. Academic Support Services (Other than Salaries)	734 (5.2)	95 (1.0)	390 (4.9)	122 (1.2)	89
iii. General Administrative Exp*	6731 (48.2)	5683 (61.7)	5198 (64.7)	7452 (70.6)	83
Total (i+ii+iii)	13978 (100.0)	9214 (100.0)	8031 (100.0)	10553 (100.0)	58
1. Teacher-Student ratio	1:11	1:11	1:15.2	1:9	
2. Teaching to Non-teaching Staff Ratio	1:1.9	-	-	1:0.4	
3. Non-teaching Staff to Student Ratio	1:5.9	-	-	1:15.5	

Note:
1. Figures in parenthesis indicate the percentage to total cost.
2. * Including payments of salaries to non-teaching staff and other non-salary items.

APPENDIX 5C-5

UNIT COSTS ANALYSIS-PER STUDENT (EQUIVALENT), 1986-87
(FACULTY OF ENGINEERING & TECHNOLOGY)

(*in Rs.*)

University Items of Expenditure	Aligarh	Banaras	Annamalai	Coefficient of variation (%)
1	2	3	4	5
i. Expenditure on Salaries of the Faculty Staff; of which:	9225 (43.5)	13670 (32.5)	3367 (29.3)	59
a) Teaching Staff	3794 (17.9)	7335 (17.5)	2468 (21.5)	56
b) Non-teaching Staff	5431 (25.6)	6335 (15.0)	899 (7.8)	69
ii. Academic Support Services (Other than Salaries)	707 (3.3)	2479 (5.9)	681 (5.9)	80
iii. General Administrative Exp.*	11253 (53.2)	25871 (61.6)	7427 (64.8)	66
Total (i+ii+iii)	21185 (100.0)	42020 (100.0)	11475 (100.0)	63
1. Teacher-Student Ratio	1:14	1:4	1:30	
2. Teaching to Non-teaching Staff Ratio	-	-	-	
3. Non-teaching Staff to Student Ratio	-	-	-	

Note:
1. Figures in parenthesis indicate the percentage to total cost.
2. * Including payments of salaries to non-teaching staff and other non-salary items.
3. (-) Not computed due to non availability of data.

APPENDIX 5C-6

UNIT COSTS ANALYSIS - PER STUDENT (EQUIVALENT), 1986-87 (FACULTY OF LAW)

(*In Rs.*)

University / Items of Expenditure	Delhi	Aligarh	Banaras	Madras	Kurukshetra	Ravishankar	Coefficient of Variation (%)
i. Expenditure on Salaries of the Faculty Staff;	1803 (47.6)	3361 (45.4)	1593 (37.8)	2637 (19.4)	3957 (28.9)	1824 (17.0)	38
of which:							
a) Teaching Staff	1085 (28.7)	2488 (33.6)	1593 (37.8)	1890 (13.9)	3112 (22.7)	882 (8.2)	46
b) Non-teaching Staff	718 (18.9)	873 (11.8)	-	747 (5.5)	845 (6.2)	942 (8.8)	11
ii. Academic Support Services (Other than Salaries)	154 (4.1)	102 (1.4)	29 (0.7)	22 (0.2)	64 (0.5)	176 (1.6)	71
iii. General Administrative Exp.*	1827 (48.3)	3935 (53.2)	2590 (61.5)	10923 (80.4)	9663 (70.6)	8706 (81.4)	103
Total (i+ii+iii)	3784 (100.0)	7398 (100.0)	4212 (100.0)	13582 (100.0)	13684 (100.0)	10706 (100.0)	88
1. Teacher-Student Ratio	1:34	1:21	1:24	1:18	1:9	1:17	
2. Teaching to Non-teaching Staff Ratio	1:1.2	-	-	1:1	1:0.4	-	
3. Non-teaching Staff to Student Ratio	1:29	-	-	1:22.8	1:12.5	-	

Note:
1. Figures in parenthesis indicate the percentage to total cost.
2. * Including payments of salaries to non-teaching staff and other non-salary items.
3. (-) Not computed due to non availability of data.

APPENDIX TABLE: 5D-1

UNIT COSTS ANALYSIS - PER STUDENT (EQUIVALENT), 1986-87 (FACULTY OF ARTS)

(In Rs.)

A. DEPARTMENT OF ECONOMICS

University / Items of Expenditure	Delhi	Madras	Ravishankar	Kurukshetra	Annamalai	Coefficient of Variation (%)
i. Expenditure on Salaries of the Department; of which:	3061 (48.2)	5348 (18.9)	2030 (16.9)	2362 (29.1)	2793 (35.2)	42
a) Teaching Staff	2151	4674 (33.9)	1318 - (16.5)	2011 (11.0)	2720 (24.8)	50 (34.3)
b) Non-teaching Staff	910	674 (14.3)	712 (2.4)	351 (5.9)	73 (4.3)	61 (0.9)
ii. Academic Support Services (Other than Salaries)	213 (3.3)	191 (0.7)	197 (1.6)	21 (0.2)	6 (0.1)	82
iii. General Administrative Exp.*	3078 (48.5)	22764 (80.4)	9773 (81.5)	5723 (70.7)	5134 (64.7)	65
Total (i+ii+iii)	6352 (100.0)	28303 (100.0)	12000 (100.0)	8106 (100.0)	7933 (100.0)	56

Note: Figures in parenthesis indicate the percentage to total cost.
* Including payments of salaries to non-teaching staff and other non-salary items.

APPENDIX 5D-2

UNIT COSTS ANALYSIS - PER STUDENT (EQUIVALENT), 1986-87 (FACULTY OF ARTS)

(*In Rs.*)

B. DEPARTMENT OF ENGLISH

University / Items of Expenditure	Delhi	Madras	Annamalai	Kurukshetra	Coefficient of Variation (%)
1	2	3	4	5	6
i. Expenditure on Salaries of the Department; of which:	2512 (49.1)	1292 (19.4)	6585 (35.2)	1533 (29.2)	83
a) Teaching Staff	2291 (44.8)	844 (12.7)	6479 (34.6)	1304 (24.8)	94
b) Non-teaching Staff	221 (4.3)	448 (6.7)	106 (0.6)	229 (4.4)	57
ii. Academic Support Services(Other than Salaries)	134 (2.6)	156 (2.4)	11 (0.1)	9 (0.2)	101
iii. General Administrative Exp.*	2475 (48.3)	5198 (78.2)	.2096 (64.7)	3706 (70.6)	58
Total (i+ii+iii)	5121 (100.0)	6646 (100.0)	18692 (100.0)	5248 (100.0)	56

Note: Figures in parenthesis indicate the percentage to total cost.
* Including payments of salaries to non-teaching staff and other non-salary items.

APPENDIX 5D-3

UNIT COSTS ANALYSIS - PER STUDENT (EQUIVALENT), 1986-87
(FACULTY OF ARTS)

(*In Rupees*)

C. DEPARTMENT OF POLITICAL SCIENCE

University Items of Expenditure	Delhi	Madras	Annamalai	Kurukshetra	Coefficient of Variation (%)
1	2	3	4	5	6
i. Expenditure on Salaries of the Department; of which:	1072 (50.5)	4035 (19.5)	4160 (35.1)	2115 (29.2)	53
a) Teaching Staff	1030 (48.5)	3397 (16.4)	4150 (35.0)	1935 (26.7)	54
b) Non-teaching Staff	42 (2.0)	638 (3.1)	10 (0.1)	180 (2.5)	133
ii. Academic Support Services (Other than Salaries)	21 (1.0)	17 (0.1)	10 (0.1)	14 (0.2)	30
iii. General Administrative Exp.*	1029 (48.5)	16655 (80.4)	7675 (64.8)	5115 (70.6)	71
Total (i+ii+iii)	2122 (100.0)	20707 (100.0)	11845 (100.0)	7244 (100.0)	62

Note: Figures in parenthesis indicate the percentage to total cost.
* Including payments of salaries to non-teaching staff and other non-salary items.

APPENDIX 5D-4

UNIT COSTS ANALYSIS - PER STUDENT (EQUIVALENT), 1986-87 (FACULTY OF ARTS)

(In Rupees)

D. DEPARTMENT OF GEOGRAPHY

University Items of Expenditure	Delhi	Madras	Annamalai	Kurukshetra	Coefficient of Variation (%)
1	2	3	4	5	6
i. Expenditure on Salaries of the Department; of which:	3799 (48.1)	5426 (18.3)	1407 (17.1)	4588 (29.0)	45
a) Teaching Staff	2168 (27.4)	3344 (11.3)	889 (10.8)	3304 (20.9)	48
b) Non-teaching Staff	1631 (20.7)	2082 (7.0)	518 (6.3)	1284 (8.1)	48
ii. Academic Support Services (Other than Salaries)	275 (3.5)	360 (1.2)	133 (1.6)	59 (0.4)	66
iii. General Administrative Exp.*	3826 (48.4)	23803 (80.5)	6674 (81.3)	11167 (70.6)	76
Total (i+ii+iii)	7900 (100.0)	29589 (100.0)	8214 (100.0)	15814 (100.0)	67

Note: Figures in parenthesis indicate the percentage to total cost.
* Including payments of salaries to non-teaching staff and other non-salary items.

APPENDIX 5D-5

UNIT COSTS ANALYSIS - PER STUDENT (EQUIVALENT), 1986-87 (FACULTY OF ARTS)

(*In Rupees*)

E. DEPARTMENT OF HINDI

University Items of Expenditure	Delhi	Madras	Kurukshetra	Coefficient of Variation (%)
1	2	3	4	5
i. Expenditure on Salaries of the Department; of which:	1543 (57.6)	5926 (18.9)	1729 (28.9)	81
a) Teaching Staff	1408 (52.5)	3794 (12.1)	1509 (25.2)	60
b) Non-teaching Staff	135 (5.1)	2132 (6.8)	220 (3.7)	136
ii. Academic Support Services (Other than Salaries)	20 (0.7)	81 (0.2)	31 (0.5)	74
iii. General Administrative Exp.*	1117 (41.7)	25451 (80.9)	4232 (70.6)	90
Total (i+ii+iii)	2680 (100.0)	31458 (100.0)	5992 (100.0)	87

Note: Figures in parenthesis indicate the percentage to total cost.

* Including payments of salaries to non-teaching staff and other non-salary items.

APPENDIX 5D-6

UNIT COSTS ANALYSIS - PER STUDENT (EQUIVALENT), 1986-87 (FACULTY OF ARTS)

(*In Rupees*)

F. DEPARTMENT OF HISTORY

University Items of Expenditure	Delhi	Madras	Annamalai	Ravishankar	Kurukshetra	Coefficient of Variation (%)
1	2	3	4	5	6	7
i. Expenditure on Salaries of the Department; of which:	1566 (50.7)	10355 (19.1)	2948 (35.2)	816 (17.2)	1580 (29.3)	114
a) Teaching Staff	1445 (46.8)	4467 (8.2)	2811 (33.6)	708 (14.9)	1147 (21.2)	72
b) Non-teaching Staff	121 (3.9)	5888 (10.9)	137 (1.6)	108 (2.3)	433 (8.1)	190
ii. Academic Support Services (Other than Salaries)	35 (1.1)	28 (0.1)	5 (0.1)	77 (1.6)	7 (0.1)	96
iii. General Administrative Exp.*	1488 (48.2)	43719 (80.8)	5421 (64.7)	3862 (81.2)	3813 (70.6)	125
Total (i+ii+iii)	3089 (100.0)	54102 (100.0)	8374 (100.0)	4755 (100.0)	5400 (100.0)	122

Note: Figures in parenthesis indicate the percentage to total cost.
* Including payments of salaries to non-teaching staff and other non-salary items.

APPENDIX 5D-7

UNIT COSTS ANALYSIS - PER STUDENT (EQUIVALENT), 1986-87 (FACULTY OF ARTS)

(*In Rupees*)

G. DEPARTMENT OF PHILOSOPHY

University / Items of Expenditure	Delhi	Madras	Ravishankar	Kurukshetra	Coefficient of Variation (%)
1	2	3	4	5	6
i. Expenditure on Salaries of the Department; of which:	2202 (50.9)	2077 (19.6)	7769 (17.2)	1806 (29.2)	83
a) Teaching Staff	2012 (46.5)	1923 (18.1)	6077 (13.5)	1514 (24.4)	74
b) Non-teaching Staff	190 (4.4)	154 (1.5)	1692 (3.7)	292 (8.4)	128
ii. Academic Support Services (Other than Salaries)	24 (0.6)	- (1.5)	692 (0.2)	14	160
iii. General Administrative Exp*	2097 (48.5)	8523 (80.4)	36615 (81.3)	4375 (70.6)	118
Total (i+ii+iii)	4323 (100.0)	10600 (100.0)	45076 (100.0)	6195 (100.0)	113

Note: Figures in parenthesis indicate the percentage to total cost.
* Including payments of salaries to non-teaching staff and other non-salary items.

APPENDIX 5D-8

UNIT COSTS ANALYSIS - PER STUDENT (EQUIVALENT), 1986-87 (FACULTY OF ARTS)

(*In Rupees*)

H. DEPARTMENT OF PSYCHOLOGY

University Items of Expenditure	Delhi	Madras	Ravishankar	Kurukshetra	Coefficient of Variation (%)
1	2	3	4	5	6
i. Expenditure on Salaries of the Department; of which:	2800 (49.1)	6027 (19.4)	2320 (17.1)	2519 (28.5)	51
a) Teaching Staff	1944 (34.1)	4395 (14.1)	1453 (10.7)	1610 (18.2)	59
b) Non-teaching Staff	856 (15.0)	1632 (5.3)	867 (6.4)	909 (10.3)	35
ii. Academic Support Services (Other than Salaries)	161 (2.8)	26 (0.1)	227 (1.7)	78 (0.9)	72
iii. General Administrative Exp*	2737 (48.1)	25026 (80.5)	11013 (81.2)	6234 (70.6)	58
Total (i+ii+iii)	5698 (100.0)	31079 (100.0)	13560 (100.0)	8831 (100.0)	53

Note: Figures in parenthesis indicate the percentage to total cost.

* Including payments of salaries to non-teaching staff and other non-salary items.

APPENDIX 5D-9

UNIT COSTS ANALYSIS - PER STUDENT (EQUIVALENT), 1986-87 (FACULTY OF SCIENCE)

A. DEPARTMENT OF PHYSICS

(In Rupees)

University / Items of Expenditure	Delhi	Madras	Annamalai	Ravishankar	Kurukshetra	Coefficient of Variation (%)
1	2	3	4	5	6	7
i. Expenditure on Salaries	3744 (44.0)	8220 (18.1)	3242 (34.2)	4711 (17.1)	8486 (26.7)	44
a) Teaching Staff	1863 (21.9)	6120 (13.5)	2637 (27.8)	2847 (10.3)	4614 (14.5)	48
b) Non-teaching Staff	1881 (22.1)	2100 (4.6)	605 (6.4)	1864 (6.8)	3872 (12.2)	57
ii. Academic Support Services (Other than Salaries)	652 (7.1)	640 (1.4)	104 (1.1)	458 (1.7)	867 (2.7)	52
iii. General Administrative Exp.*	4115 (48.3)	36420 (80.5)	6137 (64.7)	22373 (81.2)	22447 (70.6)	90
Total (i+ii+iii)	8511 (100.0)	45280 (100.0)	9483 (100.0)	27542 (100.0)	31800 (100.0)	82

Note: Figures in parenthesis indicate the percentage to total cost.

* Including payments of salaries to non-teaching staff and other non-salary items.

APPENDIX 5D-10

UNIT COSTS ANALYSIS - PER STUDENT (EQUIVALENT), 1986-87 (FACULTY OF SCIENCE)

(*In Rupees*)

B. DEPARTMENT OF CHEMISTRY

University / Items of Expenditure	Delhi	Madras	Annamalai	Ravishankar	Kurukshetra	Coefficient of Variation (%)
1	2	3	4	5	6	7
i. Expenditure on Salaries	2178 (45.7)	2837 (12.6)	3400 (29.8)	3523 (17.1)	7652 (24.7)	55
a) Teaching Staff	1530 (32.1)	2837 (12.6)	2279 (20.0)	2216 (10.8)	4509 (14.6)	42
b) Non-teaching Staff	648 (13.6)	(9.8)	1121 (6.3)	1307 (10.1)	3143	70
ii. Academic Support Services (Other than Salaries)	287 (6.0)	1577 (7.0)	621 (5.5)	341 (1.7)	1457 (4.7)	72
iii. General Administrative Exp.*	2299 (48.3)	18145 (80.4)	7379 (64.7)	16716 (81.2)	21880 (70.6)	109
Total (i+ii+iii)	4764 (100.0)	22559 (100.0)	11400 (100.0)	20580 (100.0)	30989 (100.0)	99

Note: Figures in parenthesis indicate the percentage to total cost.
* Including payments of salaries to non-teaching staff and other non-salary items.

APPENDIX 5D-11

UNIT COSTS ANALYSIS - PER STUDENT (EQUIVALENT), 1986-87 (FACULTY OF SCIENCE)

(*In Rupees*)

C. DEPARTMENT OF BOTANY

University / Items of Expenditure	Delhi	Madras	Annamalai	Kurukshetra	Coefficient of Variation (%)
1	2	3	4	5	6
i. Expenditure on Salaries	6506 (41.3)	9777 (18.7)	2931 (33.4)	3126 (24.6)	58
a) Teaching Staff	3035 (19.3)	5077 (9.7)	2500 (28.5)	2140 (16.8)	41
b) Non-teaching Staff	3471 (22.0)	4700 (9.0)	431 (4.9)	986 (3.0)	85
ii. Academic Support Services (Other than Salaries)	1646 (10.4)	454 (0.9)	161 (1.8)	620 (4.9)	90
iii. General Administrative Exp*	7611 (48.3)	42054 (80.4)	5672 (64.8)	8976 (70.5)	81
Total (i+ii+iii)	15763 (100.0)	52285 (100.0)	8764 (100.0)	12722 (100.0)	69

Note: Figures in parenthesis indicate the percentage to total cost.

* Including payments of salaries to non-teaching staff and other non-salary items.

APPENDIX 5D-12

UNIT COSTS ANALYSIS - PER STUDENT (EQUIVALENT), 1986-87 (FACULTY OF SCIENCE)

(*In Rupees*)

D. DEPARTMENT OF ZOOLOGY

University / Items of Expenditure	Delhi	Madras	Annamalai	Kurukshetra	Coefficient of Variation (%)
1	2	3	4	5	6
i. Expenditure on Salaries	6428 (41.3)	4254 (16.4)	2121 (34.0)	7240 (25.2)	46
a) Teaching Staff	2751 (17.7)	2225 (8.6)	1904 (30.5)	5246 (18.3)	50
b) Non-teaching Staff	3677 (23.6)	2029 (7.8)	217 (3.5)	1994 (6.9)	71
ii. Academic Support Services (Other than Salaries)	1614 (10.4)	814 (3.2)	79 (1.3)	1212 (4.2)	70
iii. General Administrative Exp*	7515 (48.3)	20833 (80.4)	4033 (64.7)	20271 (70.6)	112
Total (i+ii+iii)	15557 (100.0)	25901 (100.0)	6233 (100.0)	28723 (100.0)	96

Note: Figures in parenthesis indicate the percentage to total cost.

* Including payments of salaries to non-teaching staff and other non-salary items.

APPENDIX 5D-13

UNIT COSTS ANALYSIS - PER STUDENT (EQUIVALENT), 1986-87 (FACULTY OF SCIENCE)

(*In Rupees*)

E. DEPARTMENT OF GEOLOGY

University / Items of Expenditure	Delhi	Madras	Annamalai	Ravishankar	Coefficient of Variation (%)
1	2	3	4	5	6
i. Expenditure on Salaries	5462 (40.3)	9839 (18.8)	5198 (33.5)	3834 (17.1)	43
a) Teaching Staff	3266 (24.1)	7482 (14.3)	4242 (27.3)	2786 (12.4)	48
b) Non-teaching Staff	2196 (16.2)	2357 (4.5)	956 (6.2)	1048 (4.7)	45
ii. Academic Support Services (Other than Salaries)	1558 (11.5)	375 (0.7)	275 (1.8)	381 (1.7)	94
iii. General Administrative Exp*	6533 (48.2)	41982 (80.5)	10044 (64.7)	18238 (81.2)	74
Total (i+ii+iii)	13553 (100.0)	52196 (100.0)	15517 (100.0)	22453 (100.0)	62

Note: Figures in parenthesis indicate the percentage to total cost.
* Including payments of salaries to non-teaching staff and other non-salary items.

APPENDIX 5D-14

UNIT COSTS ANALYSIS - PER STUDENT (EQUIVALENT), 1986-87 (FACULTY OF SCIENCE)

(*In Rupees*)

F. DEPARTMENT OF MATHEMATICS

University Items of Expenditure	Delhi	Madras	Ravishankar	Kurukshetra	Coefficient of Variation (%)
1	2	3	4	5	6
i. Expenditure on Salaries(44.4)	3215 (18.9)	9682 (17.0)	5123 (47.2)	6713	44
a) Teaching Staff	2183 (30.2)	6817 (13.3)	3600 (12.0)	2637 (18.6)	55
b) Non-teaching Staff	1032 (14.2)	2865 (5.6)	1533 (5.0)	4076 (28.6)	58
ii. Academic Support Services (Other than Salaries)	522 (7.2)	365 (0.7)	500 (1.7)	56 (0.4)	60
iii. General Administrative Exp.*	3503 (48.4)	41308 (80.4)	24550 (81.3)	7440 (52.4)	63
Total (i+ii+iii)	7240 (100.0)	51355 (100.0)	30173 (100.0)	14209 (100.0)	57

Note: Figures in parenthesis indicate the percentage to total cost.

* Including payments of salaries to non-teaching staff and other non-salary items.

APPENDIX 5E-1

PER STUDENT RECURRING EXPENDITURE IN SELECTED CENTRAL UNIVERSITIES IN INDIA 1975-76 & 1984-85

(*In Rupees*)

University	Items of Expenditure	Salaries & Allowances to Teaching Staff		Salaries & Allowances to Non-teaching Staff		Total on Salaries & Allowances		Apparatus Chemicals etc.		Furniture	
1		2		3		4 = (2+3)		5		6	
		1975-76	1984-85	1975-76	1984-85	1975-76	1984-85	1975-76	1984-85	1975-76	1984-85
1.	Hyderabad	N.A.	5098	N.A.	8939	N.A.	14037	N.A.	4596	N.A.	343
			(1801)		(3159)		(4960)		(1624)		(86)
2.	NEHU	2349	6014	3358	5438	5707	11452	228	-	-	414
		(N.A.)	(N.A.)	(N.A.)	(N.A.)	(N.A.)	(N.A.)	(N.A.)			(N.A.)
3.	Aligarh*	2196	3935	1836	7369	4032	11304	174	269	34	83
		(1284)	(1269)	(1074)	(2377)	(2358)	(3646)	(102)	(87)	(20)	(27)
4.	Banaras*	2648	3872	3761	5071	6409	8943	790	199	81	37
		(1549)	(1249)	(2199)	(1636)	(3748)	(2885)	(462)	(6)	(47)	(12)
5.	Visva Bharti	5572	8633	3913	5414	9485	14047	251	183	250	149
		(3765)	(2868)	(2644)	(1799)	(6409)	(4667)	(170)	(61)	(169)	(50)
6.	Delhi	715	885	678	1429	1393	2314	13	43	24	32
		(447)	(302)	(424)	(488)	(871)	(790)	(8)	(15)	(15)	(11)
7.	J. Nehru	2560	7764	2301	7346	4861	15110	160	977	69	-
		(1600)	(2650)	(1438)	(2507)	(3038)	(5157)	(100)	(333)	(43)	

(*Contd.*)

APPENDIX 5E-1 (Contd.)

University	Items of Expenditure	Library		Other Misc. Items (Including grant to college)		Total on Non-Salary items		Grand Total	
1		7		8		9 = (5+6+7+8)		10 = (4+9)	
		1975-76	1984-85	1975-76	1984-85	1975-76	1984-85	1975-76	1984-85
1.	Hyderabad	N.A.	4569 (1614)	N.A.	9154 (3235)	N.A.	18562 (6559)	N.A.	32599 (11519)
2.	NEHU	-	1891 (N.A.)	3461 (N.A.)	10685 (N.A.)	228 (N.A.)	12990 (N.A.)	9396 (N.A.)	24442 (N.A.)
3.	Aligarh*	84 (49)	408 (132)	2048 (1198)	6535 (2108)	2340 (1369)	7295 (2354)	6372 (3727)	18599 (60000)
4.	Banaras*	70 (41)	247 (80)	2546 (1489)	11443 (3691)	3487 (2039)	11926 (3789)	9896 (5787)	20869 (6674)
5.	Visva Bharati	266 (180)	678 (225)	2424 (1637)	10872 (3612)	3191 (2156)	11882 (3948)	12676 (8565)	25929 (8615)
6.	Delhi	131 (82)	13 (4)	1930 (1206)	1590 (543)	2098 (1311)	1678 (573)	3491 (2182)	3992 (1363)
7.	J.Nehru	433 (271)	483 (165)	3426 (2141)	15163 (5175)	4088 (2555)	16623 (5673)	8949 (5593)	31733 (10830)

Note: Figures in parenthesis indicate per student expenditure in real term i.e. at 1970-71 prices.

* Per student expenditure for the base year for the universities of Aligarh and Banaras pertains to 1976-77.

Sources: i) University Finance: A Statistical Profile, Association of Indian Universities, New Delhi 1982.

ii) University Grants Commission, New Delhi.

APPENDIX 5E-2

PER STUDENT RECURRING EXPENDITURE IN SELECTED STATE UNIVERSITIES IN INDIA 1975-76 & 1984-85

(In Rupees)

University	Items of Expenditure	Salaries & Allowances to Teaching Staff		Salaries & Allowances to Non-teaching Staff		Total on Salaries & Allowances		Apparatus Chemicals etc.		Furniture	
1		2		3		4 = (2+3)		5		6	
		1975-76	1984-85	1975-76	1984-85	1975-76	1984-85	1975-76	1984-85	1975-76	1984-85
1.	Sardar Patel	1278	2892	831	2226	2109	5118	492	804	33	93
		(846)	(958)	(550)	(737)	(1396)	(1695)	(326)	(266)	(22)	(31)
2.	Kurukshetra	1233	2270	418	4283	1651	7093	945	177	31	5
		(806)	(764)	(273)	(1442)	(1079)	(2206)	(618)	(60)	(20)	(3)
3.	Karnataka	771	3805	537	2839	1308	6644	32	67	10	16
		(539)	(1358)	(376)	(1014)	(915)	(2372)	(22)	(24)	(7)	(6)
4.	Kerala	2556	5282	8224	25354	10780	30636	151	1024	102	64
		(1628)	(1549)	(5238)	(7435)	(6866)	(8984)	(96)	(300)	(65)	(19)
5.	Dr. H.S. Gaur	804	1575	588	1021	1392	2596	144	168	-	-
		(462)	(501)	(338)	(325)	(800)	(826)	(83)	(54)		
6.	Vikram	355	517	880	1685	1235	2202	-	-	2	3
		(204)	(164)	(506)	(537)	(710)	(701)			(1)	(1)
7.	Bombay	114	1004	1399	4194	2513	5198	199	337	79	16
		(72)	(317)	(885)	(1323)	(1591)	(1640)	(75)	(106)	(50)	(5)
8.	Poona	1348	3709	1180	4300	2528	8009	183	1404	25	27
		(853)	(1170)	(747)	(1356)	(1600)	(2526)	(116)	(443)	(16)	(9)

(Contd.)

APPENDIX 5E-2 (Contd.)

	Items of Expenditure / University	Library		Other Misc. Items (Including grant to college)		Total on Non-Salary items		Grand Total	
	1	7		8		9 = (5+6+7+8)		10 = (4+9)	
		1975-76	1984-85	1975-76	1984-85	1975-76	1984-85	1975-76	1984-85
1.	Sardar Patel	276	629	1261	2169	2062	3695	4171	8813
		(183)	(208)	(718)	(1366)	(1366)	(1223)	(2762)	(2918)
2.	Kurukshetra	155	451	490	5204	1621	5837	3272	12930
		(101)	(151)	(320)	(1752)	(1059)	(1965)	(2138)	(4171)
3.	Karnataka	140	239	838	2687	1020	2993	2328	9637
		(98)	(85)	(586)	(960)	(713)	(1069)	(1628)	(3441)
4.	Kerala	1614	3096	10056	23149	11923	27333	22703	57969
		(1028)	(908)	(6405)	(6788)	(7594)	(8015)	(14460)	(16999)
5.	Dr. H.S. Gaur	43	63	366	2085	553	2316	1945	4912
		(25)	(20)	(210)	(664)	(318)	(738)	(1118)	(1564)
6.	Vikram	86	55	792	990	880	1048	2115	3250
		(49)	(18)	(458)	(315)	(506)	(333)	(1216)	(1034)
7.	Bombay	311	349	1545	4920	2054	5622	4567	10820
		(197)	(110)	(978)	(1552)	(1300)	(1773)	(2891)	(3413)
8.	Poona	389	100	1622	5985	2219	7516	4747	15525
		(246)	(32)	(1026)	(1888)	(1404)	(2372)	(3004)	(4898)

Note: Figures in parenthesis indicate per student expenditure in real term i.e. at 1970-71 prices.

Source: 1. University Finance: A Statistical profile, Association of Indian Universities, New Delhi 1982.
2. University Grants Commission, New Delhi.

APPENDIX 5E-3

PER STUDENT RECURRING EXPENDITURE IN SELECTED INSTITUTIONS IN INDIA 1975-76 & 1984-85

(In Rupees)

University	Items of Expenditure	Salaries & Allowances to Teaching Staff		Salaries & Allowances to Non-teaching Staff		Total on Salaries & Allowances		Apparatus Chemicals etc.		Furniture	
	1	2		3		4 = (2+3)		5		6	
		1975-76	1984-85	1975-76	1984-85	1975-76	1984-85	1975-76	1984-85	1975-76	1984-85
1.	C.I.E.F.L.	7667 (5438)	6475 (2288)	6103 (4328)	10449 (3692)	13770 (9766)	16924 (5980)	85 (60)	445 (157)	-	519 (183)
2.	School of Mines	2268 (1418)	5317 (1866)	1905 (1191)	9753 (3422)	4173 (2609)	15070 (5288)	8885 (553)	-	-	-
3.	Gujarat Vidyapeeth	2013 (1333)	2808 (930)	1072 (710)	2414 (799)	3085 (2043)	5222 (1729)	-	12 (4)	-	-
4.	Tata Instt. of Social Science	2958 (1872)	531 (1677)	2391 (1513)	7743 (2443)	5349 (3385)	13058 (4120)	-	-	302 (191)	1411 (445)
5.	B.I.T.S.	1414 (943)	3884 (1221)	1205 (803)	24 (8)	2619 (1746)	3908 (1229)	283 (189)	1197 (376)	-	-
6.	Gurukul Kangri	1834 (1207)	2829 (913)	1001 (659)	2659 (858)	2835 (1866)	5488 (1771)	66 (43)	124 (40)	8 (5)	193 (62)
7.	Jamia Millia Islamia	1904 (1190)	2697 (920)	1049 (656)	1392 (475)	2953 (1846)	4089 (1395)	33 (21)	69 (24)	-	-

(Contd.)

APPENDIX 5E-3 (Contd.)

University	Items of Expenditure	Library		Other Misc. Items (Including grant to college)		Total on Non-Salary items		Grand Total	
1		7		8		9 = (5+6+7+8)		10 = (4+9)	
		1975-76	1984-85	1975-76	1984-85	1975-76	1984-85	1975-76	1984-85
1.	C.I.E.F.L.	31	189	11802	9519	11918	10672	25688	27596
		(22)	(67)	(8370)	(3364)	(8452)	(3771)	(18218)	(9751)
2.	School of Mines	308	649	7915	15863	9108	16512	1328	31582
		(193)	(228)	(5947)	(5566)	(4693)	(5794)	(8302)	(11082)
3.	Gujarat Vidyapeeth	63	9	401	5755	464	5776	3549	10998
		(42)	(3)	(266)	(1906)	(308)	(1913)	(2085)	(3645)
4.	Tata Instt. of Social Science	47	1127	1960	6730	2309	9268	7658	22326
		(30)	(356)	(1241)	(2123)	(1462)	(2924)	(4847)	(7044)
5.	B.I.T.S.	233	25	1034	1544	1550	2766	4169	6674
		(155)	(8)	(689)	(486)	(1033)	(876)	(2779)	(2105)
6.	Gurukul Kangri	34	153	647	1465	755	1935	3590	7423
		(22)	(49)	(426)	(473)	(496)	(624)	(2362)	(2395)
7.	Jamia Millia Islamia	236	425	662	2013	931	2507	3884	6596
		(148)	(145)	(414)	(687)	(582)	(856)	(2428)	(2251)

Note: Figures in parenthesis indicate per student expenditure in real terms i.e. at 1970-71 prices.

Sources: 1. University Finance: A Statistical Profile, Association of Indian Universities, New Delhi 1982.
2. University Grants Commission, New Delhi.

APPENDIX 6.1

SUMMARY STATEMENT OF EXPENDITURE ON GENERAL HIGHER EDUCATION UPTO 1995.

I. Continuing Schemes		**Rs. (in crores)**
A. Expansion and Development		
	i) Teaching and non-teaching costs	
	(a) Conventional System	92.21
	(b) Distance Education	38.56
	(c) Total (a+b)	130.77
(ii)	Quality Improvement Programmes @ 20 per cent of the total teaching and non-teaching costs [i.e. of (i) above)	26.15
(iii)	Restructuring of undergraduate and post-graduate courses Rs. two lakhs per college for 5000 colleges	100.00
	Total (i+ii+iii)	256.92
B. (i)	Development of Universities (infrastructure and research) @ Rs.2 crores for 150 universities	300.00
(ii)	Development of Colleges (Infrastructure and research) @ Rs.10 lakhs for 3000 colleges	300.00
C.	Programmes for research support	400.00
D.	Fellowships and Scholarships 10 per cent of the projected enrolment 22 lakhs for 1990-95 @ Rs. 300/- per student per month	6.6
E.	Orientation Training of Teachers 15 per cent of the total teachers @ Rs.10,000 per teacher	36.00
F.	Research Councils and Co-ordinating Agencies (Like ICSSR, ICHR, Indian Council of Philosophical Research etc.)	200.00
	Total (A+B+C+D+E+F)	1499.52 or 1500.00

(Contd.)

Appendix 6.1 (Contd.)

II. New Schemes	**Rs. (in crores)**
(a) Promotion of Research in Higher Education	75.00
(b) Modernization of equipment and other educational technologies	200.00
(c) Student support services (including hostels and other students amenities)	100.00
(d) Quarters for Teaching Staff (10,000 quarters - @ Rs.2 lakh per quarter)	200.00
(e) Development of Autonomous Colleges and University Departments	60.00
(f) Development of Rural Institutes/Universities	90.00
(g) University Adult Education Programmes	25.00
(h) Central University in Assam	25.00
(i) National Testing Service/National Evaluation Organisation	10.00
Total II	785.00
Grand Total (I+II)	2285.00

APPENDIX 6.2

SUMMARY STATEMENT OF EXPENDITURE ON TECHNICAL HIGHER EDUCATION DURING 1990-95

Sl. No.	Name of the Scheme	(Rs. in crores)
	I. Continuing Schemes	439.32
	(A) Expansion and Development	
	(B) Direction and Administration	
(i)	Reorganising, restructuring and strengthening AICTE, its Committees, Board of Studies and Bureau of Technical Education	30.00
(ii)	National Technical Manpower Information System	20.00
(iii)	Grants of autonomy to selected institutions	20.00
(iv)	Strengthening existing institutions and establishment of new institutions	30.00
	Total 'B'	100.00
	(C) Training	
(i)	Regional Engg. Colleges	55.00
(ii)	Apprenticeship Training	20.00
(iii)	Central Institutions IITs NITIE NIFFT SPA	30.00
(iv)	UGC Schemes	60.00
(v)	Advanced Technician Courses	20.00
(vi)	Restructuring Courses/Programmes	10.00
(vii)	Setting up of residential polytechnics for women, handicapped and other weaker sections of society	75.00
	Total 'C'	270.00
	D. Research and Development	
(i)	Indian Institute of Technology	70.00
(ii)	Indian Institute of Management	45.00
(iii)	Development of P G Courses	15.00

(Contd.)

Appendix 6.2 Contd.

Sl. No.	Name of the Scheme	(Rs. in crores)
(iv)	Management Education	15.00
(v)	Institutional Network Scheme	15.00
(vi)	International Centre for Science and Technology	20.00
(vii)	Research & Development in Selected higher technical institutions	30.00
	Total 'D'	210.00
	E. Development of Engineering/Technical colleges and Institutions	
(i)	Modernisation and removal of obsolescence	150.00
(ii)	Thrust areas of Technical Education, which include	60.00
	(a) Creation of infrastructure in areas of emerging technologies	
	(b) Strengthening of facilities in crucial areas of technology where weakness exist	
	(c) Programmes of New and/or improved technologies offering new courses in specialised field	
(iii)	Development of existing Community Polytechnics	30.00
(iv)	(a) Special Institute for Rural and Appropriate Technology	50.00
	(b) Experimental Pilot Projects	
(v)	Institution-Industry Interaction	15.00
(vi)	Curriculum Development	15.00
(vii)	Continuing Education	20.00
(viii)	Hostel accomodation to more students	15.00
(ix)	Providing Staff Quarters	25.00
(x)	Implementing Pay Committee Recommendations	-
	Total 'E'	380.00
	Total 'I'	1399.32

II. New Schemes

(A) Community Polytechnic

Sl. No.	Name of the Scheme	(Rs. in crores)
(i)	300 additional community polytechnics (@ Rs.15 lakhs per institution)	45.00
(ii)	Special Institute for relevant/useful Technology & Rural Development in the States	30.00

(*Contd.*)

Appendix 6.2 Contd.

Sl. No.	Name of the Scheme	(Rs. in crores)
(B)	Computerisation of Institutions for Technical & Management Education	50.00
(C)	Entrepreneurship Development Programmes	75.00
(D)	Promotion of Individual & Institutional Excellence	25.00
(E)	Implementation of Central Schemes Under AICTE	25.00
	TOTAL 'II'	250.00
III. Other Schemes		
(i)	Indian Institute of Technology in Assam	40.00
(ii)	Longowal Institute of Technology and Engineering	15.00
(iii)	Super computer at Indian Institute of Science, Bangalore	10.00
(iv)	EDCIL	7.00
(v)	New Q.I.P.	15.00
	Total 'III'	87.00
	GRAND TOTAL (I-III)	1736.32

BIBLIOGRAPHY

Altbach, P.G. and Singh, A., (1974) *The Higher Learning in India*, Vikas Publishing House, New Delhi.

Anderson, Arnold C. and Bowman, Jean M., (1971) *Education and Economic Development*, Aldine Publishing Co., Chicago.

Ansari, M.M., (1986) Flow of Financial Resources and Inter-State Disparities, *Indian Economic Journal*, April-June.

——, (1986) 'Measuring Fiscal Performance of the Centre and the State Governments in India', *Indian Economic Journal*, April-June (with M Q Dalvi).

——, (1987) *Education and Economic Development: Perspectives for Policy Planning*, Association of Indian Universities, New Delhi.

——, (1988) 'Financing of the State Plans : A Perspective for Regional Development', *Economic and Political Weekly*, Dec. 3, 1983 and also in *Budgetary Relations Betwen Centre and State Governments*, (Ed.) Gulati, I.G., Oxford University Press.

——, (1988) 'Resource Allocation for Higher Education in USSR : What can we learn from it.' *Quarterly Journal of Education, Winter.*

——, (1989) 'Resource Allocation and Financial Accountability of Universities', *University News*, Oct. 2, pp. 17-21.

——, (1989) 'Financial Health of Universities: A Diagnostic Study', *Journal of Higher Education*, Vol. 14, pp. 65-86.

——, (1989) Higher Education in India. The Implementation of New Schemes', *ABCD Bulletine*, Association of Commonwealth Universities, London, October.

——, (1990) Assessing the Extent of Use of Educational Infrastructure Facilities in the University Sector, *Journal of Higher Education*, vol.15, 1990.

——, (1991) Industry-Universities in India: Is Collaborative Effort Succeeding, *Industry and Higher Education*, Sept. (with T.C. Sharma).

——, (1991) 'University Finances: Determinants and Implications' in *Higher Education in India* by Moonis Raza (Ed), AIU.

——, (1992) *Economics of Distance Higher Education*, Concept Publishing Company, New Delhi.

——, (1993) *Unit Costs of Higher Education: An Efficiency Study of Universities*, AIU.

Association of Indian Universities, (1992) *Financial Deficits in Universities*, Author.

Azad, J.L., (1975) *Financing of Higher Education in India*, Sterling Publishers Pvt. Ltd., New Delhi.

Azad, J.L., (1988) *Higher Education in India: The Deepening Financial Crisis,* Radiant Publishers, New Delhi.

Benson, Charles S., (1978) *The Economics of Public Education*, Houghton Mifflin Company, Boston, Massachusetts.

Blaug, M., (1968) *Economics of Education* - 1, Penguin Books, New York.

——, (1969) *An Introduction to the Economics of Education*, Penguin Books, New York.

——, (1972) 'The Correlation between Education and Earnings. What Does it Signify?' *Higher Education*, 1 (i).

Bombwall, K.R., (1979) *Federal Financial Relations in India*, Meenakshi Prakashan, Meerut.

Bowen, W.G., (1972) 'Assessing the Economic Contribution of Education' in Blaug, M. (Ed) *Economics of Education*, Vol. II, The English Book Society.

Chalam, K.S., (1986) *Finances, Costs and Productivity of Higher Education*, Inter-India Publications, New Delhi.

Cohn Elchann, (1972) *Economics of Education*, Lexington Book, D. C. Heath and Co., Massachusetts.

Dean Edwin, (1984) *Education and Economic Productivity*, Ballinger Publishing Company, Cambridge, Massachusetts.

Doss, Veda, (1978) *Impact of Planning on Centre State Financial Relations in India*, National Publishing House, New Delhi.

Finis, Welch., (1970) 'Education in Production', *Journal of Political Economy*, Vol. 78.

Galbraith, J.K., (1969) *Economic Development*, Harvard University Press.

Gaundino, Robert, (1965) *The Indian University*, Popular Prakashan, Bombay.

Govt. of India, (1986) *National Policy on Education - 1986*, Ministry of Human Resource Development, Deptt. of Education, New Delhi.

——, (1986) *Programme of Action*, Ministry of Human Resource Development, Deptt. of Education, New Delhi.

——, (1985) *Challenge of Education: A Policy Perspective*, New Delhi.

Gupta, S., (1987) 'Indian Plans: Retrospects and Perspects', *The Indian Economic Journal*, Vol. 34, No. 4.

Garg, V.P., (1985) *Cost Analysis in Higher Education*, Metropolitan, New Delhi.

Harbinson and Myers, C.A., (1968) *Education, Manpower and Economic Growth*, Oxford and IBH Publishing Co., New Delhi.

Kaul, J.N., (1974) *Higher Education in India: 1951-71, Two Decades of Planned Drift*, Indian Institute of Advanced Study, Simla.

Lakdawala, D.T., (1967) *Union State Financial Relations*, Lalvani Publishing House, Bombay.

Machlup, Fritz, (1984) *The Economics of Information and Human Capital*, Vol. III, Princeton University Press.

Malik, S.C., (1971) *Management and Organisation of Indian Universities*, Vol. 19, Indian Instt. of Advanced Study, Simla.

Mathew, E.T., (1991) *Financing Higher Education: Sources and Uses of Funds of Private Colleges in Kerala*, Concept Publishing Company, New Delhi.

Mazumdar, T., (1983) *Investment in Education and Social Choice*, Cambridge University Press, New York.

Meir, G.M., (1984) *Leading Issues in Development Economics*, Oxford Univesity Press, New York.

Mishra, A., (1962) *Educational Finance in India*, Asia Publishing House, Bombay.

——, (1967) *The Financing of Indian Education*, Asia Publishing House, New Delhi.

Mridula, (1985) *State Funding of Universities: A study of maintenance Grants to Universities*, Association of Indian Universities, New Delhi.

Mukerjee, S.N., (1970) *Administration of Education, Planning and Finance : Theory and Practices*, Acharya Book Depot, Bombay.

Nanjundappa, D.M., (1976) *Working of University Finances*, Sterling Publishers Pvt. Ltd., New Delhi.

Padmanabhan, C.B., (1967) 'Cost and Financing of Education in India, An Aggregate Study', Asian Instt. of Educational Planning and Administration, New Delhi.

Panchmukhi, P.R., (1977) *Economics of University Finances: Basic Principles and Practice*, Centre for Multi-Disciplinary Research, Karnatak Historical Research Society, Dharwar.

Psacharopoulos, G., (1973) *Returns to Education: An International Comparison*, Jossey-Bass, Elsevier.

——, (1981) 'Returns to Education: An Updated International Comparison', *Comparative Education*, Vol. 17, No. 3.

Rao, V.K.R.V., (1966) *Education and Human Resource Development*, Allied Publishers, New Delhi.

Rizvi, F.H., (1960) *Financing of Higher Education in Less Developed Countries*, Aligarh Muslim University, Aligarh.

Schiefelbein, E., (1983) 'Educational Financing in Developing Countries: Research Finding and Contemporary Issues', International Development Research Centre, Ottawa, Canada.

Schultz, Theodore W., (1971) *Investment in Human Capital: The Role of Education and Research*, Free Press, New York.

Shafi, Zeenat, (1991) 'Performance Indicators in Education', *Journal of Educational Planning and Administration*, Oct.

Sharma, M.M., (1992) *Financial Management in India*, Concept Publishing Company, New Delhi.

Singh, A. and Sharma, G.D., (1981) *University and College Finances*, Association of Indian Universities, New Delhi.

Singh, P., (1982) *Financing of University Education*, B.R. Publishing Corportion, Delhi.

Singh, Baljit, (1983) *Economics of Indian Education*, Meenakshi Prakashan, New Delhi.

Sulochana, M., (1992) *Financial Management of Higher Education in India*, Chug Publications, Allahabad.

Tilak, J. and Varghese, N.V., (1983) 'Resources for Education in India' *National Institute of Educational Planning and Administration*, Occasional Paper No. 2.

——, (1991) 'Financing Higher Education in India', *Higher Education*, Vol. 21, Jan. 1991.

Vaizey, E., (1968) *The Economics of Education*, Faber and Faber Ltd., London.

Varghese, K.V., (1985) *Economic Problems of Modern India*, Ashish Publishing House, New Delhi.

Zeenat Begam, (1989) 'Facility Utilisation in University Sector', *Yojna*, Nov. 1-15.

INDEX